The Warmblood Guidebook

THE Warmblood Guidebook

CHARLENE STRICKLAND

Half Halt Press, Inc.
Middletown, Maryland

The Warmblood Guidebook

Published 1992 in the United States of America by
Half Halt Press, Inc.
6416 Burkittsville Road
Middletown MD 21769

Drawings by Heather J. Lowe

Photos by the author, except where otherwise noted.

Book and jacket design by Clara Graves.

Printed in the United States of America

Library of Congress Cataloging-in-Publication Data

Strickland, Charlene.
    The warmblood guidebook / Charlene Strickland.
        p.   cm.
    Includes bibliographical references (p.   ) and index.
    ISBN 0-939481-28-6 : $34.95
      1. Horse breeds—Europe. 2. Horse breeds. I. Title.
SF290.E85S77 1992
636.1'3—dc20
                                       92-35016
                                         CIP

Table of Contents

Acknowledgements

The following breed authorities contributed to this book: Ludwig Christmann and Dr. Jochen Wilkens, Hannoverian Verband; Louis Thompson, Jr., Hermann Friedlaender, Judy Hedreen, American Hanoverian Society; Dr. Thomas Nissen, Holsteiner Verband; Elizabeth McElvain, Doris van Heeckeren, Masu Hamacher, Dietrich Felgendreher, Janice Scarbrough, American Holsteiner Horse Association; Dr. Eberhard Senckenberg, Trakehner Verband; Joan Schlimme, Henry Schurink, Leo Whinery, Helen Gibble, American Trakehner Association; Frank La Salle, North American Trakehner Association; Mrs. Finkler, Westfalen Studbook; Lucy Parker, Westfalen Warmblood Association of America; Dr. Roland Ramsauer and Margaret Schrant, International Sporthorse Registry; Bernard Maurel, Haras Nationaux, Cecile Grosse, Union Nationale Interprofessionnelle du Cheval, Sheryl Akers, North American Selle Français Horse Association; Gert van der Veen, Rolf Brinkman, Dr. van der Meij, Gerti Nieuhoff, KWPN; Elizabeth Searle, Faith Fessenden, Cynthia Warren, Mary Giddens, NA/WPN; Koen Overstijns, Belgian Warmblood Breeding Association; Kristina Paulsen, Swedish Warmblood Association; Jean Brooks, American Warmblood Society; Sonja Lowenfish, American Warmblood Registry.

Thanks to these North American breeders: Judy Williams, Dr. Richard von Buedingen, Guenter Bertelmann, Judy Yancey, Anita Hunter, Gerhard Schickedanz, Robin Koenig, Janet Sperber, Barbara Raehn, Jill-Marie Jones, Kim Tulypin, Pat Limage, Marian Munsinger, Lilo Fore, Gerd and Yvonne Zuther, Cathy Hastings, Dale Bormann, Tony de Groot, Uli Schmitz, Dorie Vlatten-Schmitz, Jayne Ayers, Peter Lert, Peter Kjellerup, Douglas Mankovich, Kyle Karnosh, John Quirk, Patty Arnett, and June Palmer.

These riders and trainers also contributed their expertise: Kathy Adams, Hans Schardt, Jan Ebeling, Steffen Peters, Guenter Seidel, Willie Arts, Linda Zang, Nancy Chesney, Sally Graburn, Katie Lindberg, Karen Lencyk, David Wilson, Gerhard Politz, Michael Hedlund-Beining, Gwen Stockebrand, Barbi Breen, Julie Sodowsky, Leslie Reid, Cynthia Dunoyer, Pamela Nelson, Hilda Gurney, Marie Meyers, Frank Madden, Emil-Bernhard Jung, Susan Haupt, Greg Best, and Michael Plumb.

Thanks also to these authorities: Bill Nichols of Alex Nichols Agency, Jann Hasenauer of Jet Pets, Diana Clark of *Sport Horse World*, Robin Bledsoe, Pete Roper, DVM, Karen James, DVM, Edgar Hotz, Natalie Lamping, and Martha Worcester and Beth Wood, United States Dressage Federation.

PART 1

Introduction to the Breeds

The breeds discussed here are the best-known sport horses of the Continent and Scandinavia, although similar breeds do exist in Austria, Switzerland, and Hungary. In general, the horses represent only a few distinct types—Germany's Hannoverian, Holsteiner, and Trakehner, and the French horse. The breeds from other German regions and other countries have developed from these four types and the English Thoroughbred.

All breeds, except the Trakehner, have open studbooks. Associations permit the introduction of lines from certain other regions, or "approved" populations. Part II contains details of breed registries and selections of breeding and performance horses.

CHAPTER 1

Introduction

H alfblood, warmblut, demi-sang—their blood measures the same temperature as other horses, but the European warmbloods are the sport horse supreme. The elegant athletes which carry the names of European states and nations triumph in the classic equestrian sports.

These horses combine beauty with substance. They appeal to equestrians with their good looks, and they are powerful athletes under saddle or in harness. Their amenable dispositions make them willing to respond to the directions of rider or driver.

All European warmbloods resulted from blending native stock and partbred horses with fullbloods, Thoroughbred or Arabian. The warmblood is a dilution between the fullblood and the partbred, not a cross between "hot" fullbloods and "cold" draft horse breeds.

Warmblood breeds are both old and new. Some have existed for centuries; others originated after the second World War. European horse-breeding has been concentrated on the Continent and in Scandinavia, primarily in the regions surrounding the Baltic and North Seas. Horsemen have perfected the art and science of producing the qualities desired in a sport horse.

The warmblood, like the fullblood, is bred for a purpose—the purpose of sport rather than galloping at speed. The warmblood adds style, temperament, and durability to the speed and stamina it has inherited from its fullblood ancestors.

Today warmbloods produce almost all the performers who win Olympic medals and na-

The European sport horse is an attractive equine athlete. Steffen Peters on Udon, a Dutch Warmblood.

tional, European, and World championships. They dominate world-class competition of three of the four disciplines.

As an example, the 1990 World Equestrian Games hosted four World Championships. The record:

	Percent of entries	Percent in the top 10 places
Show jumping	72	70
Dressage	80	100
Driving	90	90
Three-day	30	30

In the Three-day event, most entries were Thoroughbred or Thoroughbred crosses. These

The Trakehner stallion Ibsen shows a lot of "caliber" in the dry conformation type.

continue to be the breed of choice for eventing, primarily due to their speed at the gallop. Most warmbloods which excel in eventing have a high percentage of Thoroughbred bloodlines.

To perpetuate sport horse qualities, European breeders have studied pedigrees of ancestors and progeny. They apply this data to improve the next generation. By maintaining open studbooks, they select stallions and mares to meet their goals of ideal athletes.

Europe supplies a global market with performance horses and breeding stock. Suppliers on both sides of the Atlantic aggressively market their animals as the elite sport horses.

Discriminating competitors recognize the athletic potential of European warmbloods. To compete at advanced levels, riders and drivers demand horses that will excel in the discipline. They can improve their chances of success by selecting the athletic horse that naturally fits the function. In the sports of dressage and combined driving, the equestrian cannot compete on an equal basis without a warmblood.

For the North American horseman, this book surveys the major regional breeds of European sport horses. From a few individuals to thousands of animals, the North American warmblood "invasion" has gathered momentum through the 1980s. Yet high prices, foreign terminology, and an unfamiliarity with European breeding and selling methods have limited understanding about these horses.

Chapters in three segments present an overview of European approaches, and how they influence North American trends. The book is not an exhaustive study—it begins an education through documenting facts and noting opinions from authorities on both sides of the Atlantic.

Information on breed history, traits, and selection methods introduces the basics of adapting European sport horses into contemporary American equestrianism. The book also includes information on recent European economic changes, which continue to impact upon the horse industry.

The emphasis is on the European sport horse in America and how these athletes meet American tastes. Economics and the domestic preference will cause the average rider to choose an American-born horse.

Defining the Sport Horse

The sport horse is a unique animal. Like a hunting dog or falcon, this companion assists a person in the pursuit of a sport. The horse becomes a partner, not only a beast of burden.

The sport horse combines physical with mental qualities. Its size, power, and stylish bearing predispose it to the correct movement required in the four classic sports.

Today's sport horse evolved to suit the market developed along with the sports. Horses have influenced competitions, and sports have shaped their equine competitors.

Today's sports require certain performance skills. For instance, the size of indoor arenas limits the distance between fences. Dressage tests specify certain movements and transitions. The successful sport horse meets the current demands of its primary discipline.

The sport horse has the athletic ability to move at the gait, direction, and height required to cover ground in an efficient, attractive style. It can and will adapt to the trainer's requests.

Part I of the book describes the various regional breeds of Europe. Despite their national origins, all breeds now produce a similar animal. Crossbreeding has resulted in a mingling of traits.

The modern equine athlete presents a picture of overall balance. The horse presents the appearance of symmetry, with all parts in perfect harmony.

The sport horse displays caliber—a strong physical substance. Bones and muscles are strong

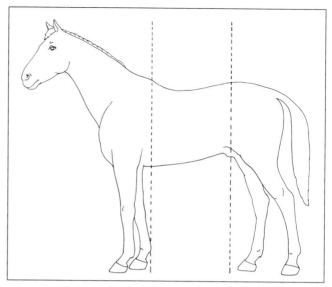

The horse's three main components—forehand, middle, and hindquarters—are in proportion and smoothly connected. The ideal sport horse type is rectangular in its body due to its length of shoulder and hindquarter, not a long back.

and solid, and tissues are firm.

Hotblooded horses like Arabians and Thoroughbreds characterize the "dry" conformation type. The animal's outlines look lean and sharp. It has a fast metabolism for efficient functions of respiratory, cardio-vascular, and excretory systems. It has a thin skin, prominent muscles, and well-defined tendons.

The ideal sport horse is of this dry conformation type. Its body forms a rectangular frame with a deep heart girth. Standing, the horse should cover a lot of ground, and its length exceeds its height.

Dr. Roland Ramsauer of the International Sporthorse Registry explained how horsemen evaluate horses by type: "We distinguish different types as a light, elegant Thoroughbred type, the heavier hunter type, the heavy carriage type, and the draft horse. Nowadays we prefer the Thoroughbredy sport horse with a high potential for performance."

This athlete moves with balance and agility. It shows natural impulsion at all gaits, and today's horses also display a unique style and appeal. They are large yet elegant.

In temperament, the sport horse is lively and energetic, yet docile and honest. It responds obediently to the demands of its rider or driver.

In Part II of this book, authorities share more detailed insights on judging strengths and faults of the sport horse's conformation and movement.

CHAPTER 2

Development of the Contemporary European Warmblood

T he supreme sport horses of today have been shaped through centuries of European civilization. Breeds of today evolved to serve man in war, transportation, and agriculture.

Today's breeds live on as legacies of the dynasties of Europe during the Enlightenment, also known as the Age of Reason. Bred and refined to please the tastes of the elite, they are living products of the feudal system which persisted through the 17th and 18th centuries.

Warmblood horses on the Continent developed parallel to the development of the Thoroughbred in England and share the same foundation sires. Their breeds, named after a region or monarchy, were created through a recipe— blending horses of various origins to produce a desired type. Over the centuries, royalty set a focus different from the Thoroughbred, with the goal excellence of performance rather than purity of blood.

Breeds developed in a slow process influenced by the fortunes of nations. As sovereigns built empires and European civilization moved toward a greater sophistication, horses also changed.

Horses of the ancien régime

Well-bred horses were important to the quasi-feudal societies of 16th-18th century Europe, known as the *ancien régime*, or the Old Order. The landed elite bred horses as symbols of their wealth, power, and divine right to rule. Horses moved across borders as dynasties flourished, intermarried, or declined.

In the 16th century, aristocrats preferred the Spanish and Neapolitan horses. These animals, progenitors of breeds such as today's Andalusian, Lipizzans, and Friesians, excelled in the stylized art of *manège*, or school riding.

In the 1500s, riding schools in France, Germany, Italy, and Spain used these horses to

The Hannoverian Gifted exemplifies the history of the European warmblood, from war horse to sport horse. This U.S. dressage champion stands 17.2 and wighs 1900 pounds but is an outstanding mover.

perform the collected movements of the manège, inspired by the teachings of the Neapolitan, Grisone. Horses with upright necks, low hindquarters, and high knee action displayed kings and nobles in heroic roles.

Noble horses also pulled the ceremonial coaches of the baroque era. With cities building broad avenues and spacious squares, royalty cultivated the pomp of the equipage in the wide streets. The state coach and bedecked horses symbolized the ruler's image of wealth and influence.

After the Thirty Years War ended with the Treaty of Westphalia in 1648, nations and prin-cipalities began to emerge as powers. Aristocrats demanded a more practical horse; royalty determined the type of horse needed to uphold its position.

Royal families considered themselves as absolute rulers. The ruler and the state merged, and despotic kings and emperors guided their dynasties toward grandeur. As the state's confidence and influence grew, the populace became used to the dictates of the state in all areas of life.

In feudalism, citizens lived under the protection of the overlord who served a king or duke. The monarch's dependents offered services in exchange for the state's protection.

Continental nations shared frontiers and had to guard against invasion. Dynasties' squabbles increased the importance of provincial and national armies, and the elite pursued the cult of war. Cavalry became both a profession and a social rank.

These soldiers required horses that would accept training and cover ground at speed. To provide such horses, 17th century rulers encouraged regional horse breeding. They realized that a reliable supply of war horses was a national priority.

France and northern Germany bred horses in the good grazing lands of Hannover, Schleswig-Holstein, Pommern (Pomerania), and Mecklenburg-Schwerin. Normandy, East and West Prussia, the lands along the Elbe and Weser rivers, and parts of Westfalia, Oldenburg, and Saxony were also traditional horse-breeding centers.

Each state determined to establish its own distinctive breed of horse. Horses became a source of national pride and a potentially profitable enterprise.

Several rulers established national studs as a long-term strategy to produce the horses they required. The states subsidized breeding by offering the use of government-owned stallions to local farmers and estate owners.

The system assured the privileged elite a reliable supply of horses for riding and cavalry. The state's stallions influenced the quality of horses breeders would produce. Breeders served their sovereign in this exchange, as part of the payment for living under his protection.

The local horse industry benefited from the military's needs. With a ready market for their stock, farmers could afford to raise their own horses.

Although the system produced horses for local use, the state frequently introduced outside blood. Many of Europe's dynasties were linked by blood or marriage, and they exchanged breeding stock among themselves. Horses also changed ownership as spoils of war, when conquering armies commandeered livestock within newly expanded frontiers.

On the Continent, horses of the early 18th century traced back to the Spanish and Neapolitan horses. However, most breeds were heterogeneous, of dissimilar type. The breeds only began to change through regular infusions of the blood of "improvement" sires.

During the years of the 18th century's Enlightenment, men sought to advance knowledge in all areas of life. They applied the scientific method to improve horse breeding.

Systematic breeding began in England, with the development of the Thoroughbred and Cleveland Bay breeds. The Thoroughbred originated through the late 17th and early 18th centuries. Native stock, already influenced by Spanish horses, formed the basis of the breed along with three famous imported progenitors—the Godolphin Arabian, Darley Arabian, and Byerley Turk.

The Cleveland Bay was established as early as the 16th century, similarly developed through the crossing of native English horses with Arabian, Turkish, and Spanish breeds. Thoroughbred sires later helped to improve this breed.

European royalty traveled in state coaches. The coat of arms of the house of Hannover adorns the doors of this elegant vehicle.

All horse breeders wanted to produce riding and carriage horses for the army, farmwork, and coaching. Most riding horses went to the military. The utility ride-and-drive horses were used both on the farm and in the armed forces.

Breeding systems began to consolidate the native stock with the better-bred English horses, which greatly influenced all horses on the Continent. To establish uniformity, governments enforced systems of selection. Authorities maintained records of pedigrees and graded the animals' quality.

Horsemen judged stock by standards of merit. Judges and breeders influenced regional breeds by selecting superior horses for desirable traits. Horses were culled from the gene pool if they failed to meet standards of quality.

Prussia's Frederick the Great emphasized cavalry's role and the importance of effective horsemanship. Under his leadership, Prussia's cavalry moved rapidly to attack and pursue its enemies.

The discipline of the parade ground set a standard of excellence. Prussian cavalry had to drill in horsemanship and endurance. One exercise required the rider to gallop long distances, with a charge lasting one mile over rough ground.

The durable cavalry horses were exercised regularly, mostly at the trot and the gallop. They had to have endurance for long marches, strength to carry the weight of rider and gear, tractable dispositions, and the ability to maintain weight while foraging. Stamina was usually more important than great speed.

Artillery horses maintained the army's mobility. To move equipment quickly, the Prussian army demanded a heavier warmblood horse, although not a cart-horse type. The ride-and-drive horse was often used in artillery, with drivers riding postillion.

The Age of Imperialism—and Industrial Revolution

Breeds continued to spread in the early 19th century. The Napoleonic wars brought many German horses to France, including a substantial number of stallions previously owned by the conquered states. Wars and the expansion of Napoleon's empire greatly reduced numbers of horses, and Continental governments imported large numbers of animals from England to help rebuild stock.

When French rule ended, Prussia emerged as the dominant state of 19th century Germany. As its army expanded and each officer demanded several chargers, the equine population grew to supply demands.

Military might generated national pride. Influenced by Germany, many monarchs began wearing military uniforms in their public appearances. (Nearly all rulers were related to Germany's elite through blood or marriage). The cult of war remained an elite pursuit that tested the prowess of both man and horse.

Away from the battleground, improved roads led to the development of transportation systems. Teams of strong, fast-moving horses pulled coaches at speed.

In the late 18th and early 19th centuries, England's Yorkshire Coach horse excelled at pulling mail coaches. Resulting from crossing the Thoroughbred on the Cleveland Bay, it became known for its speed and endurance. By 1850, teams of Yorkshire Coach horses had shortened the driving time from London to York to one-quarter the previous record.

The Yorkshire Coach was a large, powerful horse. Most had long, deep bodies on comparatively short legs, with level quarters. The horse moved with free shoulder action, and its elegance matched stylish private carriages.

Breeders on the Continent imported Yorkshire Coach horses. German and Dutch breeders also imported English Hackneys and Norfolk Trotters, which they admired for action and speed at the trot.

With all studs relying on English stock as improvement blood, most European horses were similar across national boundaries. For example, Prussian stallions since 1819 traced to 74 foundation sires—62 of these were Thoroughbreds.

Even after the Industrial Revolution brought the railroad, horses continued to transport people and goods. The railway streamlined long-distance travel. For shorter journeys, horses pulled carriages and carried riders from village to village.

Agriculture remained a major economic force, and horses worked the fields. In the late 19th century, family-owned farms dominated the agriculture-based economy.

The state continued to support landowners. The agrarian elite exercised their political power by soliciting government support, and they contributed to nations' military expansion. Farmers adapted to trends determined by the state.

Although governments began to publish studbooks, they continued to keep the books open by introducing other bloodlines. The states refined the selection of the better potential stallions, now requiring proof of pedigree.

The horses that farmers produced, sired by both private and state-owned stallions, could toil in the fields in times of peace. When war broke out, the state enlisted stock to serve on the battlefield.

In the early 1900s, the peacetime German army included 100,000 horses. Animals served from eight to nine years in the artillery, nine to ten in cavalry. Prussia supplied most horses—in 1907 the army bought 13,400 unbroken horses to train at its depots.

Horses Adapt to the 20th Century

The conservative aura of the *ancien régime* persisted until 1914. The noble estate—the dukes, princes, marquis, counts, viscounts, barons, and knights—set the standards in all areas of life. Royalty elevated notables to the nobility, according to their worth. The system, like the studbooks of Europe's regional horse breeds, was both open and closed. Barriers were adjusted so that the desirable personage could rise in social position—or the prominent stallion was invited into a breed's registry.

At the beginning of the 20th century, people depended more on horses than at any other time. Equine populations peaked in all countries.

World War I involved a million horses on all fronts, primarily as transportation. (The romantic cavalry was outdated by powerful firearms). The war greatly reduced Europe's horses, and armies were reduced or disbanded at its end.

Motorized transport replaced coach horses

The European warmblood has successfully transformed into a sport horse. At the 18th century State Stud at Celle, Germany, modern horse vans transport the Hannoverian stallions.

in most regions, although farming in Germany and France was slow to mechanize. In the years between the two world wars, Germany's horse population numbered over three million animals.

With horses needed for agricultural work, breeders adjusted their breeding programs. Most breeds in the 1920s and 1930s concentrated on the heavier type of warmblood horse. In general, these horses had longer backs and shorter croups than the types influenced by the Thoroughbred.

Modern equestrian sports developed from the traditions of military horsemanship, when officers selected the best remounts and competed among themselves. (Many nations still call the three-day event the "military" event). The Olympic Games added equestrian events in 1912, and cavalry officers dominated the Games for the next three decades. The Germans excelled in show-jumping, while Swedish officers gained most honors in dressage.

Horses were again drafted for military service in the second World War. Despite the Germans' reputation for blitzkreig invasions, they still relied on horses for transportation. Over 800,000 German horses worked during the War.

Breed populations dwindled in peacetime, when motorized vehicles replaced working horses during the 1950s. With the revival of international equestrian competitions, sport saved the breeds in their third century. The old breeds became the new rage, and regions and nations regained pride in the horses that carried their names.

The European horses shaped the sports of show jumping, dressage, and the three-day event. Within each breed, breeders culled stock to meet the new demands of the market. Horses that failed to meet the new sport horse standards went to slaughter.

Breeders built on centuries of selective breeding to produce a European warmblood. The state and private studs introduced more Thoroughbred stallions. Open studbooks encouraged exchange of breeding stock, with the goal to produce an athletic horse rather than a purebred. (The Trakehner has remained an exception). By selecting horses from a broad field, breeders were able to change direction in a short time.

Politics divided West from East. Eastern countries built on the basis of long-established breeds and studs, yet horses in the DDR (East Germany), Poland, and the Soviet Union developed separately from their relations in the West.

By the 1960s, nations had recovered from the devastation of war and its aftermath. The average person had more money, and many became interested in the sport of riding. Breed associations actively promoted their breeds in the international marketplace.

West Germany regained distinction as the supreme equestrian nation. It was one of the first countries to operate a national equestrian center, and its civilian teams mastered international competitions.

By the 1970s, riding horse sales had greatly increased. In Germany, the number of private breeders tripled in only four years. Germany now has over 55,000 registered warmblood mares and 2000 stallions.

Major national and European shows offered prestigious awards. German breeds compete at the DLG (*Deutschen Landwirtschafts Gesellschaft*, or German Agricultural Society) bi-annual agricultural exposition. Winning the championship has become a great honor for the breeder, owner, and association.

Today the horses from Germany, France, the Netherlands, Belgium, Denmark, and Sweden have successfully evolved to meet the needs of the modern equestrian. With all breeds sharing a common ancestry and producing a lighter, "Thoroughbredy" animal, horses greatly resemble one another.

The diversity which separated breeds has vanished, and breeds have few unique characteristics. Only geographic boundaries and the historic brands distinguish these regional breeds. Germany produces a "German riding horse," similar to the "European riding horse."

National pride continues to support the various breed associations. Nations boast about their equine superstars, with jumpers earning the greatest economic significance. One World Champion in dressage, Marzog, has been claimed by three countries— Sweden (his sire), Germany (his dam), and Denmark (his birthplace).

Authority Hans Joachim Köhler said, "The improvements noted in recent years in riding and performance qualities of horses are primarily the result of healthy competitive thinking. The individual breeds are forced to uphold their trademark, and breeders want to be 'in' and to operate economically and profitably."

The competition remains friendly in spirit. Authorities freely exchange information, along with horses. Breeding areas invite judges from other countries to their shows and breed selections.

Recent political events have eliminated barriers between East and West. The reunification of Germany returns five states to the nation: Saxony, Saxony-Anhalt, Thuringia, Mecklenburg-Vorpommern, and Brandenburg. Horses from the DDR's state studs enter the marketplace and show arena, along with Russian and Polish horses.

The European Community also impacts the traditions of horse breeding. Briefly, this unification of 12 European nations will transform Europe into a single open market. By December, 1992, Europe will become the world's largest economic market, with a free exchange of goods. It will overshadow the economic power of the U.S., with three times the exports.

The Community aims to end Europe's tragic history of national rivalries and the resulting conflict, bloodshed, and destruction. The unified economy intends to replace the traditional "Fortress Europe" mindset, a protectionist attitude toward guarding domestic markets from competitors.

The Community will secure and expand agricultural markets. In this "megamarket," goods can move freely, with no physical, technical, legal, or tax barriers. Common agricultural policies eliminate borders and replace national laws regarding animals. Each country will recognize every breed, assuring fair competition.

The member nations have harmonized their practices by changing their existing regulations. By 1990, Germany had repealed its animal breeding law and removed the state from stallion licensing. France is also anticipating the expanded opportunities to market its sport horses.

Every nation described in this book is a member of the European Community, except Sweden.

The Hannoverian

O f the modern sport horse breeds, the Hannoverian has exerted the greatest influence on its neighbors. The horses of Hannover appear in the pedigrees of most German breeds and the Dutch, Danish, Belgian, and Swedish warmbloods.

Walking down the aisles of the barns of *Landgestüt* Celle, the State Stud, the visitor feels an awe and a reverence for the stallions in the ancient stalls. Each of the 250 priceless sires represents generations of the best horses of Europe. The horses of today are living results of the aims of aristocrats. For the admirer of the equestrian arts, the State Stud is like touring a great cathedral, or a living museum of European history.

Hannoverian History

The horses of Hannover have been bred for 400 years in the fertile lowlands between the Weser and Elbe rivers. Hannover was one of the nine Electorates of the Holy Roman Empire, along with Bavaria (Bayern), Württemberg, Hesse-Kassel, Hesse-Darmstadt, Holstein, Saxony (Sachsen), Brandenburg, and the Palatinate.

In the 15th and 16th centuries, dukes established their own studs, and farmers also bred horses for cavalry. Hannoverian horses served in regiments from local duchies, Sweden, and England.

The local stock was improved by crosses with Spanish and Neapolitan stallions. One stud, Memsen, was founded in 1653 to provide the house of Hannover with the famous Hannoverian creams. These horses were either white or the cream-colored "Isabella" horses, that later became famous in 19th-century England. They

The traditions of breeding the Hannoverian horse continue today. The Hengststation at Bargstedt features the H symbol formed from two horseheads. Wooden shapes of crossed horseheads decorate gables of barns and homes throughout Niedersachsen.

Today's Hannoverians fall into two types: The older type (top), looks strong, solid, and reliable in body and expression. The modern type (bottom), is lighter and more elegant..

pulled ceremonial coaches during coronations and other royal occasions.

George William, Duke of Celle and grandfather of George II, owned close to 400 horses of English breeding. The stables of the Hannoverian court held 600 horses.

The breed emerged with the Hannoverian succession in 1713, when Ludwig George, Elector of Hannover, assumed the crown of England as George I. The Hannoverian connection with England and free trade between the two nations increased the exchange of horses.

George II ascended to both thrones in 1727. A respected soldier like his father, he ruled both Hannover and England until 1760. As he favored his German homeland, he determined in 1732 to improve horse breeding to benefit his subjects and to develop Hannover's power against France's growing strength.

The Elector aimed to reduce the importation of horses for the military. He also planned to sell quality horses to the military market. In 1735 he issued a decree which established the *Landgestüt*, or State Stud, at Celle. The following year, 13 (some authorities say 14) selected stallions from Holstein arrived at the stallion depot. To breed better horses, the house of Hannover would provide quality stallions at low fees to the farmers' mares.

Known for his characteristic Hannoverian obstinacy, George embarked on horse-breeding partly out of envy. He yearned to match his fellow king and brother-in-law, Friedrich Wilhelm I of Prussia, who had established the royal stud Trakehnen in 1732.

Hannover, like other independent states of the 18th century, needed a strong breeding program to sustain its position. The tradition started in 1735 continues today, with farmers producing quality foals from their mares.

"The breeding aim was determined by the army and agriculture," described Ludwig Christmann, Deputy Breeding Manager of the

A Dash of Thoroughbred

Over the centuries, the Hannoverian type has been improved through infusions of "blood." Arabian blood originally improved all warmblood breeds, yet Thoroughbred lines have been the primary crosses used by Hannoverian and other European breeders.

The Thoroughbred (in German, *Vollblüter*) adds and reinforces desirable traits. In European breeding, sires like Adeptus, Dark Ronald, Furioso, Lucky Boy, Ladykiller, Perfectionist, and Angelo have enhanced the warmblood breeds. These outcrosses "refresh" the gene pool by contributing qualities that can be lost when breeding warmblood to warmblood.

Thoroughbreds' influence helps stabilize all warmblood breeds. The cross enhances performance by improving the quality of the walk, speed, and a long-striding gallop. Regular infusions of the fullblood help the warmblood counteract its tendency to heaviness, while it adds the "interior" qualities of durability, strong constitution, and sensitivity.

As a lighter horse, the Thoroughbred can introduce negative traits. Some horsemen criticize the cross for a lack of substance and a flatter trot. The breed's temperament can be a disadvantage or an asset, depending on amount of spark and brilliance the sport and the rider demand.

Breeders control the impact of the Thoroughbred outcrosses by careful selection and balancing the amount of blood through the generations. In choosing individuals, they select for substance, movement, and soundness.

Hannoverian officials buy or lease horses according to racetrack performance. A German Thoroughbred receives a GAG-mark, or a weight handicap in kilograms. Eight kilos is the minimum requirement, to prove soundness and speed.

Dr. Wilkens of the Hannoverian Verband explained, "To find the right Thoroughbred stallions for our breed is one of the important points for us, and why we are leading breeding managers."

He noted how jumper breeders need to maintain athletic ability while refining the offspring. Authorities study prospective stallions in free-jumping and aim to choose the right Thoroughbreds to match mares of jumping lines.

Officials realize that the results might not meet their expectations. "If you need a Thoroughbred stallion, you go on a risk," said Wilkens. "It's always a risk for the breeder, but we need this risk."

Breeders blend carefully and analyze results by evaluating the offspring. Wilkens said, "When the Thoroughbred stallion comes to a station, the next year we have a big group of foals. When you see the first group, you see how it runs—if he has the basic quality or not."

Hannoverian Verband. "History determined how the aim fluctuated, when the army needed lighter horses, and the farmer needed heavier horses."

The stud set up stallion stations in 1736, to disperse stallions close to centers of farming. Farmers' mares received priority, and each *Landbeschäler* (state stallion) was limited to 40-50 mares per season.

George contributed greatly to the success of his state stud. He established a breeding season from March 1 to June 30, and he donated stallions from his private stable in Herrenhausen. He brought several stallions from England and exported the Hannoverian Creams to the British court.

Through George's influence, the Hannoverian became closely linked with the English Thoroughbred. Both horses shared the ancestry of the three foundation sires, and Hannoverians descend from the same Eclipse, Herod, and Matchem lines that dominate the Thoroughbred.

In England, George issued an act in 1740 to control racing. The act regulated horses' ownership and required certificates of breeding.

Although farmers continued to breed most mares to privately owned stallions, by 1745 the state's 50 stallions covered 2000 mares. Holstein and Denmark supplied most replacement stallions.

The Hannoverian state stud operated 17 *Hengststations*, or stallion stations, by 1748. Breeders received certificates of breeding and foaling.

The Seven Years' War (1756-1763) affected the development of the breeding program, but the stations stood over 60 stallions by 1790. In the previous decade, the state exported over 10,000 horses annually. The breed was fashionable as a carriage horse.

According to an order dated 1768, the state stud started branding horses to designate their origin. The brand was most likely the tradi-

tional Lower Saxon emblem of two crossed horses' heads—still seen in the breed's brand and logo today.

The state assumed authority from the King to operate the stud in 1776. At that time the state stud owned about 100 stallions dispersed across its 50 stations. Breeds used to improve the Hannoverian included the English Thoroughbred, Cleveland Bay, Pommern (Pomerania, now in Poland), and Mecklenburg. French occupation forced evacuation and reduced the numbers of breeding stock, but in 1815 the state and the Duke of Brunswick were operating public and private studs at Harzburg-Büntheim.

Private stallions still sired most foals, which varied in quality. Two brothers, August and Friedrich von Spörcken, worked to rebuild the stud and direct the breed successfully through the 19th century.

These brothers served succeeding terms as *Landstallmeister* (Stud Director) at Celle from 1816 to 1866. The state established in 1844 a *Körordnung* (Licensing Order) to issue breeding licenses only to stallions which received official approval. This regulation reduced the number of lesser-quality private stallions and expanded Celle.

Throughout the breeding area, the state stallions stood at stallion stations. Each consisted of a small barn, housing from two to eight stallions through the breeding season. The manager maintained close relations with local farmers, serving as a liaison between the state and private enterprise. The *Landstallmeister* regularly toured stations in a coach pulled by Hannoverians.

Over its first 150 years, the breed produced two basic types. The robust horse was ideal for driving carriages and military vehicles. The riding type served as a cavalry horse. Breeders began to refine the type by increased use of Thoroughbred and halfbred stallions.

English Thoroughbreds and Hannoverian

A Dash of Thoroughbred (continued)

German breeders tend to emphasize the second, "backcross" generation—the result of the half-Thoroughbred offspring crossed with a predominantly warmblood parent. In such blending, the strength of the warmblood lines can overcome deficiencies of a particular individual.

Dr. Roland Ramsauer, formerly Breeding Director of the Oldenburg Verband and now with the International Sporthorse Registry, advised, "If the mare is light, cross again [the offspring] with the heavier type. If a medium horse on both sides, then he can cross with the warmblood side. Three-quarters. Thoroughbred is not too much, You cannot have too much Thoroughbred in your bloodlines, in my opinion. They get heavier by themselves."

Wilkens noted, "From the point of refining, if there's a weak point in one generation, it's not a problem to breed with this mare again. It will be better in the next generation, because the basic quality is quite good."

Mentioning the cross of the Anglo-Arab, Matcho, Wilkens said, "This is a form of refinement we must do. Perhaps the top combination is this next generation." He added that judges recognize the pedigree when evaluating the first-generation offspring. In order to support the introduction of new lines, they may apply different standards.

Some horsemen advise against adding too much refinement blood. They do not want to see the warmblood lose its characteristics.

Elizabeth Searle, a member of the Dutch warmblood's jury, noted, "It has to be well-thought out with the mare. With more Thoroughbred on finer Dutch stallions, they lose the bone and the movement."

Ludwig Christmann said, "The breeding aim is not to produce Thoroughbred horses with a Hannoverian pedigree. We need all the different types. If 90 percent of our mares looked only like the Matcho daughters, we'd know we're wrong."

All breeding areas stress the more elegant riding horse rather than the large, heavy horse that some riders term "a moose." This three-year-old States' Premium mare (Abajo xx— Garibaldi II) shows an excellent walk.

halfbreds raced at Celle from 1838-1863, but wise breeders recognized that the Thoroughbred should not dominate the bloodlines. They realized that the Thoroughbred influence could improve the breed by adding elegance to shoulder, withers, croup, and length of leg. However, they determined to preserve the horse's expression and hardy character through careful, controlled introduction of such "improvement" lines. By 1840, about one-third of the state stallions were Thoroughbred, and the rest contained at least one-quarter Thoroughbred blood. Yorkshire Coach horses also contributed to the breed's heavier type.

Prussia absorbed the Kingdom of Hannover in 1866, and Prussian Stud Authorities assumed management of the province's 220 registered stallions. Duke Georg von Lehndorff served as *Oberlandstallmeister*, overseeing all Prussian studs.

During Celle *Landstallmeister* W. H. Grabensee's administration (1892-1915), the aim was to breed a strong horse that reflected the needs of the region: "Weight with nobility." The number of registered stallions was about 370, with rules intensified in 1894. Approved stallions had to meet the requirements of conformation and an established pedigree.

In 1867 breeders formed the first Hannoverian breed society, the *Verein zur Förderung der Hannoverschen Landespferdezucht*. Breeders had earlier organized into local groups, representing areas such as Lüneburg (1854) and Verden (1855).

To help consolidate the breed, a *Stutbuch* (studbook) was founded in 1888. This mare register, overseen by the Chamber of Agriculture, noted which horses bred on and graded the quality of the offspring. State stallions covered 34,000 mares in the last decades of the 19th century,

The breeding aim has changed over the centuries. At the end of the 19th century, General Freiherr von Troschke defined it, "a suitable

cavalry as well as artillery horse with straight, ground-covering gaits. Horses used on the farm must be able to pull a plow making a furrow at least 30 cm deep."

After the second World War, the breeding aim had changed to, "a strong warmblood horse, able to do all kinds of work on the farm but possessing enough blood, zest, and quality gaits to be usable as a riding and carriage horse." Hannoverians became known as a modern riding horse, blending the look of a Thoroughbred with the character, movement, and temperament of the warmblood of the pre-war years.

Shortly afterward, the aim was altered to read, "a noble, strong warmblood horse equally well suited as a riding horse as for work on the farm."

The state added a facility in Westercelle in 1907, to house the growing numbers of stallions. By 1920, it also established a stallion-raising center at Hunnesrück. The state stud could purchase colts as potential stallions, rather than compete with foreign buyers in Mecklenburg and Pommern. With close to 600 stallions in 1925, the state opened another regional stud in Osnabrück-Eversburg.

The breed society evolved into the *Verband hannoverscher Warmblutzüchter* in 1922. In 1928, the state started stallion testing at its Westercelle location. Breeders also held annual mare shows, which graded the quality of young mares and rewarded excellent breeding choices.

Like other German breeds, the Hannoverian lost its remount market after the first World War. The national socialist regime demanded horses for Germany's army, and the Third Reich issued farm production regulations requiring Hannover and East Prussia to breed riding horses again.

Politics diminished the breed during the second World War. Many Hannoverians died during the hostilities, especially on the arduous Russian front. Harsh elements and lack of feed

Celle Today

Landgestüt Celle complements the Hannoverian horse. Like the breed, this stud combines the old, established regime with the advantages of modern technology.

Celle encompasses 15 acres in the center of Hannover's medieval town, Celle. The river Fusen divides the complex of stately buildings.

The oldest building dates from 1713. This ancient stable has been modernized into a medical laboratory and AI facility. Examination chutes have replaced the walls of the original tie stalls.

Several barns house all the state stallions through the summer and fall. Many tie stalls have been modernized into boxes. Stallions are grouped by their breeding or training. One newer barn of only box stalls houses the Thoroughbred stallions; another holds stallions trained in dressage.

The state has added electricity and plumbing to the 18th and 19th century buildings, providing conveniences like heat lamps and automatic waterers. Yet a sharp contrast remains, as staff still sweep the stalls and aisles with old-fashioned brooms, fabricated from bundles of bound twigs.

Stallions are bedded deep with straw on the stalls' brick floors. In tie stalls, horses are tied with short straps to brass tie rings at the manger.

All stallions' stalls are labelled with wooden plaques. These stall markers list the horse's name, sire, dam's sire and grandsire, *Züchter* (breeder), *Aufzüchter*, and date of birth. The marker accompanies the horse when it moves from Celle to its stallion station.

The facility has small turn-out paddocks

The Grabenseestall at Celle.

caused heavy losses.

Most of Hannover became absorbed into the new state Niedersachsen (Lower Saxony) in 1946. Part of the province went into the DDR (East Germany). The state studs at Osnabrück and Harzburg were closed in 1960 and 1961, with all stallions consolidated at Celle. In 1960 only 179 stallions covered 4240 mares.

Even though mechanization replaced the Hannoverian's role on the farm, the breed had excelled in the new equestrian sports. Hannoverians won medals in the first equestrian events in the modern Olympics, and they also performed in European and World Championships.

Wise breeders focused on the new market. The cooperative efforts of the state and the Verband have established the Hannoverian as an outstanding sport horse. With a worldwide breeding population nearing 20,000 mares and stallions, the Hannoverian boasts the largest numbers of any warmblood breed.

The 1988-89 International Equestrian Yearbook, *L'Annee Hippique*, named the Hannoverian as the top sport horse. Evaluating 1988's six major competitions by the horses' origins, the Yearbook scored horses of Hannoverian breeding first. Dutch horses were second, and Westfalens third.

An all-time champion money-winner, Deister by Diskant, was one of the breed's outstanding jumpers. Deister was three times European Champion.

Ferdl by Ferdinand was on the German team that won the gold medal in the 1960 Olympics. Simona by Weingeist was on the gold medal-winning team in 1972, and won the World Championship in 1974. Warwick Rex won the gold medal in the 1976 Olympics.

Gladstone by Götz won the 1979 World Cup and the gold in the 1980 Alternate Olympics. Aramis by Argentan and The Natural by Diskus were both World Cup winners. The Natural was also a member of the gold-medal team at

the 1986 World Championships.

Mr. T by Wohlan won the World Championship in 1986. Walzerkönig by Watzmann won the individual gold medal in the 1988 Olympic Games. Other jumping stars include Special Envoy by Wettstreit and Dollar Girl by Dynamo.

In dressage, Draufgänger won the gold medal in the 1928 Olympics. Doublette by Duellant won DM 100,000 during her career in the 1950s. This mare won a record 164 Grands Prix in dressage.

Asbach by Anilin won the bronze medal in the 1960 Olympics. In 1968's Games, Dux by Duellant won the individual bronze and was on the German team which won the gold medal. Dux also placed third individually in the 1966 World Championships and was on Germany's gold-medal team.

Liostro by Der Löwe and Mehmed by Ferdinand helped win the dressage gold medal at the 1972 Olympics, and Mehmed was World Champion in 1974. Mehmed took the bronze at the 1976 Olympics, while Woyczek by Wunsch II won the gold.

In 1978, Slibovitz by Servus was second in the World Championships and on the gold-medal team. Dynasty by Darling was on Canada's team at the 1988 Olympics, which won the bronze medal. Some Hannoverian dressage champions in North America include Willie the Great by Werther, Federlicht by Federgeist xx, Gifted by Garibaldi II, Funny Boy by Furioso II, and Grundstein by Graphit.

Hannoverians also win in three-day eventing. At the 1952 and 1956 Olympics, three Hannoverians were on the teams which won silver medals. Sherry and Shamrock, both sired by Thoroughbreds, helped win the gold medal for Germany's team in the 1988 Olympics. Sundance Kid placed seventh in the 1990 World Championships.

Hannoverians have contributed to the development of breeds of surrounding regions and nations. The pedigrees of Oldenburg, Westfalen, Dutch, Belgian, and Danish warmbloods show heavy infusion of Hannoverian lines. Hannoverians helped establish the Danish, Belgian, and Dutch warmbloods.

Hannoverian Characteristics

Hannoverian authority Hermann Friedlaender said, "The whole breeding goal is oriented in the riding horse direction." A recent breeding aim was "a correctly built, noble, versatile warmblood horse, capable of superior performance under saddle, with big ground covering, yet light and elastic gaits, good temperament and an honest character." The Verband's newest breeding aim describes, "a noble, big-framed and correct warmblood horse with good rideability. A horse which, on the basis of its natural abilities, its temperament and charac-ter, is suitable as a performance horse as well as a pleasure horse."

The variety of types developed in Hannover continue today, with individual breeders producing the type of horse they prefer. As both an old and a new breed, horses display the varied characteristics of their multiple ancestors.

In general, the Hannoverian typifies the rectangular appearance desirable in the modern sport horse. Horses stand from 16 to 17.2 hands. All have good bone and muscle in proportion to their size.

The older types are majestic, heavy, and powerful, but well-balanced with springy, straight movements. Some have a large, plain head, "noble" in the classic sense, yet the poll and jaw should be light so the horse can bend its neck.

Older foundation types often tend to have

shorter necks and pasterns, with a straighter shoulder, low wither, and more compact body with a thicker flank and flatter croup. Some show a long loin and shorter croup.

These Hannoverians have traditionally been the best jumpers. They display temperament, rideability, and willingness to work.

The modern type is lighter and more elegant. These horses appeal to the current market, with their "Thoroughbredy" appearance. Contemporary riders prefer the modern horse to what some call the old-fashioned "Thudmonster—" although the heavier Hannoverians generally have a quieter temperament.

Chestnut is a predominant color in the breed. The introduction of more black and bay horses is changing the dominant colors. Grays are not popular with German breeders.

The Verband acknowledges the need for the variety of types, and they encourage the differences. "People have different demands in horses," explained Christmann. "The Verband is in the position where we can provide horses for different purposes. We need the older, more solid, well-muscled type. But we don't only want to breed that type. Compared to other breeds, we're not trying for a homogeneous type."

Whichever type the horse represents, movement is an important factor. The horse shows great freedom of the shoulder, and thrust with the hindquarters. The rider feels the Hannoverian's power and size, as the horse moves with big, springy movements with *Schwung*. In the trot, the current style is for a rounder movement, with a higher knee action and still a reaching, forward stride.

Among some riders, the Hannoverian still has a reputation for being heavy in its movements. They complain that they need to use a very strong seat and leg.

The breed's temperament is calm, amenable, and level-headed. Although some equestrians categorize the Hannoverian as "dull," individuals vary in their personalities.

Hannoverian Breeding

Tradition governs the breeding of the Hannoverian. Central to the system are the farmers of Niedersachsen who own the 15,000 mares.

These wealthy, independent farmers have bred horses for generations. Fathers passed on to their sons their knowledge of the family's mares.

Breeding horses is a sideline. Farmers raise cattle and pigs for greater profit, yet the prestige of producing quality foals makes breeding a source of pride. Breeders strive to contribute to the betterment of the breed, beyond individual accomplishment.

Christmann said, "The farmers still breed today, owning from one to three mares. The breed is in the hands of the small breeder."

The farmers' prized mares represent a link with the past, and they involve the breeder with a sense of history. Breeding horses is a passion, a pursuit of excellence. U.S. breeder Dr. Richard von Buedingen said, "In Northern Germany, they talk horse pedigrees at bars, not sports scores. These farmers are the salt of the earth. Their mares' bloodlines have been in the same family for generations, and their family has been there since 1300."

Mare owners may choose from state stallions or privately owned Hannoverian sires, *Privatbeschäler*. They trailer mares to the local stallion station for breeding and veterinary examinations. The state stallions are based at the 50 breeding stations from February to July.

With state stallions representing the best bloodlines, the state maintains the breed's quality. To encourage breeding, fees continue to be very reasonable. The standard fee is DM 580.

U.S. breeder Judy Williams explained, "The breeders pay their taxes, and they 'own' those stallions. The state supports the stud, so they own that horse at their station."

The stallions owned by private breeders are fewer in number. In order to compete for breedings, privately owned stallions must also be priced comparably.

Tradition dictates the care of breeding stock. Mares are not used as riding horses, but serve as broodmares most of their lives. Mares and foals live outside spring and summer, and in barns during the winter.

Farmers grow grass hay to feed to horses in the winter. From November to April, the old-style breeders keep horses indoors, with occasional turnout in exercise paddocks. Weanlings and yearlings live in groups, in large stalls. Many caretakers rely on the traditional method of deep bedding stalls, in thick layers of straw.

Christmann noted a recent trend, of the decrease in farm-bred horses, the traditional source of outstanding performance animals. "The number of farms is declining, and many give up breeding horses for cattle. Young farmers are told that breeding horses isn't economical, and families lack time to care for horses. The farmer's knowledge is lost in one generation."

In previous centuries, farmers raised foals as a cash crop. If they dedicated their pastures to cattle, they sold foals to landowners with sufficient pastureland to raise young horses inexpensively.

When East Germany absorbed the eastern pasturelands after 1945, equestrian entrepreneurs established a system of *Aufzüchters*, or raisers. These horsemen assumed the task of buying and raising young stallions. Some were refugee farmers from the eastern areas of Mecklenburg and Pommern.

The *Aufzüchter* system thrives in modern Germany. Unlike the typical farmer, the *Aufzüchter* specializes in raising horses. Dressage trainer Jan Ebeling said, "They usually have large farms with their own fields where they can turn the horses out. They have a large

number of horses—20 to 100—that live outside all summer day and night. In the fall they keep them in big stalls, three or four horses, sometimes more."

These equestrians have established business and social relationships with their suppliers, the local farmers. In Germany's close-knit society of horsemen, the *Aufzüchter* knows the region's breeders and bloodlines. He has the first rights to purchase many of the superior foals, even before birth.

U.S. Holsteiner breeder Elizabeth McElvain said, "The *Aufzüchter* knows where the best horses are. He knows what he wants. It's so stable there. It's not like Americans who move around. These people have lived in the same farmhouse for 400 years."

To prepare stallion prospects for the *Körung* at 2 1/2 years old, the *Aufzüchter* buys from 10 to 15 colts. This totals from 700 to 800 annually in Niedersachsen. The state stud also buys approximately 60 colts to raise at its *Hengstaufzuchtgestüt* (Stallion Rearing Center), Hunnesrück.

The system benefits the farmer, who can continue to breed foals for a high profit margin. It also provides a lucrative income for the *Aufzüchter*, who raises foals at minimum expense for sizeable profits.

The *Aufzüchter* also contributes to the sport. Dr. Thomas Nissen of the Holsteiner Verband said, "If you buy 10 colts, one or two could be good stallions. The other eight, you sell as sport horses. So you make sport horses as well as stallions."

Farmers belong to breeding clubs associated with the local stallion stations. Clubs are affiliated with district societies which are part of the 8500-member Verband hannoverscher Warmblutzüchter.

To promote the breed, the private Verband cooperates with the Chamber of Agriculture. The relationship between the state and the

Verband has been intertwined. The Verband maintains a separate office and auction facility, the Niedersachsenhalle, in Verden, yet the Chamber of Agriculture controls the Verband. The state oversees the studbook and the operation of Celle, the Stallion Training Center, and Stallion Rearing Center.

The Verband and the breeders protect the quality of the breed. This society sets the pace, according to the wishes of its members, the mare owners. It balances the breeders' demands with the standards set by tradition and the society's goals. Generally, the Verband is conservative in its decisions.

Celle's present *Landstallmeister*, Dr. Burchard Bade, works with the breeders to assign excellent stallions throughout the breeding area. The stallion's qualities complement the local mare base. Stallions generally remain at one station for several years.

The state influences the breed's future by its placements. For the last century, state involvement has helped to consolidate the breed, through linebreeding of prepotent stallions. Horses of these lines perpetuate their superior athletic qualities.

For example, the stallion Grande was placed in a station where his dam's sire Duellant had stood. The resulting linebreeding retained Duellant's genetic merit.

The Verband supports the *Landstallmeister's* assignments by recommending to breeders which type of stallion will cross best with particular mares. Breeders usually focus on either the heavier or lighter type horse, depending on their mares' lines. "In breeding, consider the bloodlines and think how to match the stallion line to the mare line," advised Christmann.

Through the centuries, regions have established reputations for particular types of horses, depending on the pasture land itself, agrarian society, and qualities of stallions over the decades. In general, the horse reflects the type of

soil of its region. Areas of heavier soil produce heavier horses (generally jumper lines), and lighter soil produces lighter horses (usually dressage lines).

For example, the Lüneburg, Verden, and Hoya areas have traditionally boasted of well-bred mares. Verden was the only area where Hannoverians were bred for racing. Cuxhaven and Badbergen were known for heavier horses, while Splietau and Oberndorf have produced numbers of jumpers.

Dr. Jochen Wilkens, Managing Director of the Verband, noted how nutrition affected mares in the Freiburg area: "It seems at Freiburg, where we have good feed conditions, our mares become heavier and heavier. So we needed to bring in Thoroughbred, a bit of Trakehner and Anglo-Arabian, but especially Thoroughbreds."

Christmann noted a change in the regional types. "It used to be that you could tell a horse's origin from its pedigree. Mares in an area *were* similar—not so much anymore."

Today the experienced breeders know the advantages and disadvantages of every stallion available. They have studied each horse's ancestry and offspring, and crave access to stallions beyond those assigned to the local station.

In the assignments of new stallions, breeders and the state stud negotiate which horses go where. Christmann related the first year of the stallion, Duellant: "The stallion station at Landesburg wanted the winner of the stallion licensing. They could only get the winner if they would take Duellant. Nobody now remembers the name of that other stallion—during his time, Duellant was the most famous producer of dressage horses in Germany."

The state does set a limit of 200 mares per stallion each season. About five get that many, with the popular young sire, Weltmeyer, receiving 500 applications in his first year at stud. Most stallions average 50 mares.

The state's stallion stations are located in the

Gralsburga

Foaled in 1981, Gralsburga is owned by Pat Limage of Bae Prid Farm, Gainesville, Virginia. The dark bay mare, standing just under 16.2, was sired by Gralsritter by Grande out of a Diplomat mare.

Limage was looking for a young stallion when she purchased Gralsburga. "She was imported as a yearling by Alex Horn of Canada. I went to see a colt, and I saw her in the broodmare band. I fell in love with her."

This mare typifies the Hannoverian's sport horse qualities. Limage noted, "She's a very nice mover, and her disposition, temperament, and desire to learn are superb. We broke her as a five-year-old, and she walked off like a broke horse. She has a wonderful attitude."

As a broodmare, Gralsburga has earned her Elite Mare status with the American Hanoverian Society. She has produced three sons, with her 1991 colt sired by Lanthan.

"She's the older type mare," said

Gralsburga and 1991 foal.

Limage. "She's full-bodied and large-boned, but she has a very nice head. That was what I was looking for, for a mare in this country. I feel we need a little stronger mare."

community, with some in residential or commercial neighborhoods. Stations like Oberndorf, Ihlienworth, and Landesbrück house several stallions in barns with box stalls facing an inside aisle. A large room serves as the breeding shed in stations using natural cover. In facilities breeding by fresh semen, a room contains chutes for artificial insemination.

Stallions are exercised in a longeing ring adjacent to the barn. After the breeding season,

they return to the central facility at Celle for a break during the summer months.

The Verband industriously assists its members in the marketing of horses. Since 1949 Verden has hosted auction sales to showcase the breed. A series of auctions attract potential buyers from around the world. The Verband also acts as a sales agent, directing shoppers to farms.

Following the state's lead, the Verband's

The state stallion, Cavalier (Cardinal xx—Ferdinand), shows the caliber desired in today's sport horse.

members have gradually accepted modern technology. Artificial insemination, initiated in 1986, will replace natural cover. All stallions are blood-typed.

AI has made it possible for popular stallions to breed large numbers of mares. It has also improved the conception rate to an average 75 to 80 percent. The stallion Weltmeyer bred 200 mares in 1989, with 92 percent in foal.

Stallions are retained in the state stud according to their potential and their individual quality. Because officials know each horse's progenitors, they consider the horse's contributions to the breed.

Dressage trainer Uli Schmitz explained, "European breeders very often think that some bloodlines carry over into the second and third generation. It's not necessarily the first offspring, but it comes out in the second or third generation."

Through the Verband the state responds to mare owners' preferences. The state moves stallions among stations or removes them from the stud. If a line has many good representatives, or

the breeders fail to utilize a stallion, the state could choose to sell it.

"Mostly a stallion goes to a station where the lines traditionally match," explained Christmann. "But you can't say the stallion wouldn't match with other mares as well. You can only say they he didn't match with the mares at *that* place."

Hannoverian officials realize that some stallions might not produce well early in their careers. Because it could take years for a horse to establish itself as a valuable progenitor, authorities try to allow stallions ample time to produce.

For example, the stallion Gotthard was not popular with breeders at his station for several years. Only later in his life did his offspring make him famous. Of his sons, most were foaled after their sire's twentieth year of covering mares.

Christmann said, "Good stallions are made by the number of mares they get. It takes a long time—you only know when the oldest offspring are 10 years old." He noted that the Hannoverian breeders tend to prefer the younger stallions.

The structure of the Hannoverian breeding program, the largest in Germany, is duplicated throughout other German breeding areas. (Not all states maintain a state stud). The German Ministry of Agriculture maintains overall control of the nation's horse breeding.

Hannoverian Bloodlines

The art and science of selective breeding has defined the modern Hannoverian. As a science, the breed's strict breeding practices, proven bloodlines, and meticulous documentation have placed the Hannoverian at the forefront of European warmbloods.

U.S. breeder Dr. Richard von Buedingen said, "The Hannoverian horse is probably the leading example of large animal eugenics in the world. You can go back 200 years to see all its characteristics in the studbooks. They list all the traits, and they carefully keep track of the animals' performance characteristics. They could come closer to breeding type, more than anyone else."

Another U.S. breeder, Douglas Mankovich, agreed. "Some horses at Celle are producers of dressage horses; some are producers of jumping horses. You can follow the pedigrees and see that a stallion has produced X number of successful jumpers, on the basis of the winnings of the offspring. You get a very good idea that when you cross that one with certain bloodlines in your mare, you have a potentially better-than-even chance that you will produce a good jumper or a good dressage horse."

To meet market demands, breeders have changed the Hannoverian type to meet new sport horse needs. They added other lines—Holsteiner, Thoroughbred, Trakehner, Anglo-Arabian, and Arabian—to refine and consolidate the breed. Few contemporary horses are of "pure" Hannoverian breeding.

Authority Hans Joachim Köhler noted, "All warmblood breeds used for producing…riding and performance horses are not able to maintain their nobility, heartiness, and good riding points without continuous additions, for improvement purposes, of Thoroughbred and Trakehner blood."

He also explained the term, improving: "It is not only pointed at the nobility and beauty of the head, but encompasses the quality of the whole unusual domestic animal which should be maintained in its nobility or made more noble if necessary. For instance, the formation of the shoulder and withers which is so important in the riding sport would soon wither away without adding more blood."

Breeders usually introduce the cross through the stallion. Breeding a finer quality stallion with a strong, well-bred broodmare, they strive to produce a superior sport horse.

The outcrosses with refinement sires have had to blend with the breed to upgrade particular characteristics. Limited by studbook regulations, the breed currently accepts stallions from the Thoroughbred, Anglo-Arab, Arabian, Trakehner, and Anglo-Norman studbooks.

To distinguish their origin as outcross sires or dams, the horses' breeds are noted on pedigrees:

Thoroughbred	xx
Anglo-Arab	x
Arabian	ox

Other European breeds are noted in parentheses:

Holsteiner	(Holst.)
Trakehner	(Trak.)
Westfalen	(West.)
Oldenburg	(Old.)
Anglo-Norman	(A-N)

Breeders consider which type to produce. They determine when to cross back to the older type, or refine with the more modern type. As advisors, the Verband's authorities assist breeders in deciding which sport they will produce: jumping or dressage. Some people consider the Hannoverian an all-around performer, but certain lines are known for particular disciplines. Hannoverians have long established a tradition in the jumping arena, and recently breeders have concentrated on lines to improve the jumper's marketability.

Breeders choose a stallion to match their mares' pedigrees. Christmann counselled, "If the mare is of a jumping line, the breeder should choose a stallion from a jumping line. He should also consider type and rideability, because you should not breed only for performance. You want a jumping horse that should become attractive and easy and comfortable to ride."

Hannoverians are grouped by stallion lines, with horses named after the initial of the sire. Duplicate names are allowed—Roman numerals distinguish stallions with the same name.

Horses are described by the sire line, often carried to the third generation. For example, a horse by Wendekreis out of a Bolero mare, herself out of a Grande mare, would be known as Wendekreis—Bolero—Grande.

Stallion lines endure by developing strong characteristics. Lines help group horses into types and ancestry, but Christmann cautioned against over-generalization. "The lines' characteristics change very much through the years. Each stallion has his own characteristics, and so does the mother line. You should always consider the individual characteristics of stallion and mare, no matter what the line.

World Cup I is the heavier, older type of Hannoverian stallion.

"The stallion is the most important step to make progress in breeding. The influence of the individual stallion on the progress is much higher than the mare. Don't put too much emphasis on the pedigree, if there is not much influence from a distant generation."

Famous stallions established and consolidated their lines, known in general for certain traits of conformation and performance. Lines are constantly in transition, as breeders develop the breed depending on current conditions.

A line may become prevalent when one or more sires gain popularity. Many sons and daughters increase the sire's dominance. Or, a line may add few sires and dams to the breed, and a sire's influence gradually dissipates.

Some sires establish reputations for high heritability (consistently passing their characteristics to a large percentage of their offspring). A prepotent sire can be known primarily for his performance horses, which implies that he gives good riding qualities to his offspring. He might sire more performers than breeding stock who can perpetuate his line. For instance, Watzmann, sire of the jumper Walzerkönig, was second in the list of Germany's top money-winning sires in 1989, with 155 offspring competing.

"Every stallion has the potential to produce good horses," noted Christmann. One may sire many, to carry on his line. Another could sire only one or two outstanding horses in his career. The jumpers Deister and Mr. T are examples of such offspring.

Other stallions may pass characteristics on to the succeeding generations, when their sons and daughters cross with complementary lines. For example, the sire Werther (Wendekreis-Marcio xx) shows the influence of his dam's line more than his sire. Wendekreis exemplifies a famous sire whose sons have not eclipsed their sire's reputation. Yet the following generation can outproduce the previous horses, with greatness occasionally skipping the son in favor of the grandson—and incorporating the influence of the dam's line.

Authorities rely on documented facts about stallions. They describe individuals and lines with candor. They discuss a stallion's strong points and faults in terms of his individual excellence and how he passes on his characteristics. Such honest, objective descriptions benefit the breed as a whole. These horsemen admit their continual efforts in search of the perfect sport horse.

Lines fall into old and new lines (introduced after World War II). Because the Hannoverian has influenced so many other European breeds, this chapter discusses important lines. All lines incorporate outside blood, of stallions imported into the breed from other areas or studbooks. Dates indicate the years the horse stood at stud in the Hannoverian breeding area.

Old Lines

In the latter half of the 19th century, four stallions stamped the breed: Zernebog and Jellachich (both from Pommern), and Norfolk and Flick. Up to 1914, two-thirds of the Hannoverians traced to Flick or the Thoroughbred, Adeptus xx. Many Hannoverians were inbred to these foundation horses, although later infusions of outside blood have replaced their influence. *Landstallmeister* Grabensee introduced horses from other Prussian studs to offset the effects of inbreeding.

The A-line. Adeptus xx (1884-1904) added blood to maintain courage and action. He influenced the breed through his descendant Agram (1942-1962). Agram sired jumpers more than breeding stock. On his dam's side, Agram traces back to Amurath I, which Grabensee brought to Celle from Austria as an improvement stallion in 1902.

Another branch has bred on through Eindruck II (1955-1972). ("E" names were added

to the A-line in the 1950s). His son Einblick (1973-), more refined that his old-type sire, sired good performance horses.

Eisenherz I (1972-1990) had a great influence on the A-line, producing many sons and daughters. His son Eiger I (1979-) is known as a consistent producer and one of the best state stallions today.

The F-line. This line originated with the foundation stallion Zernebog (1849-1871). This part-Thoroughbred founded the F-line through his son Flick (1865-1887) and great-grandson Fling (1913-1922).

Fling's sons Feiner Kerl and Flavius have continued the line through many outstanding performers. Feiner Kerl (1922-1943) sired jumpers, and his great-grandson Ferdinand (1944-1967) became famous as one of the best producers of jumpers in the world. His offspring were known for the courage and athletic ability which he contributed.

Ferdinand's three most influential sons were Winnetou, Wedekind, and Wendekreis. Wendekreis (1971-) has sired many stallions who continue to pass on the dressage and jumping abilities of the F-line, including Werther and Wendepunkt.

The Wendekreis grandson Wanderer (1984-) is one of Hannover's most popular stallions. He produces jumpers, and his outstanding son, Wanderbursch II, represents the athletic, older type Hannoverian.

Another descendant of Feiner Kerl is the jumper sire, Watzmann (1972-). Also a heavier type, he produces riding horses and requires refinement on the dam's side. His best-known son, Walzerkönig, is out of such a mare by the sire Absatz.

Flavius (1918-1935), son of Fling, founded another branch of the F-line. From this sire has come Woermann, sire of Wenzel I, Wenzel II, and World Cup I.

A States' Premium Mare, Grandizza (Grande—Ladykiller xx)

Woermann (1975-1988) currently has a major influence on the breed as a dressage producer. His sons breed on, although they are of different types. Wenzel I produces very good conformation and dressage horses; World Cup I is known for powerful movers and jumpers. Wenzel I (1980-) is more refined, while World Cup I (1981-) crosses best with mares of Thoroughbred blood. World Cup sired Weltmeyer (1988-) out of an Absatz mare.

Due to the spread of the F-line, the Verband's Board of Directors have decided to divide it into two parts. Horses tracing to Feiner Kerl will resume the initial F. The descendants of Flavius will retain the initial W.

The D-Line. Devil's Own xx (1894-1906) founded this line through his descendant Detektiv (1926-1943). From this line came the jumper Deister, and the renowned sire, Duellant (1946-1965).

Duellant produced many sons and outstanding dressage horses. Although neither of his influential sons, Duft I (1961-1981) and Duft II (1962-), resembled their sire, they carried on the D-Line. Duft II's son Darling sired the Canadian dressage star, Dynasty, and Duerkheim sired two sons who stand in the United States: Diamont and Domingo.

The D-line has a jumping part, represented by the stallions Diskus (1974-1986) and Don Carlos (1966-1980). Diskus sired The Natural. Don Carlos is known for siring attractive performers, like the German jumper Diablo and the sires Dynamo, Drosselklang I, and Drosselklang II.

The G-line. Currently the most successful line, the Thoroughbred stallion Goldschaum xx from Mecklenburg founded the "G" horses. The stallion Goldfisch II (1939-1958) produced its two primary names.

Grande (1962-1987) by the Goldfisch son Graf is described as a phenomenon. Christmann noted, "Grande produced such good horses. When you look at his pedigree, on the sire's side he has the jumping part—Graf by Goldfisch II. On the mother's side he's Duellant, a very big dressage influence.

"His production is versatile—excellent dressage horses and jumping horses as well. His offspring want to work, and they have a lot of suspension."

Siring 40 approved sons, some of Grande's offspring include the son Graphit (1968-1987), sire of the U.S. horses, Grundstein I and Grand Canyon (Old.). Grennus (1978-) is one of the top jumping sires in Germany, along with Landgraf I (Holst.) and Pilot (West.)

Grande's line continues to dominate the sport of dressage in Germany. His son Garibaldi II (1978-1988) also sired excellent jumpers and dressage horses, including the U. S. champion, Gifted.

The Grande grandson Grenadier (1978-) produces dressage horses such as Golfstrom, on the 1990 German team at the World Championships.

Another Goldfisch II son, Gotthard (1953-1978), also sired many famous jumpers and stallions in the state stud. His dam was sired by Amateur I, a renowned sire of broodmares and performance horses. Gotthard produced athletic types rather than horses with attractive conformation and movement.

With over 20 approved sons, the Gotthard line has bred on to produce contemporary sires. His son Gardestern (1978-83) sired Glückstern and Gimpel, while Gardeoffizier (1979-) sired Glockenklang (1986-).

Rather than import stock from England, *Landstallmeister* Grabensee brought in sires from Trakehnen, Beberbeck, and Graditz. Of the 300 stallions at Celle in 1911, 19 were Trakehners, 8 Thoroughbreds, and 1 Arabian. Thoroughbred sons and grandsons totalled 40, and Trakehner sons and grandsons over 100. Horses from this improvement period influenced the breed in succeeding generations, with some observers considering their effect a reconstruction of the breed.

New Lines

These lines were founded after World War II, based on stallions brought to Hannover from other breeds. Two Trakehners, refugees from East Prussia, helped improve the modern Hannoverian.

After the war, author Hans Joachim Köhler recalled that *Landstallmeister* Korndoff considered two Celle stallions as prototypes for the future Hannoverian: Goldfisch II and the Trakehner, Semper Idem.

Semper Idem (1946-1951) sired Senator (1954-1973), who added several stallions to the state stud. In 1954, breeders at first resisted the refined son of Semper Idem. "He didn't breed very much his first year," said Christmann.

"The breeders didn't want such light types. There were only seven foals born in that first year. Six of those foals became stallions in the state studs—five to Celle and one to Warendorf."

This horse illustrates the gradual transition through the cross with improvement lines. Generally the generation after the outcross produces horses which impact upon the breed. By tradition, the new blood is "diluted" by the familiar Hannoverian lines.

Senator's son Sender (1959-1978) and Sender's son Servus (1965-) established the Semper Idem line. Servus sired the dressage champion, Slibovitz.

Another influential Trakehner was Abglanz (1946-1964). "His line almost created a new Hannoverian after World War II," said Christmann. "If he hadn't come, the Hannoverian would look much different. Horses of this line stamp their type more than any other

The state stallion, Wanderer.

line...Abglanz was very responsible for the change in type from the farm horse to the modern riding horse."

Köhler noted, "The Trakehner sires became a very high influence since the Arabian and English Thoroughbred intake had already been consolidated within the noble Trakehner horse. The Trakehner Abglanz now carries the most important sire line in Hannover. He is incomparable in his type."

Absatz (1964-1982) was Abglanz' most famous son, who stamped his type on generations to come. The line is known for producing typy horses with good heads, necks, and movement.

The Absatz son Argentan (1971-) also gives his offspring the Abglanz head and neck. His son Aramis competed in the 1976 Olympics, and his son Airport is a popular stallion. Argentan sires good jumping and dressage performers, and his mares are reliable producers.

Other Absatz sons are Akzent I (1977-) and Akzent II (1978-). In the U.S., Armin and Ansas are two representatives of the A-line.

In recent years, Thoroughbreds have replaced Trakehners as improvement sires. Marcio xx (1953-1965), a descendant of the foundation sire Eclipse, sired good dressage horses. His grandsons Maat I and Maat II are both out of Absatz mares, and the sire Werther is out of a Marcio mare. Marcio's brother, Trapper, has also produced excellent breeding stock.

Der Löwe xx (1957-1973) was the most important Thoroughbred used after World War II. His sons Lugano I and Lugano II have produced many approved stallions. The Lugano II grandson Lanthan is one of the state's most popular stallions. Christmann noted, "He produces good dressage horses. All of them can jump with good style. That is something unique at the moment—a stallion that produces light horses very good in jumping."

Pik As xx (1953-1969) sired jumping and dressage horses. His son Pik Koenig (1972-1984) is also a prominent stallion in the breed.

Bolero (1979-1987) by Black Sky xx out of a mare by Bleep xx had a powerful impact upon the breed. This three-quarter Thoroughbred stamped his offspring during a short career at stud, producing many good sires and dressage horses. Bolero crossed well with Grande mares. The U.S. stallion Banter exemplifies this cross of a good mover that passes on his traits.

Cardinal xx (1970-1976), grandson of the famous racing sire Nearco xx, is one of Germany's top sires of dressage horses. This line crosses well with Bolero, Grande, or Duellant mares.

A new, promising sire is Matcho x (1983-). This Anglo-Arabian, imported from France as a refinement stallion, sires elegant offspring. He stamps his get with a distinctive look and outstanding movement, including excellent walks, impulsion, and suspension. His sons and daughters have already begun to influence the Hannoverian.

With all lines, breeders aim to maintain the Hannoverian types. Christmann added, "The different type is important, because it shows the character of the breed. We don't have a uniform type of horse."

He explained how the different types are important for breeders and buyers in North America. "You need modern stallions for the lighter horse, so you can make progress. You must have the movement as well as the conformation. People in the United States don't understand that the Hannoverian has so many varieties. In ratings, U.S. horses with light types are penalized. It's not only the light bone, it's the movement and type that qualify horses."

A challenge to all sport horse breeders is how to preserve the quality in the next generation. By producing a horse that meets a high standard of conformation and movement, the breeder has to consider what cross to choose in

Hannover's Relations with Other Prussian State Studs

Landgestüt Celle functioned as a stallion depot of the Prussian state studs. This system flourished through the 18th and 19th centuries. By 1939, Germany operated 26 *Landgestüte* and *Hauptgestüte* (main studs).

Celle participated in exchanges with other studs such as Mecklenburg, Graditz, and Neustadt. From the late 18th century through the end of the first World War, Hannover bought stallions from the provinces of Mecklenburg and Pommern.

By 1838, most of Hannover's stallions came from Mecklenburg. Horses have been bred for over 600 years in the grazing lands of Mecklenburg, formerly the two grand duchies of Mecklenburg-Schwerin and Mecklenburg-Strelitz. Its Redefin stud was first established in 1715 and became a *Landgestüt* in 1832.

Mecklenburg's vast estates served as stallion-raising sites for as many as 3000 Hannoverian foals each year. Farmers traveled west to Hannover to buy colts to raise; Hannoverian authorities went east to purchase two-year-old stallion candidates. Those not chosen were sold for military or farming uses.

The Mecklenburg horse changed its type through the centuries. Highly esteemed for its sturdy quality, the horse's reputation declined in the later 19th century. The horses were improved by the Hannoverian's influence, and by 1895, most stallions at Redefin were of Hannoverian lines. Mecklenburg started its studbook in 1906.

The Mecklenburg stands about 16 hands and closely resembles the Hannoverian. It has a strong neck and a more compact body.

The Prussian main studs, the *Hauptgestüte*, included Graditz, Neustadt am Dosse, Beberbeck, and Trakehnen. These studs produced stallions for the *Landgestüte*.

Graditz was founded in 1722 and bred Thoroughbreds and warmbloods, concentrating on fullbloods after 1866. Unlike other Prussian studs, Graditz did not produce horses for both military and farm work. In the mid-19th century, the stud specialized in breeding carriage horses. Graditz became part of the DDR after the second World War.

In the province of Brandenburg, the stud at Neustadt am Dosse bred horses from both Hannoverian and East Prussian lines. In 1694, the Elector Frederick II of Brandenburg founded a court stud at Neustadt. He was to become King Frederick I of Prussia. By 1724, over 2600 horses were in the king's stud farms of Neustadt, Trakehnen, Graditz, and Vessra.

Frederick Wilhelm II expanded the stud in 1787, adding buildings including the "Frederick Wilhelm stud." Horses included stock of the Trakehnen,

Hannover's Relations with Other Prussian State Studs (continued)

Mecklenburg, and Zweibrücken studs, along with imported stallions from England, France, Spain, Italy, and Arabia. The blood of the Arabian stallion Turcmain Atti influenced horses in all Prussian studs in the early 19th century.

The stud was reorganized in the DDR after World War II. Neustadt continued as a state stud, breeding a warmblood herd of almost 300 animals. Neustadt has depended on stock from Hannover and Trakehnen since the early 20th century.

Located south of Hannover in Hesse, Beberbeck first bred horses in the late 15th century. It became the Court Stud of Hesse-Kassel in 1724. In 1826, Prussia elevated Beberbeck to a *Hauptgestüt*. This stud supplied hundreds of stallions to other Prussian breeding areas before its closure in 1929.

With Germany's reunification, horses from Celle continue to influence Mecklenburg and Brandenburg. In 1990, two young stallions went to Redefin and one to Neustadt.

order to produce offspring of equal quality.

North American Hannoverians

There are about 3000 Hannoverians in North America. Most are of imported stock, brought to this continent within the last 20 years.

Two associations register the breed. The American Hanoverian Society (AHS) was organized in 1974. The Purebred Hanoverian Associaion of American Breeders and Owners, Inc., was formed to preserve bloodlines of Hannoverians which could trace their lineage to foundation stock in Germany.

CHAPTER 4

The Holsteiner

The second of the three distinctive provincial breeds from Germany, the Holsteiner claims to be the oldest of the sport horse breeds. The horses trace their history back to the fourteenth century.

Located on the northeastern bank of the Elbe, Schleswig-Holstein is today a German state. In the Middle Ages, Schleswig and Holstein were two separate duchies of the Holy Roman Empire. Schleswig was a Danish duchy from the 11th through the 19th centuries. For 400 years, Holstein was ruled by Germany's house of Oldenburg, and it belonged to Denmark for part of the 19th century.

A monastery near Uetersen began breeding horses for local farmers in 1328, using stock descended from French horses. The horses traced to Oriental, Andalusian, and Neapolitan lines.

Schleswig-Holstein developed into an important center of cattle and horse breeding. The weather conditions helped determine the Holstein horses. As farm horses, the Holsteiner worked the fields in hard-to-plow soil—deep and muddy when wet, hardened into a rocklike surface when dry.

The Holsteiner had to have the strength and power to plow in such terrain. A long-time supporter of the breed, Emil-Bernhard Jung, credits the soil for developing the horse's characteristic action: "The early Holsteiner was forced to plow and work in the field in a trot which gave the animal the elevation and hock action. Necessary for that hard work was a horse with superb action and a powerful hindquarter."

The large, robust horses from Holstein also served in wars since the 1500s. After the Reformation in the early 16th century, the crown assumed the breeding of horses. In 1680, the duke of Holstein issued regulations for their breeding while breeding stock at the royal stud at Esserom.

With their combination of power, majesty, and elegant action, Holsteiners attracted the attention of warring monarchs. They were exported to Spain, England, Italy, and to neighboring Denmark, to influence many other European breeds. Crossed with Andalusians, Spain's war horses of Holsteiner bloodlines helped conquer the Americas.

George II brought stallions from Holstein to help found his stud in Hannover. France also imported Holsteiners, with many commandeered by Napoleon's invading troops. To differentiate the breed, Holsteiners were first branded with the shield and crown in 1781.

Holsteiners excel in combined driving. Steve Roach competes in the final phase with a pair of Holsteiners.

The horses of the 18th and 19th centuries were crossed with English and French stock in order to produce elegant riding and driving horses. Thoroughbred and Cleveland Bay stallions helped improve the type. Yorkshire Coach horses added the characteristic gait, compact conformation, and reliable disposition. Some mares came from Hannover to cross with the Holsteiner stallions.

Denmark's King Christian VIII annexed the duchies in 1846 to initiate the Schleswig-Holstein question. Saxon and Hannoverian troops occupied Holstein in 1863, and Prussia annexed Schleswig in 1864. Prussia had acquired both regions by 1866, ending Danish rule.

Schleswig established a state stud in 1864. The state stud moved to Traventhal in 1874.

Holsteiner breeders organized in 1883, naming the breed after its traditional birthplace, "Kremper Marsch." For many years, breeders operated as two independent groups, of the West (Marsh) and East (*Geest*) districts.

Breeders issued the first Holsteiner—also the first German—studbook in 1886. The Holsteiner was the first breed to record both mare and stallion lines. It was recognized by the United States government in 1892.

To consolidate the breed, English and French horses brought refinement to the farm horses. They added more elegant heads and longer necks, while the Holsteiner retained its powerful hindquarters, natural cadence, and strong, solid conformation.

U.S. breeder Masu Hamacher explained how the outside blood enhanced the Holsteiner's riding horse qualities: "The Thoroughbred added good hip angles and slope to the shoulder. In its gaits, it brought a better canter. The earlier horses were influenced by the Yorkshire Coach, which had an up and down gait and no canter."

A stud farm at Elmshorn was built in 1895. This establishment today remains the Verband's stallion and training center. In 1897, the state stud began to expand the stock of breeding stallions.

After World War I, the changing market demanded that the breed return to the heavier farm horse. The Third Reich's farm production regulations ordered Holstein's farmers to breed work horses for pulling heavy artillery.

Masu Hamacher noted how the breed has changed in the last century. "It was like a wave, light, then heavy, then light again. They were heavy as caisson horses, and lighter in sport."

Careful selection maintained the breed's soundness and willingness to work under hardships. In the years just before the second World War, Holsteiners showed a strong Thoroughbred influence.

Along with other breeds, the Holsteiner declined in numbers after World War II. Due to the war's impact and the economic state of the country, the 20,000 mares of 1947 dropped to only 1300 by 1960. The state disbanded the stud at Traventhal in 1960.

The modern Holsteiner Verband was formed in 1935, when the two districts joined into one society. With the state stud's closing, the Verband determined to purchase the state's stallions at auction in 1961.

This bold action saved the breed and helped it to reorganize into a world-class sport horse. Holsteiner authority Dr. Dietrich Rossow wrote, "With a state stud, the Holsteiner breed would never have been able to occupy the commanding stature it has now achieved. This is simply because state studs are for the most part cumbersome mechanisms of government. Whereas, corporate or private stallion ownership and management can orient itself more quickly to market demands and can operate with much greater flexibility." (Translated by Kaye Norment-Smarslik.)

By 1980 the breed had rebounded to include 3100 mares—still a small population compared to their Hannoverian neighbors. Holsteiners account for approximately 5 percent of sport horse competitors, yet they win 35 percent of the prizes.

Famous contemporary performers excel in jumping, dressage, and eventing. The jumper Meteor won two Olympic gold medals, the individual bronze, third in the 1956 World Championships, and 150 Grands Prix. Other winning jumpers include Calypso I, Farmer, Livius, Silbersee, Lavendel 48, The Governor, Chin Chin, Lassandro, and Sedac. The Dutch horse Saluut II is one-half Holsteiner.

Holsteiners have succeeded in the International Jumper Futurity. In 1989, Calvin by Chin Chin won first place. Nicholson (by Chardonay) was third, and Orlando (by Othello) was fifth.

In dressage, Granat by Consul won 18 medals in the Olympics and World Championships. He won gold medals in the 1976 and 1980 Olympics and 1978 World Championships, along with the silver in the 1982 World Cham-

pionships. Venetia by Anblick was on the gold medal team and took the individual bronze in the 1972 Olympics. Montevideo by Marlon xx was on the gold-medal winning team in the 1984 Olympics, and also won the bronze medal at the European Dressage Championships. Corlandus by Cor de la Bryere won 1988's silver medal and was the European Dressage Champion.

Despite a reputation for stamina rather than speed, Holsteiners also excel in eventing. The German team of three Holsteiners won the silver team medal at the 1974, 1978, and 1982 World Championships. In the 1976 Olympics, Madrigal won the bronze individual medal, and helped win the team silver. Foliant, Fair Lady, and Freedom won the team bronze for Germany at the 1984 Olympics. At the 1990 World Championships, the Holsteiner Chagall by Cor de la Bryere competed for the U.S.

Holsteiner teams won the World Championship in driving in 1976, 1980, and 1984. Emil-Bernhard Jung's team won a silver medal in the 1976 World Championships and placed eleventh in 1990.

American drivers choose Holsteiners to compete in international events. At the 1990 World Championships, Deirdre Pirie and Bill Long both drove all-Holsteiner teams.

Holsteiner Characteristics

Holsteiners are sturdy, durable horses. They combine an impression of strength and solidity with fineness.

U.S. breeder Dietrich Felgendreher explained, "The Holsteiner is one of the few breeds that tries to remain true to type. Unlike the Hannoverian, Westfalen, and Oldenburg, it is one of the most identifiable horses."

Horses stand from 16.1 to 17.1 hands. The breed has a bold, expressive face, with a deep body and a short, strong, flexible back. The topline is smooth, with a strong connection from the long, muscular neck to hindquarters.

The Holsteiner has large joints and abundant bone. It has strong, low-set hocks on hind legs set well under the body, which contribute to its natural balance.

The Holsteiner is handsome, but not characteristically "beautiful." Some consider the breed plain or even common in its appearance.

Due to the influence of history, today's Holsteiner falls into two distinct types: "old" and modern. In general, the old type retains its massive bone and large, square knee and hock joints. It has a shorter leg length.

The modern type is lighter and more refined. "It is good that breeders modernized the Holsteiner in the 1950s," said breeder Elizabeth McElvain. "They kept the strength, movement, and disposition, and the breed has never lost those characteristics."

No matter what the conformation, horses of the breed share a consistent look. McElvain recalled her first visit to Elmshorn: "I looked at 300 horses who all looked alike. I was incredibly impressed with the consistency of the breed. Walking up and down the aisles of the barn, the horses were tied up outside the stalls, being shod and tacked up and groomed, and not one horse tried to bite your nose off as you went by. They stood there calmly accepting what was being done to them."

Holsteiners move in round gaits with high knee and hock action. "They are born light, never heavy in the forehand," explained Masu Hamacher. "The knee action is up and out, not daisy-cutting. They are extremely agile and they like to work."

Breeder Doris Van Heeckeren praised the Holsteiners' natural balance. "You don't take two years to train a Holsteiner how to go around a corner without falling to the inside."

The Holsteiner naturally works off its hindquarters. This reliable characteristic makes the horse easier to train for jumping and dressage,

as the trainer does not have to urge the horse's head up while driving it to engage the hindquarters.

Hamacher added that the breed has a wonderful sense of humor. "They are not dull warmbloods, but fun warmbloods. They like to touch you, to nose you. They're very tactile, and they have an interest in life. They have a lot of brilliance and zip, out of fun."

McElvain agreed that the Holsteiner is a sensitive horse. "My horses are so easy to ride, even the big ones. They are light in hand. They are sensitive to the leg; they are easy to collect."

Bay is the predominant color, with few chestnuts and grays. German breeders generally dislike the chestnut coat color.

Holsteiner Breeding

The Holsteiner mare population in Schleswig-Holstein is approximately 4600 mares, producing about 2000 foals each year. Most of the 3100 breeders are farmers who own a few mares. Like their neighbors in Niedersachsen, they raise horses as a proud tradition.

McElvain said, "Breeders have the same *stamm* [mare] lines, and everybody knows about those mares. Schleswig-Holstein is a tiny place. You can drive across it in half a day. The breeders know everything about their horses—the knowledge they have of their horses is just staggering."

The Verband has about 2500 members. They may choose among the 60 breeding stallions owned by the Verband, and some privately owned stallions. The Verband stations its sires throughout the district during breeding season, with one to five stallions at each site. Stallions return to Elmshorn when breeding is completed.

The Verband sets stud fees of DM 40 to 1000, and breeders may use stallions from February 1 to the end of October. Stallions are limited to 130 mares. The Verband continues to receive some financial support from the state.

Holsteiner Trend

Along with the modernizing of the breed, two stallion lines have dominated all others. Of the Ladykiller xx and Cor de la Bryere (A.N.) lines, Dr. Nissen noted, "In decades, breeders will use certain stallions very heavily. We often discuss about the concentration of Ladykiller and Landgraf in the bloodlines." He mentioned that in the 19th century, Achill also predominated, and in years to come, breeders will look for the Landgraf and Cor de la Bryere lines.

The Verband is concerned about the overwhelming popularity of these stallions. Because almost all breeders wanted to breed to these sires, the Verband has limited the numbers of mares. Mares born in an even-numbered year are eligible to choose to breed to Landgraf or Cor de la Bryere; those of odd-numbered years may choose Lord or Capitol. To breed to Landgraf, a mare must meet certain re-

quirements. She must be registered in the Main Studbook and stand at least 165 cm. Landgraf may breed to only 150 mares per year, and the owners must apply for the privilege. Applications are drawn by lot.

Nissen said, "You contract with the Verband when you breed to Landgraf. If you get a colt, you may sell it to the association. If the stallion makes a good performance test, the breeder gets money from the Verband."

He felt that the breed has benefited greatly from its few superior sport lines. "The problem in every other breed is a lot of stallion lines—like in the Trakehner, Hannoverian, and Westfalen. Our success is the small population and very strong lines." He mentioned two lines which will bring some variation—Cottage Son (through Capitol) and Silbersee.

Like their Hannoverian counterparts, Holsteiner breeders have adopted modern technology. Of the Verband's stallions standing at Elmshorn, about one-third breed only by artificial insemination, using fresh semen. Breeders can also use other top Holsteiner stallions stationed across Europe, such as Ramiro (standing in Holland).

As in Hannover, *Aufzüchters* contribute to the success of the breeding program. They buy approximately 90 percent of the foals—mostly

colts—sold by farmers.

Many Holsteiner stallions stand a year or two at stud, then enter training for competition. In 1990, over 40 stallions competed on the European jumping circuit. The stallion Silbersee recently completed a successful Grand Prix career.

The Verband maintains a database of Holsteiners' winnings in sport. Stallions receive an "elite" designation when they have the largest number of offspring who are winners.

Chagall competed in the three-day event at the 1990 World Equestrian Games. Mike Plumb up.

Holsteiner Bloodlines

For over a century, breeders have blended the coach horses of the 19th century with English bloodlines. Responding to the demands of the market, breeders began to restructure the Holsteiner in the decade from 1960 to 1970. During the years between 1945 and 1980, the Verband used over 50 stallions from the Thoroughbred and Anglo-Norman breeds, acquiring them from Germany, England, and Ireland.

"We've refined the Holsteiner a little more slowly than some of the German breeds, introducing French, English, and German Thoroughbreds," explained Emil-Bernhard Jung. "This is why we've been able to maintain such consistency, and why it's not easy to 'type' Holsteiners by jumping or dressage lines. We've kept the bouncy gaits and a good hind leg, which is the motor, after all."

Colts take the first initial of their names from the sire. Fillies are named after a designated initial for each year. In 1989, all fillies had "D" names.

Like other breeds, a stallion's success has depended on the breeders' acceptance. With the breed controlled by the Verband, members could not rely on the state's resources to wait for stallions to produce.

The Verband leases some young stallions to different breeding associations. If the horses produce, the Verband incorporates them into the breeding program in Schleswig-Holstein. The Verband sells sires unpopular with breeders. In some cases, officials have sold horses that had limited opportunity to breed with complementary mare lines.

As the Verband introduced new stallions, breeders chose which mare lines would nick with certain sires. They could cling to tradition and stay with proven lines, or they could breed more experimentally. As the new lines succeeded, the older Holsteiner type became unpopular.

Like the Hannoverian breeders, the Verband describes its stallion lines with candor. Authorities note both positive and negative heritable traits, which persist through the generations. The best sires have been able to produce both performance horses and approved breeding stock.

Stallions which contributed to the breed included Thoroughbreds, an Anglo-Arab, and Anglo-Normans. Of the 60 Thoroughbreds the Verband introduced, only a few founded stallion lines: Trebonious, Anblick, Cottage Son, Frivol, Manometer, Marlon, and Ladykiller.

Anblick xx (1954-1964) was sired by Ferro, a winner of the German Derby. From the Graditz stud, Anblick was unsuccessful in the Hannover breeding area but established a line in Schleswig-

Holstein. This stallion was prepotent with the old-style Holsteiner mares, and he produced 40 sons.

The English import Cottage Son xx (1959-1964) produced 40 sons. However, now only one stallion, Capitol, represents his line.

Manometer xx (1962-1968) was sired by Abenfrieden, a full brother to Anblick. This horse influenced the breed by producing jumpers. The sire Midas carries on this line.

Marlon xx (1965-1981), an Irish Thoroughbred, produced performance horses in all three riding disciplines. His son Madrigal won the individual bronze in the three-day event at the 1976 Olympics. Although he sired 30 sons, few maintained the line beyond the first generation.

Ladykiller xx (1965-1979) has made a major impact on the breed. The Verband's Dr. Thomas Nissen speculated, "Ladykiller was the best Thoroughbred we had not only in Holstein, but all over the German breeding area—maybe in all of Europe. We find his sons in every pedigree. They are the basis for the breed's success now and in the future."

Ladykiller's offspring excelled as jumpers. Dr. Rossow wrote, "He had first rate legs and feet for a Thoroughbred and was an elastic mover."

His most famous of 35 sons is Landgraf I, foaled 1968 out of an Aldato (by Anblick) mare. Landgraf has also sired 35 sons.

Dr. Nissen said of his offspring, "The riding horses by Landgraf, in their younger years they are not easy. The rider needs to learn about the horse's jumping ability."

In 1989, Landgraf stood at the top of the German list of money-winning sires. He is considered the most important sire of jumpers in the world. The lifetime earnings of his 580 offspring was DM 2 million.

Landgraf has made his name through passing on his athleticism. His interior qualities have made him a great sire. He is prepotent,

Guenter Seidel warms up Excalibur for the Grand Prix Special.

crossing with many lines, especially with mares carrying Thoroughbred blood.

Dr. Nissen noted that this elderly stallion still has "a lovely face, big neck, and a very compact body. He does have leg problems now—when he was a younger stallion, you could see his problems." He added that in the stallion selection, judges need to compromise between a horse's leg conformation and its abilities—its will to work.

Landgraf continues to sire both performance and breeding horses. His stud fee is the highest of any of the Verband's stallions.

Other Ladykiller sons have included Lord, Lorenz, Lagos, and Ladalco. At 21 years of age, Lord is one of the most popular sires. He is out of a Cottage Son dam and has sired 15 sons and many world-class jumpers.

An American-bred Holsteiner, Fogata (Columbus-Fasolt), Champion Mare at a 1989 Breeding Stock Approval of the American Holsteiner Horse Association.

A famous progenitor in the 1960s was Ramzes, an Anglo-Arabian who also sired offspring in the Westfalen breeding area. "The breeders were skeptical about him, but his sons and daughters are very good jumping horses," said Nissen.

Although Ramzes stood only two years in Schleswig-Holstein, he sired five sons, including Rigoletto and Raimond. Probably his most famous grandson is Ramiro, out of a Cottage Son daughter. A prepotent sire of jumpers, Ramiro has contributed to the Hannoverian, Dutch, and Westfalen breeds.

Another wave began in 1970, when breeders modified the results from the latest influx of Thoroughbreds. Eighty percent of mares were covered by Thoroughbred stallions, causing breeders from surrounding areas to view the Holsteiner program with skepticism.

Around 1970, the Holsteiner breeders began to consolidate the breed in succeeding genera-

tions, and to emphasize jumping ability. Dr. Nissen explained, "Because we had a lot of Thoroughbreds, we had many Thoroughbreds in the backgrounds of horses. We returned to our older stallions with little Thoroughbred, to get the characteristic points. We couldn't do it all with Thoroughbreds."

In recent decades, the breed has introduced some Anglo-Norman stallions. Cor de la Bryere, Almé, and Silbersee are the most successful French stallions.

Cor de la Bryere (1971-1984, 1986-) has sired 33 approved sons for the Verband. He sired the dressage champion Corlandus out of a Land-graf I mare. His sons include Calypso I, Calypso II, Caletto I, and Caletto II. Calypso I and II are prepotent sires of both jumpers and dressage horses.

"The Cor de la Bryeres have beautiful form," said McElvain. "They inherit it—it is just so beautiful to see it one after the other. Some people say that Cor de la Bryere would have been nothing if he had stood in France, that it was the Holsteiner mares that made him."

Holsteiner breeders rate the *stamm* (mare line) equal in importance to the stallion. Breeder Masu Hamacher believes that mares can also be prepotent. She has a mare that produces similar foals each year, regardless of the stallion. "Bred to three different lines—the R, C, and M lines—all the foals look alike," she reported.

Three stallions of the 19th century established reputations as mare line sires: Ethelbert, Achill, and Farnese. Ethelbert was foaled in 1874. Only mare lines represent his blood in today's Holsteiner.

Yet the breeders continue to respect the history of the breed by retaining families of pure Holsteiner lineage. The Achill line, undiluted for 150 years, remains an important cross within the breed.

Of the Achill line, Farnese established a family added to the breed, the F-Line. Farnese passed on traits of bone and jumping ability to many sons in Germany. Dr. Nissen said, "Fleming is the hope for Farnese now." Offspring of the Farnese son Fasolt represent the line in the United States.

Like Ethelbert, the Adjutant line is now represented only in mare lines. With the breed's modernization, many old bloodlines became rare when hundreds of mares went to slaughter. Old lines disappeared as new ones flourished.

The market demands Holsteiners as superior jumpers, so breeders concentrate on specific, popular jumper lines. "The Holsteiner is the only horse that is bred for jumping, and they are extremely good jumpers," said McElvain.

She admires the breed for its prepotency. "The breeders took this relatively small group of horses and kept it clean genetically while they added what they needed to make it saleable all through the years. They have maintained the type, and it is so strong that the horses pass on their characteristics." She described Holsteiners as predictable, even when crossed with Thoroughbreds. Offspring reflect the Holsteiner type in size and conformation.

North American Holsteiners

Iowa horseman A. B. Holbert imported the first Holsteiners to North America in the late 19th century. The contemporary breed was imported and promoted in the late 1970s by Jung, under contract with the German Verband. He

Elizabeth McElvain is greeted by friendly youngsters.

founded the American Association of Breeders of Holsteiner Horses (AAOBOHH) in 1977.

The American Holsteiner Horse Association, Inc., was also established in 1977. The two associations merged into the current American Holsteiner Horse Association, Inc. in 1987.

CHAPTER 5

The Trakehner

T he Trakehner has survived four centuries of history. This horse shared the glories of Prussian victories—and the agonies of German retreats.

With its supporters terming it the oldest and noblest German warmblood, the breed earned its name after the famous Trakehnen stud, home of the elite horses of East Prussia. Its full name is the East Prussian Warmblood Horse of Trakehner origin.

Trakehner History

The province of East Prussia was a traditional location of horse-breeding for centuries, home of a native breed, the Schweiken. The wars of the Middle Ages introduced other breeds. When the Knights of the Teutonic Order conquered Prussia in the early 13th century, they established one of Europe's earliest stud farms in 1264, at Georgenburg. In the following decades the Order built over 60 studs. The Order required that landowners provided cavalry, which supported their goal of spreading Christianity and civilization.

Centuries later, in 1731 King Friedrich Wilhelm I (1730-1740) founded a Royal Stud Office. He sought for his troops a lighter, faster horse with style and stamina, and he combined the best horses from seven existing farms into a state stud in Litauen, in the northwestern part of East Prussia. The King chose a site near Gumbinnen for its rich soil and deep grass. In 1732, 1100 horses, including 500 mares, comprised the royal stud named Trakehnen.

Friedrich II (1740-1786), known as Frederick the Great, was an ambitious ruler. His reign built Prussia into a first-class power. He considered the army the foundation of the state and saw that most of the state's revenues supported the army.

Frederick intended that Trakehnen would supply his royal stables and army with quality remounts. The stud would also show a profit.

For its first 50 years, the stud refined the type of the sturdy Schweiken. Over 350 stallions of varied breeding helped develop the breed, of English, Arabian, and Spanish lines, with horses also originating from Turkey, Bohemia, and Denmark. Many were obtained as spoils of war, captured during Frederick's campaigns.

Frederick admired the English horses, which added size to the East Prussian. Arabian sires contributed beauty and natural balance, while both fullbloods improved the breed's courage and nobility.

At Frederick's death, Trakehnen transferred to state ownership. Count von Lindenau as-

The Trakehner is the lightest of the German warmbloods. This horse shows the modern type, with a flatter hindquarter.

sumed management and organized the Prussian State Stud Administration. Under his administration (1786-1808) the *Hauptgestüt* Trakehnen served as the Royal Prussian Main Stud. He declared that the stud's future sires should be "pure gold," or Thoroughbreds and Arabians.

In 1787 Trakehnen began branding horses on the right hindquarter with its exclusive mark, the single seven-pointed moose antler. (This moose, *Alces alces alces*, roamed the forests of northern Europe).

The Stud added the objectives to improve the provincial horse breeding industry and raise stallions for the Prussian State Studs. Early in its history, Trakehnen initiated the system of breeding state stallions to mares owned by farmers and landowners. Other German studs patterned their own state-run stallion stations after those in East Prussia.

East Prussian farmers owned from one to five mares, which worked the land in addition to raising foals. A few landholders owned herds of a hundred mares, but 80 percent of the foals were born at farms with only one or two mares.

In all districts of East Prussia, breeders could ride or drive their mares to a stallion station. Several hundred stallions, provided by the Main Stud, stood at low fees during the breeding season. They spent the fall and winter at Trakehnen.

The breed developed into an elegant, versatile horse, the product of typical German thoroughness. Officials at Trakehnen selected mares for conformation and bloodlines. Von Lindenau divided the stock into three herds by color, grouped by black, brown, and chestnut. (Prussian royalty traditionally preferred blacks as carriage horses.) He also organized the program by riding and carriage horses.

Trakehnen became the most significant German horse center. In 1791, East Prussia began selling horses as remounts for the cavalry. Up through the second World War, the region would continue supplying Prussia and later Germany with the largest number of remounts of any breeding area.

In the years before the Napoleonic wars, influential stallions included Arabians, Anglo-Arabians, and a very few Thoroughbreds. The smaller, lighter horses continued to increase in size and bone through the late 18th century.

Trakehnen itself encompassed a series of spacious estates. At its height of prosperity, the stud spread over 14,000 acres. It supported a village of 3000.

Trakehnen had almost 400 buildings, huge fields for mares and foals, and farms for raising young horses. Cattle shared the lush pastures with horses, grazing in fields bordered by evergreen hedges.

Mounted herdsmen watched over horses grouped as mares and foals, or as one-, two-, or three-year-olds. Stock grazed outside in the days and spent the nights in covered paddocks adjacent to the stud's spacious barns.

Trakehnen produced docile, well-behaved young horses. Workers treated horses with kindness and calmness, handling youngsters daily. Horses learned to enjoy human contact during grooming sessions.

Indoor arenas allowed staff to exercise horses during inclement weather. Over 350 permanent obstacles dotted the countryside's excellent hunting territory. The region gave its name to the famous Trakehner post and rail fence.

The stud's location, close to Russia, was politically insecure. In 1794, the threat of Polish insurgents forced the first of a series of evacuations. When French troops invaded East Prussia in 1806, the Prussian studs of Trakehnen and Neustadt were removed to safety in Russian Lithuania.

When French troops sought to capture the prize stock, State Stud Administrator W. von Burgsdorff moved horses to temporary quarters in Silesia. The devoted staff cared for close to 800 state-owned mares and stallions in temporary quarters in 1812.

Besides the evacuations, the Napoleonic wars reduced the equine population. Prussia lost 90,000 horses between 1806 and 1813.

The stud again flourished with the end of the French occupation. Trakehner breeder Patricia Goodman wrote, "During the twenty years from 1817 to 1837, select English Thoroughbred and Arabian stallions were purchased and added to the breed, a practice that is still followed today under strict approval conditions by the West German Trakehner Verband. It is this carefully controlled addition of 'hot' blood that has given the Trakehner its characteristic breediness and refinement—the elegance and beauty that gives it the edge in stiff competition, and sets it apart from the other European warmblood breeds."

Starting in the 1830s, Trakehnen's public auctions attracted buyers from around the world. Like England's Newmarket, the stud became a social center for equestrians. Breed-ers, Prussian noblemen, cavalry officers, and horse dealers flocked to the stud to sort through the culls—riding horses, mares, and stallions no longer needed at the stud. They enjoyed Trakehnen's gracious hospitality as they toured the sale barns and watched staff walk and trot horses down the aisles.

At the day-long auction, the *Landstallmeister* acted as a royal merchant. The best animals were offered for sale with an unannounced reserve, and the *Landstallmeister* could enter the bidding to raise prices toward the reserve.

The stud's administration continued adding sires from French, English Thoroughbred, and Arabian lines. Trakehnen supplied horses to the stud at Georgenburg and sent Thoroughbred and Arabian mares to Graditz. Both Graditz and Beberbeck sent stallions to Trakehnen.

The Trakehner achieved recognition as the premier military mount in the late 19th century. Some breeders expressed concern about the amount of "blood" in the horse, but the highest quality East Prussian horses continued to excel in the cavalry.

Authorities praised the breed for its endurance and ability to work under demanding conditions. For example, in an 1871 winter campaign, a regiment of Prussian hussars covered 35 miles a day through ice and snow.

In 1878, the first studbook was published, followed by the first studbook for halfbred Trakehners in 1890. The East Prussian Stud Book Society was founded in 1888.

By 1899, the province had 5 major stud farms, 16 provincial studs, and 15 remount stations. The total horse population was over half a million head. East Prussia contributed 12,000 remounts to the German army, 7000 to Prussia itself.

Trakehnen supplied lighter army remounts during the decades of Prussia's greatest influence. With Thoroughbred stallions covering 80 percent of the broodmares, the refined blood horses closely resembled Thoroughbreds.

Trakehnen's fourth evacuation occurred in 1914, with horses fleeing Russian troops. Along with Prussian citizens, Trakehnen's horses remained refugees until the stud returned in 1919. World War I reduced the number of horses by one-half.

After the Treaty of Versailles disbanded Germany's cavalry, Trakehnen reduced its mare herd. Although the cavalry returned in 1920, the stud reorganized its breeding and modified the breeding goal. The elite horses of East Prussian breeding, those bred as officers' mounts, lacked the substance and bone required for farmwork. The market demanded a warmblood horse of more caliber, which could serve on the farm as well as under saddle.

The goal read, "The horse must be perfectly suitable as a military and utilitarian horse. To reach such a goal the state breeders must not raise a specialized breed. The model broodmare must have a medium-sized rectangular frame, short legs, with a low and broad rump, of a noble expression. She must move straight and in natural balance with good mechanics and much impulsion. She must have a quiet temperament, be willing to work, and have a healthy and hard constitution. A medium size of 156 to 162 cm should correspond to a girth from 180 to 200 cm, the cannon bone should not be less than 20 cm. The stallion as the embodiment of masculine strength must be more imposing in all respects."

Trakehners began to show more substance, resembling heavy hunters. The cavalry resumed buying approximately two-thirds of East Prussian riding horses. Although many horses went to farms, fortunately the breed was able to retain its type. Some riding horses moved into the new sports of jumping and dressage, or went into racing.

In 1922, the East Prussian Stud Book Society adopted the double antler brand on the near

hip. This marked all horses of Trakehner origin born in the province, with the single antler reserved for those born at Trakehnen.

By 1936, the breed was the most populous in Germany. Over 1200 stallions covered almost 90,000 mares in that year. The East Prussian studbook alone showed 20,000 registered mares in 1937.

Trakehners established themselves as performance horses before World War II. In the Olympics of 1920, a Trakehner won the silver medal in dressage. Trakehners won the gold and silver in dressage in 1924; the bronze in 1928. At the Berlin Olympics, they repeated their win of gold and silver in dressage and took the individual gold in three-day eventing. Germany also won the team gold in eventing, with two Trakehners on its team.

The breed's turning point was its abandonment of its homeland, in the final year of World War II. With the Russian armies threatening invasion, officials dispersed much of the stud to various locations in Germany. In 1944, authorities evacuated over a thousand horses from Trakehnen, by rail and on foot. Horses transferred to studs such as Mecklenburg and Georgenburg were eventually captured when Soviet troops occupied the areas.

When Russia did take over the province, millions of refugees, including 15,000 East Prussian breeders and their beloved mares, fled to the safety of Allies in the west. The Germans feared the Russians under the Stalin regime. Families had to retreat west as Russian troops killed or imprisoned Germans who chose to remain in their villages. The march to Germany was one of the most strenuous tests of equine performance.

In the famous Trek, the noble horses pulled wagons on journeys from 500 to 900 miles to reach British forces. Harsh weather, lack of food and shoes, and the stress of crossing difficult terrain caused many horses to die. Those that survived received credit for their endurance, as they rescued their families from Russian capture.

Out of over 50,000 horses, fewer than a thousand Trakehners escaped to the new West Germany. Through the war, one and a half million German horses died.

The war's end did not signal the breed's rebirth in the west. With their homeland in ruins as politics separated West from East, the horses of Trakehnen were scattered through Germany, mostly in Hannover and Holstein. Alongside their displaced owners, the horses helped rebuild their conquered nation. Hardships continued as they worked in the fields.

The Trakehners gained the admiration of German farmers during the hardships of the Trek. One refugee recalled, "One farmer in Mecklenburg remarked, 'Look at those Trakehners! They've been pulling wagons for so long and they're still on the bit. They can go like that until they reach the Rhine River.'...The farmers admired the Trakehners' strength and endurance, which often exceeded that of the native Holsteiner horses."

The fortunes of war banished the breed from its birthplace. Once the most populous breed in Prussia, the Trakehner's numbers dwindled to mere hundreds.

The breed's admirers tried to gather the scattered survivors. They vowed to rebuild with the horses which had proved their worth through the test of the Trek. The Trakehner Verband was founded in 1947 by members of the former East Prussian Studbook Society. The first West German Trakehner foals were born in 1948.

In 1950 the West German government recognized the Verband's efforts. To help preserve the horse, the state helped fund a Trakehner farm near Hunnesrück.

With 40 stallions and 700 mares (including Thoroughbred and Arabian stock), the Verband increased the breed's numbers to register 650

mares and 50 stallions by 1954. In a miraculous comeback, the breed numbered 1600 registered mares and close to 200 stallions throughout Germany by 1970. The Verband operated three studs at Hunnesrück, Rantzau, and Birkhausen.

The displaced Trakehner stock refined other German breeds and the Swedish warmblood. Trakehner stallions helped transform the heavier Oldenburger and Hannoverian breeds into sport horses.

U. S. breeder Robin Koenig explained, "The other warmblood breeds use the Trakehner for its elegance and prettiness. They use the Trakehner to help refine the heavy warmblood."

Canadian breeder Guenter Bertelmann added, "They use in Germany a lot of Trakehner stallions—to get more charm into their horses. Today if you want to go in hunter competition, you cannot go with a Holsteiner or Hannoverian. You have to show a pretty horse."

Politics separated Trakehners east and west. Poland gathered herds of stallions and mares left after the war, identified by their brands or registration papers. Poland re-established many of the East Prussian studs to continue the breed. (Trakehnen itself no longer functions as a horse-breeding farm). To preserve the heritage of East Prussian breeding, the Polish Ministry of Agriculture registers Trakehners in its *Great Polish Horse Stud Book*. State studs breed the Polish Trakehner, registered in the studbook along with the Wielkopolski, a name for the Polish warmblood horse.

Russia claimed many Trakehner mares and stallions. From Mecklenburg and Neustadt/Dosse, hundreds were shipped to the Soviet Union. Breeding continues at the Kirow stud.

Frank LaSalle explained how the horses changed ownership after the second World War: "The majority of East Prussian horses, as contrasted to Trakehnen's, were gone. The breeders who had one to three horses left East Prussia with their mares. Russia took them, all the stallions [from Trakehnen], but they didn't want the German breeds. They hated anything that was German, and they would even change the names of streets if the names were German."

Recent political changes have "liberated" Trakehners from behind the Iron Curtain. Guenter Bertelmann noted how Russia is an important source of Trakehners. "They have today, in a stud in Lithuania, 950 purebred Trakehner mares which they'd like to bring in, to get the same contract like the American Trakehner Association has with the German Verband. It looks like they will get their own brand. They want to join the family of the worldwide Trakehner breed.

"Their sport horses are all Trakehner, dressage and jumping. In Russia, the Trakehner brings seven times the price of any other horse."

Today Trakehners maintain a reputation for versatility. As the preferred military horse, they continue to excel in all disciplines. At the 1956 Olympics, three Trakehners were on the German team, which won the silver medal in dressage. Pepel, a Russian Trakehner, won the gold medal in dressage in 1968. Another Russian horse won the silver medal in dressage in 1972, while a half-Trakehner won the gold in the three-day event.

In 1976, the Trakehner Ultimo was a member of the German team that won the gold medal in dressage. Abdullah won the individual silver medal in show-jumping at the 1984 Olympics. This stallion also won the 1985 World Cup. In 1986, he was second in the World Championships and on the gold medal team. Amiego, out of the same dam as Abdullah, won the bronze medal in three-day eventing at the 1987 Pan-American Games. Another jumper, Livius, also represents the Trakehner in international competition. And in 1990, a Russian Trakehner, Prints, has become one of the top open jumpers in Germany.

At the 1990 World Championships, the Rus-

sian Trakehner, Dikson, placed seventh individually, the highest score for the silver-medal Russian dressage team. Dikson placed second in the 1991 World Cup finals.

Trakehner Characteristics

Trakehner fanciers emphasize the breed's distinctive type. They consider the Trakehner unique among all other German warmbloods, comparing it to the Thoroughbred.

Dr. Eberhard von Velsen described the type as "conformation, harmony, and nobility. The horse must be 'dry' in appearance, that is the skin is fine and thin, the veins are close to the surface, and the skin lies close to the bone, resulting in a well-defined musculature with hocks and other joints that are not puffy. Type is what makes the Trakehner easily distinguishable from all other breeds."

The horse displays a compelling presence— a picture of refinement and elegance. It combines the classic beauty of blood with size, bone, and substance.

Like the Thoroughbred, the Trakehner is a rectangular horse. It stands from 16 to 17 hands, with a deep girth and round, full ribs. It has a length of leg shorter than the Thoroughbred. The horse does not have a long body, but a more compact leg.

In general, the Trakehner has a flatter hindquarter than other German breeds, and its tail is set higher. Horses are well-ribbed, with medium frames and strong backs.

Compared to the heavier warmbloods, the Trakehner has lighter, medium bone. Breeder Judy Yancey commented on the quality of bone. "Because of their Arabian background, these horses have a greater density of bone. If you did a cross section of cannon bone, the density would be very great, second only to the Arabian horse."

The "breedy" head of the Trakehner is distinctive in its charm and nobility. Its shape

The Trakehner's Reputation

Despite the Trakehner's success as an improvement sire in Germany, currently few stallions are being used in studs in Hannover, Holstein, and Westfalia. Thoroughbred sires are more popular, with officials citing faster improvement.

In Europe, the Trakehner sport horse has gained a reputation similar to the Arabian's in North America. Like the Arabian, the breed's spirit and temperament can make them slower to train. Riders consider the Trakehner a "hot" breed.

Few Trakehners compete on the international jumping circuit. Riders tend to restrict them to dressage, and some criticize the Trakehner for its lack of power over fences as compared to the heavier warmbloods. Drivers seem to prefer stronger breeds for combined driving.

Some critics claim that the breed has lost its character in recent decades. They say that the Trakehner no longer looks distinctive, due to crosses with Arabians and Thoroughbreds after the war. Yet, concentrating on conformation and movement has also compromised the breed's reputation as an athlete.

Trakehner fanciers support the breed enthusiastically. Some tend to describe themselves as "hard-core," or feeling like "the underdog." The Trakehner's history appeals to dedicated protectors. Many breeders and owners describe a responsibility toward perpetuating this breed.

A California breeder, Kim Tulypin, said, "I want to preserve the history. The horses went through so much. It's the history of the Lipizzans intensified."

reflects its Arabian ancestry, with many showing a slightly dished profile. The forehead is wide, with large, kind eyes. The Trakehner has a slim, defined throatlatch and a graceful neck.

In motion, the Trakehner's gaits are light and flowing. The breed characteristically thrusts from the hindquarters, while moving its shoulders freely and swinging its back. "Look for an elongated, floating trot, with more extension than in other breeds," explained long-time breeder Leo Whinery.

The horse has a reputation as a lady's mount due to its light, responsive nature and its aptitude for dressage. Its smooth elegance captivates admirers.

Breeder Barbara Raehn explained how the breed differs from the typical German warmblood. "I feel they're easier for a woman to ride. They're not as hard to drive forward. They're a little lighter on the front end and easier to engage. The Trakehner is light and airy."

Yancey looks for movement to originate from a good hip. A longer hipline can balance the movement in front and behind, instead of the horse being a "front end mover" that lacks sufficient impulsion. Yancey described how a hip can limit a horse's power at the trot: "Some Trakehners do what I call a cheat. They have a wonderful shoulder and can throw their front legs out, but not necessarily follow through behind. The flip of the front foot, in German, *antreitt*, is almost a moment of suspension before the foot comes back to the ground."

Admirers agree that the Trakehner has a more alert temperament than some other breeds. Some credit the Arabian ancestry for the horses' dispositions. "You can't bully these horses," explained Hunter. "They're intelligent and sensitive. They require an intelligent and sensitive owner."

Although some horsemen describe the breed's temperament as hotter than a Hannoverian or Holsteiner, supporters praise the Trakehner's reliability. Robin Koenig said, "The Trakehner takes more of a patient, thinking rider. You don't put him in a situation that he can't get out of—you allow him the opportunity to do the job. With that elegance from the Thoroughbred and Arabian, he's a little hotter, too."

Riders agree that the Trakehner is willing to cooperate. The horse seems to have a "built-in" connection with its rider. Today's Trakehner also has stamina to respond with courage and style.

The Polish Trakehner differs slightly from its German relatives. These horses are larger and heavier, with more substance. In general, the Polish horses seem to have calmer dispositions.

Breeder Frank LaSalle explained the background of the Polish type. "Trakehners weren't different right after the war. The Poles needed horses to pull wagons and plow fields, so the breeding went in that direction."

"The Poles look for a three-day type horse— a big, strong, galloping, free-moving horse that has jumping in its heart, not a dressage horse character. They don't go for a pretty head. They know you need a good-looking horse to sell, but it first must move."

He noted how the West German breeders preferred more refinement, with a dished head. To him, this horse is more of a "model" horse, rather than a bold, big-moving performance horse.

Trakehners mature slower than other breeds. Breeders estimate that these horses are fully mature at ages five through seven.

Trakehner Breeding

Although "Trakehners Worldwide" is the breed's theme, the Verband is the center of Trakehner breeding in Germany. (The Verband's full name is *Verband der Züchter und Freunde des Ostpreussichen Warmblutpferdes Trakehner Abstammung e. V.*)

The Verband hosts shows, the *Körung*, and gala auctions in Neumünster. Six associations cooperate with the Verband—the American Trakehner Association and groups in Switzerland, Australia, Denmark, Yugoslavia, and Great Britain. Only Trakehners bred in West Germany may wear the brand which signifies the direct descendants of East Prussian horses. The Verband has 4000 members and 2300 breeders. Most breeders own only one or two mares.

Germany has a population of about 22,000 Trakehners. Breeding stock includes 4500 mares and close to 300 approved stallions. In 1989, the Verband registered approximately 1500 foals. The most popular stallion covered 90 mares.

Today the Verband aims for "the production of a high-quality, multi-purpose horse for all disciplines of a demanding sport," according to Trakehner authority, Dr. Fritz Schilke. Central to breeding is the preservation of type.

"The Trakehner is the only warmblood breed that is a true breed type," explained Judy Yancey. "The others are sport horses, and they are excellent sport horses. The Oldenburg, the Hannoverian, the Holsteiner—they're breeding societies, not really a breed."

Trakehner stallions continue to be famous for their ability to perpetuate the unique Trakehner type. "It's my opinion that if you have a good Trakehner stallion, you have much more of a chance of producing what you want because of their genetic purity," said Yancey. "They don't have a smidgen of this and a smid-

Samurai II

Eventers continue to debate the abilities of warmbloods in their sport. The Trakehner stallion, Samurai II, has excelled in this discipline since 1986.

The bay stallion was foaled in 1982, bred by Egon Hoerdemann of Rheinland. Mackensen, a grandson of Flaneur, sired the colt out of Sarika, an Ibikus daughter. At the *Hengstkörung* in Neumünster, Samurai II was 1984 Reserve Champion. He was imported to the United States in 1985 and is owned by Leo and Doris Whinery of Cedar Crest Farm, Noble, Oklahoma.

After Samurai II completed the American Trakehner Association's (ATA) performance requirement at a horse trial, Whinery placed the horse with eventer Michael Huber. The stallion was USCTA Area V Reserve Champion, Novice, and Champion, USCTA Area V, Training. He also won the Championship in Training Division for ATA.

Samurai II moved up to Preliminary in 1988, again winning the Championships for USCTA Area V and ATA. In 1989, he was Champion of AHSA Zone VII in Preliminary. He competed in Preliminary and Intermediate in 1990, with two more ATA championships (Preliminary Champion and Reserve in Intermediate).

Of his stallion's success, Whinery noted, "His breed characteristics of good temperament, size, bone and substance, excellent movement at all three gaits, and endurance have made him a good candidate for eventing. As an individual within the breed he excels in all four of these qualities.

"A talented individual in temperament, conformation, and movement, a careful and precise early development of the horse under saddle, and maturation of the horse slowly under an excellent trainer and competitive rider have all made the difference in Samurai's success to date as an event horse. How much further he will go remains to be seen. Many eventers believe that warmbloods lack the speed and stamina that is essential for three-day eventing, particularly at the advanced level.

"Whether Samurai represents an exception to this generally held view is yet unanswered. Mike says he has learned to run and enjoys competing."

Samurai II. Photo by Judy Huber.

gen of that."

Unlike other breeds, the Trakehner maintains a closed studbook. However, a closed registry does not imply that the breed is pure. At different times in its history, the breed mixed halfbreds and horses from other Prussian studs. Like the "purebred" Thoroughbred, outside infusion did occur in earlier generations.

With its registry controlled for over a century, the Trakehner has not changed its type as quickly as other breeds. Breeds like the Holsteiner were able to react to changes in the market by crossbreeding to modify their type.

Yancey described what some breeds have produced as "an end product—a filial first cross. It generally doesn't reproduce itself. The Trakehner has gone on very ploddingly through history. It takes many more generations—20 years—to change the type of the Trakehner."

The Trakehner breeders could produce variations of the type. "You can change things relatively easily within the warmblood business, because there's no such thing as a purebred," said Frank LaSalle. "If you breed size to size, sooner or later you have a bigger horse. All breeders understand that you can breed anything you want, even within a closed studbook."

Anita Hunter described different types within the breed. "The old style tends to be larger, more rectangular, with heavier bone. New styles are more compact and tend to be shorter-coupled."

Breeders have maintained the horse as a unique warmblood, to influence other breeds. The American Trakehner Association's Helen Gibble said, "From the start, the Trakehner was bred as an improvement horse. It was bred as a refinement breeder for other breeds."

In Poland, LaSalle noted how the breed has adapted to the market for sport horses: "The East Prussian horses stayed in Poland—on the big farms, the horses never left. The same Polish

workers stayed, and they knew the horses and the pedigrees. The Poles never had a market for riding horses, because they didn't have the money. They started breeding riding horses to export as a commodity to sell for hard currency."

He noted the relationship between breeders in West Germany and Poland. "In the 1950s, Germany bought mares from the Poles, and the Poles bought stallions from the Russians. When the Poles began selling horses to Sweden, Holland, and North America, then the Germans stopped buying horses from Poland. The Poles don't have the expertise [in marketing], but they have the numbers to produce good horses."

Trakehner Bloodlines

The Trakehner consolidated the Arabian and English Thoroughbred. It provided an ideal cross with other German breeds, as less of an outcross. The Trakehner sires Abglanz and Semper Idem greatly influenced the modern Hannoverian.

With careful and strictly controlled crosses, breeders in Germany follow the practice of infusing Thoroughbred and Arabian lines into the Trakehner breed. These fullbloods are the only outside blood allowed, to refine the breed without losing its longstanding traits. (In Germany, these offspring out of studbook Trakehner mares are registered as full Trakehners. Thoroughbred or Arabian mares which are approved for breeding to Trakehner stallions are registered in the German Appendix).

U. S. breeder Robin Koenig explained, "The Trakehner has used the Thoroughbred and Arabian to keep its elegance. If inbreeding, the selection process would push you back to the old type."

Of Trakehnen's main stallions in the late 19th century, the total number of sires have had as high as 90 percent Arabian or Thoroughbred ancestry. Some authorities consider the

Trakehner to be an Anglo-Arabian horse. The Arabian and Thoroughbred lines complement each other.

Arabians contributed to the sires of Trakehnen. The stallion Turcmain Atti ox, main stallion at Neustadt, sired 16 sons. He passed on desirable riding horse attributes rather than strictly Arabian characteristics, and his sons sired 141 broodmares for Trakehnen.

Dr. Schilke noted, "The purpose of adding Arabian blood is primarily not because of the exterior but the interior characteristics of the Arabian horse, mainly its easy keeping and adaptability to all conditions, its endurance and hardiness, its health and its excellent, easily managed temperament. Of the exterior characteristics one would also like to take the exquisite beauty of the Arabian and inscribe it onto the larger frame of our horses. One would like to have the head set of the Arabian, the dry, noble head, the fine harmony of its entire body which imparts a natural balance to the horse at any time and in any position."

Nana Sahib x stood at Trakehnen from 1908 to 1921, imported from France to stand a year at Celle. This Anglo-Arabian produced 10 stallions, 15 studbook mares, and many outstanding sport horses. His daughter Cymbal foaled the stallion Cancara.

Fetysz ox came to Trakehnen from Poland's Janow Podlaski stud in 1937. He and several other Arabian stallions and mares influenced the breed, despite the contemporary demands for horses with rectangular frames.

Fetysz sired 6 approved stallions and 22 mares. He established his line through the son Famulus, and his son Termit sired Abglanz.

Famulus influenced the breed through sons and daughters. His son Maharadscha sired 10 approved sons, including the famous producer Flaneur. Flaneur sired 13 approved sons. His line has carried on through the daughter Maharani, who foaled the sire, Mahagoni. Flaneur's

The stallion San Remo shows the breed's refined expression. Shown by Judy Yancey.

son Troubadour excels in dressage, and the Flaneur son Arogno was champion of the German 100-Day Testing at Adelheidsdorf.

The Maharadscha daughter, Abiza, foaled Abdullah and Amiego. Another daughter, Fawiza produced the dressage stallions, Falke and Fabian.

Some breeders argue that the breed needs to bring in another dose of Arabian blood. Horses of today can lose the interior qualities of hardiness and endurance through a less-demanding environment—yet the logistics of adding such blood causes debate.

Judy Yancey said, "Ideally the Arabian is good, back in the fourth generation. The type of Arabians they have in Germany are really nice. They have performance horses, strong-boned horses standing 16 hands."

Adding Arabian blood does involve risk. Breeder Henry Schurink noted that the Arabians' conformation and head carriage is detrimental to a sport horse. "Arabian blood becomes useful only in about the fourth or fifth generation. The difficulty is you've got to get it in the first generation to get it in the fourth generation. It takes a long time. If for a long time you don't infuse that blood, you might be too late. The real Trakehner head comes from the Arabian."

He prefers crossing with the Thoroughbred, to bring the quality of toughness. "Eventers like a Trakehner sired by a Thoroughbred. It gives them the hardness, the cross-country speed. You really have to push the warmblood to get the speed, and the Thoroughbred does it easier."

Dr. Eberhard von Velsen, Breed Director of the Trakehner Verband, supported the Thoroughbred as improvement blood. "The warmblood breeds, due to the fact that in the course of their breed histories have always been adapted to changing economic demands and have therefore been selected according to varying criteria, are not so well balanced in their performance traits. To obtain and further enhance performance capability and aptitude in a warmblood horse, which is also to have good riding horse characteristics, the selection process customary to warmblood breeds according to conformation, way of going, pedigree, and constitution alone is not sufficient."

Canadian breeder Guenter Bertelmann said, "Overall, you need a percentage of Thoroughbred blood. I like the most 12 to 25 percent in the modern Trakehner sport horse. The combination with the modern type stallion gives excellent sport horses that the market is asking for."

One of the most influential Thoroughbreds was Perfectionist xx (1903-1906), of the Eclipse line. Of 131 foals, Perfectionist sired 32 stallions and 37 broodmares. He was known for his substance, unusual in a Thoroughbred. Perfectionist sired the influential stallions Tempelhüter, Jagdheld, and Irrlehrer. His broodmares included Posthalterei, dam of the main stallion Parsival. Most of today's Trakehners in Germany, Poland, and Russia trace to this Thoroughbred.

Foaled in 1903, the legendary sire Tempelhüter sired 54 stallions and 60 broodmares. He passed on his type, substance, high withers, and long stride. After his death in 1931, officials added a life-sized, bronze statue of him to the grounds at Trakehnen. Four sons of the Tempelhüter son Poseidon were rescued to the West.

The Parsival line was often crossed with Tempelhüter or Dampfross mares. Parsival's son Kupferhammer was Trakehnen's main stallion, 1931-1940. Another son, Hirtensang, was important in the last years of Trakehnen. His influence continues today due to his son Altan out of a Dampfross daughter. Hirtensang's offspring excel over the founder, Parsival, in type and character, and he is known for producing broodmares.

Jagdheld sired Humboldt, who sired Impuls. Impuls was also known as a broodmare sire, passing on substance, correct conformation, and good character. Jagdheld also sired Kadett and Kassim.

Humboldt also sired Thor, who in 1989 led all German Trakehner stallions as a producer. Thor's get had won more money than any other Trakehner sire.

The Dingo-Dampfross line is prominent today. Known for harmony and balance, substantial bone, and excellent movement, these horses are willing to work and have excellent character. The line produces very good riding horses. The champion dressage horse, Marzog, traces twice to Dampfross.

Pythagoras was by Dampfross out of a Tempelhüter mare. This line carries on Dampfross' ideal legs, light movement, and excellent temperament.

Totilas by Pythagoras founded a new line after World War II. He sired five sons and more

Anita Hunter, Trakehner Breeder

At her Moonlight Farm, Redlands, California, Anita Hunter aims for type and rideability. She feels the Trakehner is the ideal warmblood for American riders.

"We grew up on Thoroughbreds, Arabians, and Quarter Horses. The Trakehner is this wonderful, blessed combination of the old warmblood with a splash of Thoroughbred and Arabian. It makes him an attractive horse, not so bulky. It's a horse that's much easier to ride with much less effort. They're considered the warmest of the warmbloods in Germany, but for the Americans they're a piece of cake."

She likes the cross between the older, heavier Trakehner and the more modern mare, looking for an "in-between" horse. She describes her stallion Tropez (Schwalbenzug—Pregelstrand) as this type. "I'm trying to breed a horse that's big enough, with big feet, big bone, and the movement, without petiteness. I want you to look and know that's a Trakehner." She stands two other stallions, Sigurd (Pergamos—Wirbelwind xx) and Fabius (Memelruf—Persaldo).

Hunter sees the breeder's role as an educator. With only 120 approved stallions in North America, the Trakehner still comprises only a small percentage of American sport horses.

"I spend lots of time with people who come visit the farm. We're such a small breed, and I feel that for me it's an obligation. Gerda Friedrichs told me the Trakehner horse was a responsibility, not a gift. The Trakehner has a rather emotional and romantic past. When you read the accounts of their survival over the last couple of centuries, you get very possessive about them.

"You really get hooked on them. I don't ride anything else now, they're just such a joy."

than 80 approved broodmares. His offspring are recognizable due to the expressive Pythagoras head. Pythagoras was also the grandsire of Pepel, a stallion which won the Olympic gold medal in dressage.

Komet, the great-grandsire of Amiego, was also of this line. He was foaled out of the mare Kokette, sired by Cancara.

Pregel, by Tropenwald and out of a mare with Fetysz as a grandsire, sired Donauwind, the sire of Abdullah. Both Pregel and Donauwind have strongly influenced the breed's regeneration.

Before World War II, other Thoroughbreds influenced the breed. Sahama xx sired Vorwarts, who sired Flugel out of a Dampfross mare. Flugel was main sire, 1873-1887. He passed on Trakehner type through succeeding generations, through the main stallions Eberhard, Discant, and Passvan.

Thunderclapp was the son of Mickle Fell xx. A main stallion in 1844-1864, he founded the chestnut herd, considered Trakehnen's best herd. Dampfross also contributed to the chestnut herd, along with Poseidon, Hyperion, Airolo xx, Hirtensang, Termit, and Lowelas ox.

After the war, Thoroughbred sires included Stern xx. He had good bone, and crossed with mares from consolidated lines to strengthen desirable and eliminate undesirable Thoroughbred qualities. Horses of this line include Preussengeist and Trautmann.

Pasteur xx was used by Trakehner and Rhineland breeders. His son Mahagoni was champion of the 100-Day Test at Adelheidsdorf and has added elegance to North American Trakehners. The Mahagoni son Donnerfurst, an outstanding Trakehner stallion in North America, passes on the smoothness, elegance, and temperament of the Mahagoni line.

Few Thoroughbred or Arabian stallions are currently being used in Germany. In 1980, 40 Thoroughbred and 12 Arabian sires covered only five percent of all Trakehner mares. Breeders do realize that with the small population, the gene pool can become too small.

Robin Koenig explained, "The Trakehner Verband gives its breeders the Anglo-Trakehner and says, 'Run with it. We'll look in three years to see if it's what we want.' They let the line die out if it's not what they want." In 1990, five of the 15 stallions approved were Anglo-Trakehner, and two were in the premium group.

Three stallion lines now dominate the breed—Pregel, Impuls, and Flaneur. Representing other lines, Malachit is also a sire in Holstein. Caprimond was the champion at the 100-Day test in Adelheidsdorf in 1988.

Trakehner stallions continue the tradition of taking the first initial of their names from the dam line. Breeders recognize the importance of the dam. For example, dams are credited for certain lines of sport horses, such as the jumpers Saaleck and Zauberfee.

The mare Heraldik was very influential in Trakehnen's black herd. Her descendants in later generations have names beginning with the prefix, Herbst. Many mares were known for producing main stallions, such as the Tempelhüter daughters, Pechmarie (produced Pythagoras), Technik (produced Termit), Kronhuterin (produced Kupferhammer by Parsival), and Palasthuterin (produced Pilger by Luftgott).

Trakehners in North America

Trakehners came to North America when Gerda Friedrichs imported breeding stock to Canada in 1957. A German immigrant, she started a breeding program with four stallions and 12 mares.

The Trakehner has flourished in North America, with over 4000 registered horses. The American Trakehner Association (ATA), founded in 1974, is the only German-recognized Trakehner registry in North America. In 1977, some members who disagreed with changes in ATA regulations formed another registry, the North American Trakehner Association. This group accepts Trakehners not born in West Germany, or out of horses other than those accepted by the German Verband.

The split has affected the breed's reputation. Some North American equestrians criticize the Trakehner as lacking a unified breeding program, and too much "politics."

CHAPTER 6
The Westfalen

Prussian horses were bred in the province of Westfalia, originally a duchy. In this traditional breeding area, farmers maintained their own breeding records. Horses' bloodlines dated back through the generations of both human and equine families.

When Westfalia became part of Prussia in 1815, breeders organized into the *Züchter Westfalens und der Rheinprovinz*. A *Landgestüt* was founded at Warendorf in 1826, started with 13 East Prussian stallions. Like Celle, *Landgestüt* Warendorf added stallion stations. By 1830, there were 50 stallions throughout the province, and 100 stallions by 1878.

Located south of Hannover, the breed relied on a Hannoverian foundation. Horses of Westfalia earned a similar reputation as an older type of foundation horse. Some Thoroughbred, East Prussian, Beberbecker, and Graditzer horses were also used. The animals intended for farm work had straight shoulders, short pasterns, and straight hind legs.

The breed did not gain its own identity until the 20th century. In 1904, breeders founded the *Westfälisches Pferdestammbuch* (Westfalian studbook). When the Rheinlander state stud at Wickrath closed in 1956, it consolidated with Warendorf to form the Nordrhein-Westfälisches

Landgestüt. The Westfalen brand was established in 1966.

Today the Westfalen is the second largest breed in Germany, with 11,000 registered mares and over 200 stallions. The association has 8000 members, with farmers owning most of the mares.

The modern breed began in the 1920s with Hannoverian lines. Recent infusions of Thoroughbred and Trakehner blood have been very influential on the breed's conformation.

U.S. breeder Jayne Ayers explained, "The breeders organized their association to model on Lower Saxony. Their breeding aim is equal to the Hannoverian. They have both state and private stallions. They have a lot of the older style mares, and also Thoroughbred stallions."

Westfalen horses have achieved memorable successes in recent years. Ahlerich by Angelo xx won the gold medal in the 1984 Olympics and was World Champion in 1982. His full brother Amon was on the Dutch team at the 1984 Olympics.

The World and Olympic Champion Rembrandt demonstrates the traits of a world-class dressage horse. Rembrandt by Romadour II won the gold medals at the 1988 Olympics and the 1990 World Championships. His score in Stockholm was 1569

At the 1990 World Equestrian Games, USET rider Anne Kursinski schools the stallion Starman before a jumping round.

in the Grand Prix Special—the highest score ever awarded in the World Championships. Other dressage champions are Ganimedes (gold medal team 1988 Olympics and individual bronze medal winner 1990 World Championships) and Malte (team bronze in 1986 World Championships).

Two Westfalens have carried riders to individual wins at the World Championships. Roman was the 1978 World Champion. Fire II won in 1982, and in that year both Fire II and Roman were on Germany's silver medal team.

Chef was on the 1986.U.S. team that won the World Championship in jumping. At the 1988 Olympics, Starman helped win the team silver medal. McLain was fourth in the individual competition.

Pedro by Pilot was on the gold medal team in 1988. Pamina by Polydor was on Germany's silver medal team at the 1990 World Championships. Alabaster placed eighth individually in the 1990 World Championship of Three-day eventing.

With the achievements of Westfalen horses, the state has gained a reputation as a superior breeding area. In a 1990 rating of studbooks, the Nordrhein-Westfalen horses placed first.

Contemporary breeders emphasize rideability. The horse has a reputation for athletic ability, good character, and a reliable temperament. It resembles other German breeds, although it is known for lighter bone and a sensitive yet amenable temperament.

"They are breeding in more Thoroughbred, so the horse has a lighter type and is easier to ride," explained Lucy Parker of the Westfalen Warmblood Association of America. "My understanding is they wanted to breed a lighter type overall...The demand structures the horse. They breed what wins, because everyone wants to ride a winner. They're interested in breeding what is in demand, and what might be easier for more people to ride."

The Westfalen breed enjoys a prime equestrian location. Its stud shares the premises of the *Deutsches Reitschule* (German Riding School), and the offices of the *Deutschen Reiterlichen Vereinigung* (FN, or German Equestrian Federation) are also nearby.

Warendorf has become a center for German riding and training, which has enhanced the growth of the Westfalen. Prominent trainers have established barns in the area and naturally use local horses.

The state stallions are stationed throughout the Rheinland-Westfalen region. Like Celle, Warendorf breeds stallions to mares both naturally and with artificial insemination.

The association conducts an aggressive marketing effort. Auctions at Münster-Handorf sell foals and riding horses. A stallion parade at the state stud attracts enthusiastic audiences.

Westfalen Bloodlines

Like the Hannoverian, the Westfalen has incorporated sires of several breeds. The Anglo-Arabian Ramzes was a prominent sire based in Westfalia. He was used as an improvement sire in breeding areas such as Schleswig-Holstein, Bayern, Rheinland, and Hannover, along with the Trakehner, Danish and Dutch breeds.

Ramzes was foaled in Poland in 1937. He stood in Austria-Hungary before coming to Germany. In 1948, this gray stallion came to Westfalia to stand at the stud of Clemens von Nagel.

Von Nagel was an outstanding breeder, who produced five horses that won medals in Olympic Games. His father had directed the Beberbeck stud, and von Nagel bred sport horses in Westfalia for 40 years.

Ramzes x was sired by Rittersporn xx out of a Shagya Arabian mare. His dam Jordi traced twice to Amurath ox, a foundation Polish sire. This prepotent stallion stamped his get and succeeding generations with a distinctive head and neck. He also passed on his endurance, willingness, and jumping talent.

Von Nagel crossed Ramzes with mares of Beberbecker and Holsteiner breeding. He used this stallion to refine old-style mares, to add more expression with a elegant head and longer neck set higher on the shoulder.

Ramzes produced outstanding competition horses and breeding stock. His son Robin was on Germany's gold-medal winning team in show-jumping at the 1972 Olympics. Remus won the silver medal at the 1964 Olympics in dressage, and the silver medal in the 1966 World Championships. Another son, Mariano, was the first World Champion in dressage in 1966 and fourth in 1970. Both brothers helped win the team gold medal for Germany at the 1966

The Westfalen Future has a desirable expression— a large, clear eye that reflects a calm yet alert character.

World Championships.

The Ramzes sons Radetzky and Raimond were Ramzes' most famous breeding stallions. Radetzky (1954-1974) was out of one of Von Nagel's Beberbecker mares. This gray stallion produced 20 approved sons, including Remus I and Remus II, and Raimondo. He also sired 29 State's Premium mares.

A grandson of Remus I was Romadour II (1972-1983). This influential contemporary sire was a champion in-hand and under saddle. He won the stallion testing at Warendorf in 1973. His son Rembrandt is out of a dam by Angelo xx.

Signor Fagotto

Foaled in 1979, this gray Westfalen gelding came to the U.S. as a four-year-old. His sire was Damokles and his dam Connue by Condus traces back to Ramzes through Radetzky.

He was imported from Germany by his owner, Colorado dressage rider Cynthia Dunoyer. She gave him his name after the operetta, *Il Signor Fagotto*, by Offenbach. Dunoyer and her trainer Nancy Chesney have both ridden and shown the horse.

Dunoyer recalled that on first sight, Chesney predicted the horse would advance through the levels to Grand Prix. Dunoyer said, "He is very bright and very kind." However, she found working with the young horse was "slow and difficult. He was a four-year-old, and just begin-

ning to walk, trot, and canter."

Chesney described Fagotto as "a kind of a lazy horse. But he's consistent, like the Rock of Gibraltar. He never takes faulty steps...he always hangs in there. He is an exceptionally good horse about putting up with the back and forth. Cynthia and I could both ride him at the same show."

Signor Fagotto won the 1987 AHSA Western Regional Championships Fourth Level Finals with a score of 62.71 and was third in Horse of the Year. This talented horse is now showing Intermediare I and II, and in 1990 he won both championships in the Rocky Mountain Dressage Society.

Romadour II also sired 13 approved sons and 56 State's Premium mares. His grandson Royal Angelo is out of the same dam as Rembrandt.

Raimond (Holst.) sired 6 sons and 122 daughters for the Holsteiner breed. His most famous son was Ramiro, a champion jumper and prepotent sire. Out of a Cottage Son xx mare, this stallion has sired offspring for the Holsteiner, Westfalen, and Dutch breeds. His get excel in competition and as breeding stock.

Thoroughbreds have contributed to the Westfalen's success. Angelo xx (1967-1982) sired Ahlerich and Amon. Papayer xx sired Paradox I and Paradox II. Paradox I (1967-1987) sired 18 stallions and 34 State's Premium mares.

Pluchino xx sired Perseus, whose son Pilatus was out of a Duellant mare. Pilatus (1968-1985) has three prominent sons: Pilot, Polydor, and Roemer (Dutch). Pilot, out of a Graphit mare, is currently one of Germany's top jumper sires. Pilot stood third on the list of Germany's top money-winning sires in 1989. In his age group of 652 stallions, he was first with 109 offspring competing. Polydor sired breeding stock and performance horses. His daughter Pamina won the 1990 Spruce Meadows Masters. Roemer, by Pilatus, was approved in Holland and is now a dressage horse and sire in the U. S.

Hannoverian state stallions are noted in the Westfalen stallion book with "Celle" after their names. Sires represent the familiar bloodlines, such as the G-line, F-line, and D-line. The stallion Fruhling (1963-1986), a descendant of Feiner Kerl on both sides of his pedigree, sired 14 approved sons and 24 State's Premium mares. The jumper Fire is of the Fruhling line.

A current prominent sire is Der Clou, foaled in 1981. Of Hannoverian breeding, this stallion by Diadem has produced sons for both the Westfalen and Rheinlander associations.

North American Westfalens

Admirers founded the Westfalen Warmblood Association of America in 1987. This club recognizes the horses' achievements and promotes the breed in America.

Breeder Jayne Ayers sees many Westfalen horses in competition. "In judging, I see almost as many Westfalen as Hannoverians in the U.S. There are very few Westfalen mares here, because few breeding stock have been imported."

The German sire Der Clou displays balanced conformation. Photo by Sangmeister; courtesy of Westfälisches Pferdestammbuch.

CHAPTER 7

The Oldenburger

T he Oldenburger has undergone substantial modifications since it developed in the County of Oldenburg, a fertile area on the West Bank of the Weser river. Originating in Northern Oldenburg, in the area known as the "Oldenburg Weser Marsh," horses were sometimes called the "Marsh horse."

The breed traces its ancestry back to Count Johann XVI (the Younger) von Oldenburg (1573-1603). He used the large, strong Friesian horses as a basis for a lighter riding horse. His successor, Count Anton Günther von Oldenburg (1603-1667), solidified the breed.

The Count established stud farms and breeding stations, along with a royal stable at Rastede. He imported breeding stallions from Spain, Naples, Poland, and Turkey, to cross with the region's strong mares.

The Count's stock included over a thousand attractive riding and carriage horses, and he sold horses to rulers across Europe. The large, heavy, yet elegant coach horses became known for their beauty and strength.

His efforts established Oldenburg as a prosperous breeding area of the 17th century. In accordance with royal custom, the Count also used horses as diplomatic exchange. His offer

The Oldenburger Walzertakt competed for the U.S. at the 1990 World Equestrian Games, ridden by Robert Dover.

Landfurst, sired by the Holsteiner Landgraf I, is branded Oldenburger and now stands in Hannover. German rider and breeder Paul Schockemöhle bred the stallion.

of royally bred horses reportedly helped to prevent the invasion of Oldenburg in 1623.

Denmark ruled Oldenburg from 1667-1713, and horse breeding continued under King Christian V von Denmark. By 1784, there were over 16,000 horses in the North marshlands and the sandy regions (*Geest*) of South Oldenburg.

In this uniform breeding area, the first official Stallion Certification occured in 1820. The state's selection commission began applying strict guidelines to its choice of breeding stock. Examiners had noted the breed's decline, with stock showing coarseness. Many horses had long backs, short necks, and Roman noses.

In the 19th century, royalty transferred responsibility for the breeding to the private sector. Unlike the Hannoverian and Westfalen areas, Oldenburg had no state stud. Farmers followed the popular trends of crossing with Hannoverian, Cleveland Bay, and English Thoroughbred horses.

One prominent stallion was the "Stäveschen

Stallion," foaled in England in 1806 and imported to the breeding district in 1820. This stallion sired two famous sons, Neptun and Thorador.

In 1861, the farmers of Oldenburg established a studbook to register the strong, muscular breeding stock. They maintained their breeding aim of a heavy carriage horse, despite the introduction of Thoroughbred and half-bred bloodlines.

The breed gained a reputation as an excellent coach and farm horse. It had strong legs, powerful muscles, and a good neck. The robust Oldenburg boasted plenty of bone and moved with high action. Maturing early, horses were able to work at the age of two. They were also known as easy keepers, despite their size.

The breed worked the fields, served in Oldenburg's cavalry, and pulled mail coaches between Oldenburg and Bremen, a journey shortened to only four hours. Oldenburg became a Prussian state in 1871. In 1897, a new law governed the licensing of stallions and mares, in addition to establishing awards for outstanding breeding stock. Hannoverian and Anglo-Norman stallions contributed to further improvement of the breed.

A breeders' association was located in two areas—in Rodenkirchen for the heavy carriage horse, and in Vechta for the lighter farm horse. The breed became known as the heaviest of the German warmbloods. Horses continued to earn praise for strength, with a good neck, wide chest, and strong thighs. The best of the breed combined the impression of power with nobility. Horses were refined, yet massive and kind.

When North and South joined to form the *Verband der Züchter des Oldenburger Pferdes* in 1923, their breeding aim described a "new" Oldenburger: a horse that was "strong-boned, full-bodied, efficient, light on feed, fertile, and long-lived." No longer needed as a carriage horse, the Oldenburg area produced all-around

East Friesian

An old breed, the East Friesian (Ostfriesland) is closely related to the Oldenburger. Based on the Friesian horse, it includes ancestors from the Andalusian, Neapolitan, and Yorkshire Coach breeds.

Ostfriesland established regulations governing stallion selection in 1715. For-mal stallion inspections began in 1814, and mare inspections in 1859.

These coach horses also incorporated Thoroughbred and Arabian blood. To-day a riding and driving horse, they stand from 15.3 to 16.3 hands. The horses are now bred in the state of Thuringia.

---

artillery horses according to the Third Reich's farm production regulations. After World War II, the association was faced with a dramatic drop in the number of horses, from 55,000 to 10,000 between 1945-1984.

Oldenburg is now a small city-state surrounded by Niedersachsen. To continue the Oldenburger's long tradition and to compete with neighboring breeding areas, breeders determined to change the horse. In a radical change beginning in the 1960s, the Verband transformed the carriage animal into a modern riding horse.

A high percentage of Thoroughbred stallions entered the breeding program to refine the breed. These sires lightened the heavy, agricultural mares. The resulting generation of mares was crossed with improvement stallions from the Thoroughbred, Hannoverian, and Trakehner breeds, and also from Thoroughbred-influenced breeds such as the Anglo-Norman and Anglo-Arabian. To consolidate the breed, breeders crossed the third and fourth generations with stallions of desirable bloodlines from the improvement stock.

Dr. Roland Ramsauer was Breeding Director of the Verband for 18 years. He explained,

"When I started my job in 1971, we had 60 percent Thoroughbred stallions in our breeding area, to get the better type on the coach horse. In this first generation, we call the first filial generation, we cross with the Hannoverian, Westphalian, and French stallions to put more foreign blood from outside into the Oldenburger population.

"Then in the third generation, it depends from the size and the type of the horse if we cross them again with a more Thoroughbredy looking stallion, or a heavier stallion with good performance bloodlines in the pedigree."

The Verband's aggressive marketing approach altered the breed's appearance within two decades. Breeders succeeded in the aim of a taller, lighter, and more elegant sport horse. Today's Oldenburger stands from 16.2 to 17.2 hands, with a strong back, deep girth, and muscular hindquarters. The horse displays the plain head and shorter leg length of many German warmbloods, and it retains its good bone.

Oldenburg remains a separate breeding area within Lower Saxony. Other areas also breed Oldenburgers, including the former DDR, Denmark, and the Netherlands.

Grand Canyon

Sired by the Hannoverian state stallion, Graphit, the Oldenburger Grand Canyon was bred by Anton Fischer. Gunter Kraut, an *Aufzüchter*, bought the colt as a foal in 1984 and raised him at his farm in southern Germany.

Dr. Ramsauer recalled branding two outstanding colts at Fischer's farm. "I branded two very famous horses, Grand Canyon and Pasquinel. Grand Canyon was number one when presented, and Pasquinel is also a champion." Kraut's manager took dressage lessons from Gerhard Politz, and he invited Politz to view the stallion prospects before they went to the *Körung*. Politz preferred Grand Canyon and Pasquinel. He recalled, "This one [Grand Canyon] appealed to me because he would be the 175 cm that the Holsteiners liked. I turned the horses out to check their temperaments. In the field, these two were playing. Pasquinel was more Thoroughbredy-looking, but in this country [the U.S.] we need a good cross with the Thoroughbred mares. Grand Canyon has good bone, a good topline, and the best Grande lines."

Politz offered the horse to Cinema Farms Breeding Corporation, Rowland Heights, California. They were captivated by him and agreed to buy him. Grand Canyon was sold on contingency that he would pass the licensing and performance test in Germany. He received his stallion license at the Oldenburger *Körung* and passed the 100-Day test at Marbach. He also won the gold medal breeder award for Herr Kraut at Marbach.

Because this stallion did not enter the Hannoverian licensing at Verden, the Hannoverian state stud did not have the opportunity to claim him. Cinema Farms imported the stallion in January, 1986, and Grand Canyon sired his first U.S. foals in 1987. At ISR approvals, five of five foals presented received the First Premium award in 1989 and 1990.

Standing 16.2 hands, Grand Canyon is a deep-bodied dark bay. Cinema Farms' David Wilson has shown the stallion at first level dressage, winning two AHSA high point awards of 75.416 and 70.833 points. Grand Canyon also won Champion Stallion at the 1989 Los Angeles Breeders Classic.

With the horses sharing backgrounds with their Hannoverian neighbors, the modern Oldenburger strongly resembles other breeds. It has become one of the German riding horses, a correct riding horse with energetic, ground-covering movement.

The term Oldenburger no longer describes a specific type, but a geographic origin. Trainer and breeder Gerhard Politz said, "The diversity of the breeds before the war is gone. Oldenburgers and Holsteiners are not heavy any more." The changed market led to the disappearance of the old, solid horses, which some equestrians consider a loss to the horse world and a warning to other breed societies.

Oldenburger sport horses include the world-class jumpers Grand Slam, Waldkanzler, and Playback. Warwick Rex won the individual gold and team silver medals in the 1976 Olympics. In dressage, Olympic Petit Prince competed in the 1988 Olympics, and Walzertakt competed in the 1990 World Championships. The eventer Volturno won the team silver medal at the 1976 Olympics, and was 1978 World Champion.

Donnerhall (Donnerwetter-Markus) was the Champion Stallion at the prestigious DLG show in 1986. He was the first privately-owned stallion to achieve this honor. A German Champion mare, Ausnahme, is also an Oldenburger.

In Oldenburg, all horse-breeding is in private hands. The 2800-member Verband maintains the registry of 4500 horses, with about 100 stallions in 20 private farms. Auctions at Vechta attract enthusiastic buyers.

Prominent lines feature French imports, such as Almé and Inschallah X. The Anglo-Norman Condor sired Consul. Zeus is a famous sire throughout German breeding areas. Foaled 1972, Zeus is of Anglo-Arab lines. Besides siring horses in Oldenburg, he is recognized by the Hannoverian, Hessen, Rheinlander, and Westfalen associations.

A famous sire of the breed is Furioso II, foaled 1965. Sired by France's prominent Thoroughbred, Furioso, this stallion was a champion in the 100-Day Test. He was a prepotent sire of 55 stallions, and also the leading sire of German sport horses in the 1980s.

In Oldenburg, Furioso II produced well with the Thoroughbred-cross mares. His success encouraged other societies to add French blood, and his get were accepted by all German associations. A prominent son is Freiherr, who has produced the stallion Feiner Stern. Another son of Furioso xx in the Oldenburg breeding area is Futuro.

Most Thoroughbred lines are now two or three generations back from today's Oldenburger. Hannoverian lines are also prominent, due to the proximity of the two breeding areas. Oldenburger pedigrees often include horses of the familiar A-, D-, and G-lines. Pik Bube represents the Pik As xx line.

In North America, the International Sporthorse Registry represents the Oldenburger Verband. Its Breeding Director, Dr. Roland Ramsauer, actively adds quality North American mares to the Verband's Main Mare Book. Foals by Oldenburg-approved stallions can receive the Oldenburg brand.

CHAPTER 8

Warmblood Breeds of Central and Southern Germany

G ermany's traditional horse-breeding areas have been in the agricultural North. However, famous studs also exist in the central and southern regions. Today each state has developed its own breeding area, to compete with the better-known horses of Hannover, Westfalia, Oldenburg, and Schleswig-Holstein.

Like the North, all areas have changed from breeding utility animals to sport horses. Although most areas have long histories of horse breeding, in recent decades all have developed their contemporary stock through use of Hannoverian and Trakehner horses.

These breeding areas participate in the breeding goal of German associations, as described by Dr. Roland Ramsauer: "A noble, large-framed, and correct riding horse, with elastic and extensive movements. The horse should be qualified for all kinds of riding based on its temperament, its character, and rideability.

Based on this, the breeding organizations remain on one hand independent, and on the other hand they created the conditions to use the breeding capacities in common."

Rheinlander

In the province of Nordrhein, breeders share the Warendorf state stud with the Westfalen. Their traditional stud Wickrath, named after Count von Wickrath, was founded in 1839 and closed in 1957. The studbook was begun in 1892, and the first breeders' association organized in 1902.

Breeders of the Rheinland used the Trakehner stallions Garamond and Patron, along with representative Hannoverian and Westfalen lines. Romadour II sired Rheingold, champion of the Rheinland stallion testing and a prominent sire. The Olympic competitor Romantico was a Rheinlander.

Robert Dover schools the Rhinelander gelding Romantico before their competition at the 1984 Olympics.

Rhineland-Pfalz-Saar

Along the fertile plain of the Rhine was the Rhineland Palatinate, a principality of the Holy Roman Empire. Its state stud, Zweibrücken, was established in 1755 by Duke Christian IV von Pfalz-Zweibrücken. The stud traded over 100 stallions with Trakehnen.

In the Napoleonic wars, many stallions were taken by the French. A famous painting portrays Napoleon mounted on a gray Zweibrücken stallion during the Battle of Austerlitz.

Approximately 30 Zweibrücken stallions stand at the State Stud today. The *Pferdezuchterverband Rhineland-Pfalz-Saar*, formed in 1977, maintains the registry. This Verband amalgamated separate associations in Rheinhessen-Pfalz-Saar and Rheinland-Nassau.

Bayern (Bavarian)

Bavaria was an electorate of the Holy Roman Empire. Its state stud Landshut has been replaced by Schwaiganger.

There are about 2000 mares in the state. The recently-established studbook relies on Hannoverian stock. Bavarians have been major buyers of Hannoverian stallions in recent decades. The stallions also include Thoroughbred and Trakehner sires. The Trakehner Maharadascha stood many years in Bavaria. At the 1990 World Championships, the Bayern gelding Nepomuk was on Germany's silver medal jumping team.

Hessicher (Hessen)

In Hesse were the Beberbeck and Ulrichstein studs, producing stallions and cavalry horses respectively. Another royal stud in the Nassau area produced horses known as the "Dillenburger Ramsnasen," bred by the Dillenburg dukes. These horses were popular across Europe in the 18th and 19th centuries.

State studs appeared as early as 1737 when Count Wilhelm VIII established the Kassel Stud. Other studs followed in Darmstadt, Weilburg, and Arolsen. In 1870, Prussia brought many stallions to a provincial stud in Dillenburg.

The Hessiche Studbook was published as early as 1903. Like other breeds, the Hessiche developed from a working warmblood horse into a sport horse after World War II.

The *Verband Hessicher Pferdezüchter e. V.* organized in 1960. Breeders concentrated on using stallions from Hannoverian, Holsteiner, Thoroughbred, and Trakehner lines. In 1988, breeders could choose from 63 state-owned and 72 privately owned stallions. The State Stud at Dillenburg maintains 18 stallion stations throughout Hessen.

The jumper Halla, World Champion in 1954, is the most famous horse of Hessen breeding.

Sired by the state stallion Oberst, she was out of a French trotter mare.

The breed's recent jumping stars include the World Cup finalist Intermezzo (Imperial-Lotse). Antaris (Almgold Z-Faffnir xx) won the German Federal Championships of 1988, over Holsteiner, Hannoverian, and Westfalen horses.

In dressage, Floriano (Fiothor-Halali) won the highest prize money of any dressage horse in the world in 1987. Nektar (Nelson-Radetzky), a former sire at Dillenburg, competed in the World Cup and was chosen for the Olympic team in 1988.

The breed has grown to become Germany's fourth largest in terms of active broodmares. Approximately 1200 foals are born each year, and the Verband markets horses through auctions in Darmstadt-Kranichstein.

The state stud opened a stallion-raising farm in Altefeld, site of a former Prussian stud, in 1987. It also operates a state riding and driving school, founded in 1930.

Baden-Württemburg

This provincial breed originated at the one of the oldest state studs, Marbach, originally founded 1552. The stud was later developed by the kings Wilhelm of Württemburg. Breeding stock included Arabian, Anglo-Norman, and East Prussian horses.

Through the centuries, the stud produced horses according to local needs. The Württemburg horses were bred for farm work.

They resulted from blending oriental lines, including Marbach's famous Arabian stallions, with local mares and breeds such as the East Friesian, Anglo-Norman, Holsteiner, and Hungarian.

In the early 20th century, the typical Württemburg was a medium-weight horse of cobby appearance with short legs, known for hardiness. It stood about 16 hands.

The studbook opened in 1895. In 1952, the two areas were merged into one, and the *Pferdezuchterverband Baden-Württemburg* was established in 1978.

Through the 1960s, the breed regenerated into a performance horse through the use of Trakehner blood. The average height of three-year-old mares increased from 158 cm in 1972 to 164 cm in 1983. Today the horse stands 15.3 to 16.2 hands, and is the third most populous breed in Germany.

The Trakehner sire Julmond is considered the foundation of Württemburg sport horses. This sire and his sons Ikarus, Taifun, and Lothar added refinement. Marbach continues to utilize Trakehners, with one-third of its sires tracing to this breed. Württemburg stallions also represent Hannoverian lines such as the F-line, along with sires of Westfalen and Thoroughbred breeding.

Marbach still breeds purebred Arabians. The stud's 100 horses include warmblood stallions and mares. A site for warmblood stallion testing, the stud also maintains raising farms and almost 30 stallion stations.

CHAPTER 9
The Selle Français

I n horse-breeding as in empire-building, France has rivalled its neighbor Germany. Its Anglo-Norman, now known as the Selle Français, influences many breeding areas on the Continent, and France rated second in the 1990 rating of sport horse studbooks. With characteristic Gallic aplomb, French horses today continue the triumphs of *la belle France*.

France's breeding blends a long history with a strong bureaucratic structure. Like Germany, France's empire depended on horses to perpetuate its glory. The nobles' sovereignty relied upon the feudal system, and the rivalries of monarchies and duchies required cavalry.

Geography placed France close to Europe's horse-breeding centers. Wars of the 16th and 17th centuries brought Spanish and Neapolitan horses to the French kingdom. The state began its involvement in France's horse industry in the 17th century, when King Louis XIV (1643-1715) aimed to enlarge France's kingdom abroad. Louis epitomized the royal prerogatives during a magnificent era of French history. This absolute ruler built Versailles and expanded France's military might.

The king's administrator, Colbert, cemented the state's power over daily life and commerce.

One of his products was France's *Service des Haras* (Stud Service). In 1665, the state established a series of *Haras Nationaux*, or National Studs. Its stallion depots stood horses purchased by the state in order to improve horse production. A royal stud was founded at Montfort-l'Amaury. Others included the Haras du Pin (1714-1728), Pompadour (1761), and Rosier du Sellin (1768).

France's extravagance was emulated by German princes and dukes, who admired Louis XIV and wanted to establish similar courts. After state visits to France, the courts of Celle and Hannover were modeled on the style of Versailles. The state studs in Germany copied the French concept, while the French imported stallions from Holstein, Mecklenburg, and Denmark.

France's famous cavalry school, Saumur, opened in 1771. Saumur relied on remounts from the state studs. The French Revolution (1789) destroyed the school, but it reopened in 1815.

After the Revolution and the abolition of feudalism, France became a nation of free farmers. The Revolution closed the studs, but Napoleon Bonaparte (1804-1815) re-established the state's horse-breeding. In 1806 the Emperor created six national studs, 30 stallion depots, and three riding schools. Under his rule, 1500 stallions stood at stud, and cavalry become the elite of the French army. The Napoleonic wars added new blood from the far-flung empire when troops captured horses from Egypt, Prussia, and Austria.

Breeding declined in the 1820s, although Louis XVIII (1814-1824) supported the industry. Le Pin became an *École des Haras* (school for breeding) as well as a stallion depot. The Stud's director, Gayot, founded principles of selection and crossbreeding. By the 1830s, French studs had begun adding the blood of English Thoroughbreds. The country established its Ministry of Agriculture in 1836, which has continued to direct, control, and encourage the horse industry.

Breeders continued to cross native horses with other breeds.To develop horses for military and coaching uses, the government imported Thoroughbred and Norfolk Trotter stallions. France's coach horses, in turn, later influenced the regional breeds of Westfalia, Oldenburg, and Hannover.

The *demi-sang*, or halfbred, horses took their names from their respective breeding areas. Each regional breed varied in its type and background. The Anglo-Norman was the most popular.

Traditionally a center of horse-breeding since the Middle Ages, Normandy produced substantial horses. The Anglo-Norman's ancestry included the Norman war horse, Arabian, Thoroughbred, and Norfolk Trotter. The breed was developed as a coach horse, and it also served as a light draft and heavy cavalry horse and produced the French Trotter. The Norman studbook was founded in 1949 for saddle horses.

Other regional riding horse breeds included the Vendéen, Charolais, Breton, Limousin, Corlais, Cotentin, Angevin, and northern Britanny. Breeders in the southern provinces tended to breed more Arabian and Anglo-Arab lines.

After another decline during the reign of Napoleon III (1852-1870), Bocher encouraged the industry by re-establishing the stud's administration and defining breeding areas. A remount service with 15 depots operated from 1831 to 1945. In 1905, France's horse population numbered over 3 million. The studs, located in 23 central towns, housed 3200 stallions representing all breeds. About 18 percent were Thoroughbred, Arabian, or Anglo-Arab. These were sent to 690 stations.

The state fostered Europe's largest horse population, and the Ministry of Agriculture provided the greatest support of any government. The state awarded premiums to owners of the best stallions and mares, totalling over £300,000 a year. (England's awards totalled £5000, and Germany's £190,000).

Until 1958, several regions bred light horses under the name demi-sang. In 1958, the new name of Selle Français consolidated all crossbred, regional types of riding horses. The Anglo-Norman, which strongly influenced all other regional breeds, formed the basis for the Selle Français. France published a studbook containing the Arabian, Anglo-Arab, and Selle Français in 1965.

France is now home to one-third of all horses in the European Community. Since World War II, the French have actively sought to produce superior jumpers such as the 1954 World Champion Halla. Other world-class jumpers include Galoubet, on the World Championship team in 1982, Noren, and I Love You, who won the World Championship in 1983. Idéal de la Haye won the team gold and individual bronze medals in the 1982 World Championship.

Jappeloup de Luze was the gold medal winner in the 1988 Olympics and has been an international champion for seven years. He was 1987 European Champion and fourth in the

1986 World Championships. Quito de Baussy won the individual gold medal and the team gold at the 1990 World Championships. The 1990 French team included three Selle Français and an Anglo-Arab.

In North America, the World Cup winner Big Ben was sired by a Selle Français. Other prominent French jumpers include Janus de Ver, Wotan, Webster, Babette VII, and Make My Day.

Until recently, France has not emphasized breeding for the dressage discipline. Breeders have concentrated on jumpers, although the Cor de la Bryere offspring excel in all three Olympic sports. His son, Corlandus, placed fourth at the 1990 World Championships.

Selle Français Characteristics

Today's Selle Français is a noble riding horse standing from 15.3 to 16.3 hands. Its conformation resembles the Thoroughbred's, with more bone and muscle, but not the substance of the old-style German warmbloods. The breed has become more elegant, but still retains its robust, muscular strength.

The horse has a strong frame and sturdy joints with largish feet. Horses vary according to their breeding, but most have long necks. The head might be heavy, yet still charming in its expression. Many influential sires have been chestnut, and the color still predominates.

The Selle Français with a strong concentration of Anglo-Arab breeding may look more like a square-framed rather than rectangular horse. The Arabian influence tends toward the close-coupled body, with a short back.

The North American Selle Français Horse Association, Inc., describes the breed as "a big horse with good movement, capable of covering ground, with a big-boned Thoroughbred conformation and a calm temperament."

The horse moves in balanced gaits with agility. Its natural galloping and jumping ability

The Selle Français Noctuelle III represented France in the three-day event at the 1990 World Equestrian Games.

give it the desirable attributes for eventing and Grand Prix jumping.

The French prefer a sport horse with nerve. The horse courageously performs to meet any challenge, with some authorities noting greater willfulness than horses of German breeding. French authority Bernard Maurel said, "French horses are one of the best in the world at jumping. But they are maybe not always so easy to ride. You need a good technique, different from German horses.

"They are more sport horses, not horses to go hacking. You don't have to push them. You just have to ride. They have more power of themselves."

The breed is grouped by size (height) and weight-carrying ability. Its five categories include medium weights with small sizes, medium sizes, large sizes, and heavy weights with small sizes and large sizes.

Horses also fall into three classes: the competition horse, the race horse, and the riding horse.

The race horse qualifies for races for *Autres Que Pur Sang* (AQPS), or horses other than pure English blood (Thoroughbreds). The AQPS is a crossbred with a higher percentage of Throughbred blood, bred for AQPS racing.

Selle Français Breeding

The government manages horse breeding, along with education, research, and shows. The racing industry supports these activities, through pari-mutuel funds. *The Ministere de l'Agriculture et de la Foret* oversees the *Haras Nationaux* (HN) and the *Institut du Cheval* (Equestrian Sports Department). The HN manages the breeding, marketing, and uses of horses in France. It maintains studbooks and organizes horse shows.

The nation is divided into two *arrondissements*, roughly north and south, with a total of 23 *circonscriptions*, or districts. Each district has its stud.

The HN now maintains only stallions, with breeds of all types based at the studs. Each district has a number of breeding stations, ranging from 7 in Uzes (in the south of France) to 49 in Hennebont (in the west). Le Pin and Pompadour each have 25 stations, and Saint-Lô has 43. During the breeding season, February through June, over 2000 stallions stand at the 383 breeding stations. Like German stallions, the French horses match mares in their local areas.

The *Service des Haras* has applied techniques proven in the racing industry to the development of the sport horse. Regional services oversee all activities, especially the production and registration of foals.

Government regulations have continued to affect breeding in recent decades. The *Service des Haras* applied a 1966 law on breeding, in cooperation with the *Institut du Cheval*, which requires a graphic description of each animal. Laws regulate breeds, names, stallions, identification procedures, selection, and breeders' premiums.

Every stallion may breed mares according to a printed list of mares. If a stallion receives applications to serve many mares, officials may draw lots to limit the number of mares covered. Quotas apply, limiting younger stallions to 35 mares and mature animals to 40 mares. Mares are selected in categories by age, earnings, conformation, performance, and selection indexes of their performance and their descent.

French breeders rely on producing winning athletes through pedigree research. A top performer represents proof of its ancestry, and breeding by pedigree gives the breeder an advantage and eliminates much of the risk.

The *Institut du Cheval* in Pompadour maintains the computerized SIRE, or *Systeme d'identification reportoriant les equides*. Since 1974, this computerized identification system manages data on horses' registration and performance records. The HN and *Institut* rely on electronic databases to aid the success of France's horse industry. Recently they initiated a public information service, HARASIRE. Users can access data from HN and SIRE computerized files.

French horses are named alphabetically, with the first initial changing each year. For example, horses foaled in 1985 had names beginning with T. The initials W X Y and Z are not used.

Government-owned stallions account for almost half the breeding in France. A special commission buys the national stallions, selecting the best three-year-olds. Recently the HN also tested four-year-olds on jumping ability, and they occasionally buy four- and five-year-olds with sport records. They choose horses by conformation, heredity, gaits, and performance of the individual and its ancestors. Stallions must also pass a veterinary examination.

The government owns most of the Selle Français stallions. In 1989, national stallions totaled 264, with an additional 161 private stallions. There were 13,073 Selle Français mares, with 8654 of them bred to Selle Français stal-

The Anglo-Arab

France has bred *l'anglo arabe* since the early 19th century. The breed was defined as a horse with a minimum of 25 percent Arabian blood. Today's horses are usually the result of crossing an Anglo-Arab sire with a Thoroughbred or Arabian, rather than the one-half Thoroughbred, one-half Arabian.

The horse combines the Arabian's durability and courage with the Thoroughbred's speed and will to win. Horses stand from 15.3 to 16.1 hands, smaller and less substantial than the Selle Français. The horse is known for its energy, agility, sensitivity, and grace. Horses are either bay or chestnut.

Bernard Maurel described the breed: "It's a very old breed, more than 150 years, with the Arabian and Thoroughbred stallions used with the same objective of selection—to have riding horses. Now it's like the best of the Trakehner, some very good in jumping, in military, also in dressage. They have a good temperament, a lot of personality, and are good to cross. I like them very much."

Anglo-Arabs continue to excel as international competitors. In jumping, Morgat carried his rider to third place in the 1990 World Championships. He was also on France's bronze-medal team in the 1988 Olympics. Ali Baba won the individual gold medal in the 1952 Olympics. The U. S. jumper Junipérus is an Anglo-Arab.

Anglo-Arab dressage horses included Linon (silver medal in 1928 and 1932 Olympics) and Harpagnon (medals in both the 1948 and 1952 Olympics). The breed also excels in combined training, with winners like Aiglonne (gold medal at the 1948 Olympics), Harley (team silver medal in 1986 World Championships and fourth individually), and Newlot (tenth in the 1990 World Championships).

In three-day eventing, Nos Ecus (Anglo-Arab) was second place Horse of the Year in the United States Combined Training Association, 1989. Two Anglo-Arabs were on France's team at the 1986 World Championships, winning the silver medal.

A substantial number of contemporary French horses trace back to an Anglo-Arabian grandparent or great-grandparent. Anglo-Arabs are crossed with the Selle Français to add brilliant movement, courage, strong tissues, and athletic ability.

The Anglo-Arab stallion Matcho is a state stallion in the Hannoverian breeding area.

The stallion Bonjour stands in the U.S. at Hamilton Farm. Photo by Margaret M. Douglas-Hamilton.

lions that year. In 1989, 8600 Selle Français foals were registered.

Most mares live on small, mixed farms. Farmers breed horses as a sideline, and the average French breeder owns from one to seven mares. In Normandy, some own as many as 15. Breeding is concentrated in the Manche district and around Normandy.

The number of privately owned stallions doubled between 1985 and 1989. French law requires that owners declare stallions for breeding, and a commission examines the horse. The director of the *circonscription* presides over the commission.

The best horses receive the designation "approved" if the commission judges them to improve the breed. Stallions of lesser quality, judged to maintain the breed, receive a license as "authorized." These sires can stand at stud for a determined, renewable period, and their offspring are eligible to compete in French shows. The get of a third category, "accepted"

stallions, can receive a certificate of origin.

The government is actively involved in *Élevage France* (French breeding), providing subsidies and premiums. A special program prior to the 1988 Olympics encouraged the top 10 French performers to remain in France.

France exports significant numbers of riding horses, including close to 1000 in 1988. Over 200 went to Switzerland, with Italy and Belgium second and third in numbers of imports from France.

France still stands second to Germany in its reputation as an equestrian nation. Bernard Maurel said, "The French people are not as good at horse dealing as the Germans. The quality can compete with Germany, but the French breeder is not as professional."

One factor may be the mutual influence between the breeder and the equestrian. As riders have sought horses with natural aptitudes for sport, they used existing animals. Competitors have voiced their needs, and breeders have responded. Many riders became breeders themselves. An outstanding example is Eric Navet, whose father Alain Navet bred the current World Champion jumper stallion, Quito de Baussy.

Breeders generally market foals as weanlings, as three-year-olds, or as four- and five-year-olds when they begin to compete over fences. Horses are sold at farms, through dealers, and at shows.

In 1949, a nonprofit promotional organization was founded: *Union Nationale Interprofessionelle du Cheval* (UNIC). Unique on the Continent, UNIC is a union of 38 associations, recognized by the government to assist horse buyers. UNIC markets French horses worldwide. It provides information, advice, and services to potential importers and handles details of exporting horses, including accreditation of pedigrees, transportation, and veterinary regulations.

Rockwell

"Generous, smooth, incredibly athletic" are some of the words Dale Bormann uses to describe the Selle Français stallion, Rockwell. Registered as Ouragan du Vouge, this 16.2 liver chestnut by Tigre Rouge out of Fanchon is the property of the Rockwell Syndicate. Bormann, of Spokane, Washington, rides and shows him in Fourth Level dressage.

Rockwell was imported from France for the American Sporthorse breeding program. Before his dressage career, the stallion was shown as a jumper on both West and East Coast circuits.

Rockwell's athletic ability and his courageous personality help him excel in both disciplines, which Bormann considers complementary. She called him an "overachiever" about learning new things, as he seems bothered by imperfection. "He can get hot on occasion, but by and large he gives me the benefit of the doubt. If I ask him correctly, he does it correctly. He's capable of doing any of the movements that I ask him for.

"Rockwell is a very listening horse, and he's very generous. I guess I would call him a complicated horse to ride to the upper levels. But I can put students on him and he will do anything he knows for them, if they simply use the aids."

Bormann also praises Rockwell's gaits. She finds it easier to ride him quietly, easier than on a big mover that can overwhelm the rider. "He makes it easy. He doesn't move me around or jar me. I think in the beginning it's better to ride a smooth horse, to get a feeling for the movements."

Rockwell. Photo by Patty McClure-Hosmer.

French Bloodlines

The foundation bloodlines of the Selle Français echo names of progenitors familiar in German sire lines. French breeders credit the Thoroughbred for adding distinction and nerve to the Anglo-Norman, while coach horse ances-tors produced endurance, substance, and soundness.

All Selle Français trace back to the renowned Thoroughbred sires Eclipse, Herod, and Matchem. Eclipse is represented by three contemporary lines. From the stallion St. Simon

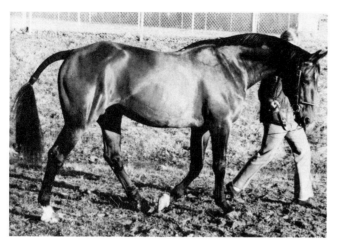

The stallion Galoubet has sired champions in both the U.S. and France. Photo by Margaret M. Douglas-Hamilton.

came Orange Peel xx (1925-1940), sire of 19 sons. Considered the founding Thoroughbred sire of the Selle Français, Orange Peel's most renowned descendant was Ibrahim (1956-1973), by the Anglo-Norman, The Last Orange. Ibrahim sired more than 50 sons in various European studbooks.

Ibrahim's son Almé sired such contemporary stars as Galoubet A, I Love You, and Jalisco B, sire of Quito de Baussy. Galoubet won the French jumping championship as a five-year-old, and in 1989 he sired 20 six-year-olds qualified for that championship.

Almé also stood in the Netherlands and Belgium. His brothers Double Espoir and Elf III are also prominent sires, with Elf III's son Kaoua an Olympic competitor.

Another branch of the St. Simon line, sired by the Anglo-Arabian Israël, produced Oldenburg's Inschallah x. Inschallah has also sired horses in the Hannoverian, Hessen, Rheinland, Westfalen, and Trakehner breeds.

A second Eclipse line, Touchstone xx, produced sires such as the popular Selle

Français Royal Chestnut, Bois Rouaud xx, and Rantzau xx. Rantzau (1951-1971) sired Cor de la Bryere.

The third Eclipse line, Irish Birdcatcher xx, includes such stars as the Selle Français Noren, Laudanum xx, and Ultimate xx. Ultimate sired the stallions Diable Rouge and Prince du Cy. His daughters have crossed successfully with Ibrahim to produce the sires Almé and Elf III. Other horses from this line are the Selle Français Silbersee (a winning jumper and Holsteiner sire) and Night and Day xx (1962-1984), a race winner and prominent sire. A grandson of Irish Birdcatcher, Fra Diavolo xx, sired Nankin, whose son Uriel is one of the most popular contempory sires of show jumpers. The famed Thoroughbred sire Nearco also represents this line.

The Herod line has been known more for its performers than its breeding stallions. Velox x sired many good jumpers. His descendant Jiva competed in the 1984 Olympics. Other sires from this line include Dollar, Tourbillon, and Popof (1955-1979), a sire in Vendée.

In France, the Matchem line is credited with producing an offshoot of the Anglo-Norman, the French Trotter. As a cross with French horses, the Trotter has produced the outstanding performers Galoubet, Jappeloup de Luze, and Halla. The cross adds honest character and energy to Thoroughbred lines.

The Matchem line also became famous due to the reputation of Furioso xx (1946-1967), an Irish Thoroughbred by Precipitation. Purchased by the *Haras Nationaux* soon after World War II, this stallion's accomplishments rebuilt the breeding center at Haras du Pin.

Furioso sired over 300 foals, of which 30 were champions of international events. His daughter Pomone B was World Champion in 1966. Lutteur B won the gold medal in the 1964 Olympics, in which 10 Furioso offspring competed.

Other Furioso descendants include Jexico du Parc by Mexico (sixth at the 1984 Olympics), Belle de Mars (gold medal at the 1976 Olympics), and J'T'Adore (a competitor in the 1984 Olympics).

Furioso has four prominent sons in France: Mexico, Questeur, Surioso, and Vurioso de l'Isle. He also sired stallions at other European studs, including Germany's Futuro and Furioso II.

As a crossbred, the Selle Français continues to incorporate a limited amount of outside bloodlines. A Selle Français stallion can sire Selle Français foals out of registered mares of Thoroughbred, Arabian, French Trotter, and Facteur Selle Français lines.

The Facteur Selle Français mare can be a riding horse brought into the studbook—a horse of another warmblood breed, or the produce of an unregistered mare by a fullblood sire. Sheryl Akers of the North American Selle Français Horse Association defined it as "a horse who is not of 'pure' Selle Français parentage or whose parentage contains horses other than those approved for use in the Selle Français breeding program but who is deemed to be of a quality which could be useful in the breeding program."

With strong stallions in its own studbooks, the Selle Français has produced outstanding sires in recent years. Also, France's aim to promote the industry from within has influenced the development of homebred stallions. Ap-proximately two-thirds of current breedings are Selle Français to Selle Français, with the most popular stallions Royal Chestnut, Ibrahim, and Uriel.

A Selle Français mare may produce a Selle Français foal sired by a stallion of one of these breeds: Thoroughbred, Arabian, or French Trotter. A Selle Français can also result from these crosses: Trotter/Thoroughbred, Trotter/Arabian, and Trotter/Anglo-Arab.

France has influenced horse-breeding in other nations on the Continent, especially its neighbors to the east. French horses contributed to the Hannoverian, Holstein, Oldenburg, Dutch, Danish, and Belgian breeds.

In the 20th century, the French have introduced bloodlines only from English and Irish Thoroughbreds. France has become self-sufficient in that it no longer needs to import outside blood. By restricting importations, the French have maintained an ardent nationalism unique in warmblood breeding. Only recently, in 1989, did France allow a non-French stallion (the American Trakehner stallion, Abdullah) to obtain a breeding permit to breed French mares.

French horses now have a registry in North America. Formed in 1990 after years of negotiation, the North American Selle Français Horse Association, Inc., promotes and registers the Selle Français, Anglo-Arab, and other French horses.

CHAPTER 10
The Dutch Warmblood

The Dutch farmer is known the world over for successful nurturing of livestock and crops. The Netherlands has thrived on an agricultural economy, including one of the world's most successful sport horses.

Dutch History

Like the German warmbloods, Dutch horses developed from an amalgamation of breeds. One ancestor, the Friesian, was unique to the Netherlands. Descended from Andalusian stallions and named for the province Friesland, Friesians carried knights in the Crusades. The strong, agile horse was used in farmwork and coaching. It was known for its high action at the trot, its upright neck, and its trademark black color with feathers on its lower legs. Friesians were the basis for Prussia's East Friesian breed.

Unlike their German counterparts, Dutch farmers did not concentrate on breeding horses for military use. Breeders developed a tradition of independent enterprise separate from any government program. They selected farm horses for the qualities of soundness, character, and willingness to work and also produced carriage horses, which they exported to France and England. The coach horses had high action, reminiscent of the Friesian.

The foundation stock of the contemporary Dutch warmblood were the Gelderlander and Groningen horses. Both breeds descended from heavier horses of Friesian origin and were influenced by Thoroughbred, Cleveland Bay, Hackney, Holsteiner, and Anglo-Norman stock. After 1850, Holland imported many stallions from Oldenburg, Holstein, Hannover, and France, to begin the transition to the modern Dutch warmblood. The first studbook, the *Warmbloed Paarden Stamboek*, was published in 1887.

The southern Gelderland province produced the Gelderlander as a farm horse. Due to the region's sandy soil, the horse was lighter than its neighbor, the Groningen. Most Gelderlanders were chestnuts and had stylish action at the trot.

The Groningen originated in the northern Groningen area, a region of dense clay that required more of a light draft horse. This breed also showed a high action with expressive, substantial conformation. Farmers crossed the two types, refining the Groningen with the Gelderlander and adding bone to the Gelderlander with the Groningen.

Holland and its agriculture endured massive setbacks during World War II. With mechanization, some farmers decided to keep their horses. The sport of horsemanship established riding clubs throughout the country, and shrewd breeders realized they could adapt their native breeds into a riding horse type.

The Dutch breeds had already changed in the direction of the modern horse, with the Gelderlander more popular than the heavier Groningen. Marketwise farmers crossed the established bloodlines with stallions of Thoroughbred, French, Hannoverian, and Holsteiner bloodlines. They aimed to retain the traditional qualities proven on the farm in a riding horse with smooth gaits and a competitive spirit. Selection retained the horse's hardiness, temperament, and soundness.

The farmers experimented with the first post-war generations of crossbreds. They "cleaned up" the gene pool by strict culling, slaughtering those horses which did not meet sport horse requirements. With the goal of breeding jumpers, the Dutch introduced more German and French lines. A substantial percentage of today's Dutch horses are based on stock imported from these two countries.

The Warmbloed Paardenstamboek In Nederland (WPN), which existed before World War II, was reorganized in 1970. This association combined regional studbooks, and it adopted a brand of a rampant lion.

Dutch horses excel in equestrian sport. In the 1980s, they dominated the international jumping circuit. Calypso, Box Car Willie, Ardennes, Larramy, Linky, Shining Example, and Apollo II were world-class competitors. The Freak helped win Germany's gold medal in the 1988 Olympics. Current Grand Prix jumpers in North America include Northern Magic, Corsair, Eastern Sunrise, V.I.P., Lego, Zadok, Volan, Voilà T, Medrano, Maybe Forever, Saluut II, Warrant, and Zulu.

The breed also produces world-class dressage horses. Ideaal was on Germany's gold medal team at the 1990 World Championships. Limandus won the individual bronze medal at the 1984 Olympics, while Duco and Ampere were on the team placing fourth. Andiamo won the World Cup final in 1990 and was third in 1991. Dutch Courage, Orpheus, Rubinstein, Dimitrius, and Pascal are also world-class competitors.

Dutch horses excel in combined driving. All-Dutch teams won the World Championships in 1982 and 1986.

Holland's network of riding clubs provides a market for its horses. Although the average person cannot afford to buy a horse, the high quality of life does allow many to join a riding club and enjoy the sport.

In 1988, Queen Beatrix granted the WPN the title *Koninklijk*, or Royal. The designation honors the Dutch horse for its century of contributing to the nation's prestige and the Dutch economy.

Dutch Characteristics

The contemporary Dutch warmblood resembles all other sport horse breeds. The horses are bred as a sound performance type, not particularly for appealing conformation. Some are attractive, while others have plain heads with Roman noses and big ears. The breed has rounded, muscular hindquarters and substantial bone. Most Dutch horses have large, durable feet.

They are average in size, from 15.2 to 16.1 hands. "The Dutch aren't for big," explained breeder and judge Elizabeth Searle. "They don't think the bigger the better at all. They feel that some horses are too big and aren't going to be sport horses."

Many have white markings. The KWPN's Chief Inspector, Gert van der Veen, said, "People liked white, especially on the coach horses. Influential French stallions were chestnut, and chestnuts normally have more white."

The Dutch horse naturally moves freely from its shoulders with power from behind. It trots with animated action, with its strength matching from hindquarter to forehand. Moving in long, springy strides, its joints articulate at knee, hock, and fetlock. The horse reaches its hocks up and forward, and most Dutch horses demonstrate a natural jumping ability.

Trainer Willie Arts looks for a "lightfooted" Dutch horse. "I like a horse that still has the character of a warmblood but the athletic ability from refined horses."

Dutch horses are known for tractable dispositions. They are easy keepers with great stamina. "I think that characterwise, they are most pleasant and easy to work with," said Arts. "Especially in the last 10 or 15 years, the breeders have worked hard on that in Holland. The stallion testing, the mare testing have kept 'the cob of the corn,' choosing the best. If they have a bad character, they aren't allowed to breed."

U.S. Dutch enthusiast Cynthia Warren said, "These horses don't throw tantrums when you ask them to work. They respond without fighting you."

Dutch Breeding

The breeding program remains in private hands, although the KWPN does receive some government support. The Netherlands has never had a state stud.

The KWPN oversees breeding, and Searle praised the association for its objective support of the horse industry. "The KWPN is a separate organization, and they want to keep the industry clean. They want it right, and they concentrate on breeding."

The KWPN has divided the Netherlands into 12 departments. It lists over 240 Dutch stallions around the world, covering more than 14,000 mares annually. Stallions stand at large and small farms, and approximately 9000 foals are born in Holland each year.

The Dutch originally separated horses into three categories: *Rijpaarden, Basispaarden,* and *Tuigpaarden.* The KWPN intends to preserve these distinct types.

The modern riding horses are the *Rijpaarden.* Bred from the Gelderland or Groningen, they resemble a big-boned Thoroughbred. Breeders produce these attractive animals with the aim of a lighter, quicker horse over fences. They comprise about 80 percent of the Dutch warmbloods.

The *Basispaarden* (basic type) is a heavier-boned animal. Larger and more old-fashioned like a light draft horse, it lacks the streamlined appearance of the sport horses. The type has produced jumpers and dressage horses.

"They were all heavy, big plow horses that worked on the farm," described Rolf Brinkman, member of the KWPN stallion approving committee. Describing a Dutch mare sired by a Thoroughbred out of a basic type, he said, "This horse has enough bone. Her body type is nice, but her legs are not strong enough. Her hind leg goes up and down, but it needs to go forward more."

About the basic type, Willie Arts noted, "Movement is more difficult. The horse has to do a lot more work to do the same thing that another one does naturally."

A Dutch mare and foal.

Dutch horses excel in combined driving. U.S. driver Bill Long competes with a Dutch four-in-hand.

Dutch authority Dr. Van der Meij said that few breeders produce this type. "The basic horse is dying out. There's no market for the Gelderlander or Groningen, and they aren't real riding or driving horses."

Uniquely Dutch is the *Tuigpaarden*. Rarely seen outside of Holland, this driving horse is carefully bred for its extreme knee and hock action. The horses are dark, with white blazes, and have massive shoulders and hindquarters. Approximately 20 percent of the Dutch horses are of this type.

Although the KWPN aims at an all-around horse, Holland's 28,000 breeders are independently minded. They tend to target horses for a specific discipline.

"The Dutch are good husbandmen," said Elizabeth Searle. "They apply themselves, are meticulous, and perform research in their animal husbandry—their parrots, macaws, cattle, goats, and chickens. This applies to horses as well.

"They've always been close to the land. They are strong on genetics, and they have a certain feel for breeding. They breed plants like you can't believe—their nursery stock is out of this world. They decided to get into ponies and went to England to get New Forest ponies. Now England goes to them to get stock to take back."

Searle added that the Dutch enter a field to produce the best, in whatever type of agriculture. "When you ask them about their open studbook, they say, 'We're not trying to promote a breed. We're trying to promote the best sport horse in the world. We don't care where the breeding comes from.' Their goal is the end result, not something along the way."

In this small country, livestock raising contributes two-thirds of the gross value of agricultural production. The clever Dutch breeders know all the horses and bloodlines of their fellow farmers. Shows are social occasions, often with long dinners afterward, where horsemen listen to speeches about the horses' accomplishments.

Farmers raise horses as a hobby. Most own two or three mares, and they enjoy breeding successful sport horses. Small breeders have produced stallion candidates, although the Netherlands does have some large horse farms.

As in Germany, certain horsemen also purchase young horses as yearlings, to raise as stallion prospects. An active network of dealers also buy and sell young horses.

The Dutch cull strictly to improve the breed. Farmers sell inferior young horses for meat to buyers in France and Italy, to make up the cost of breeding horses that don't meet the standard.

Discipline applies to all areas of horseman-

Zulu

John Quirk, Editor and Publisher of *Horses Magazine*, bought the jumper Zulu as a five-year-old. He changed the horse's name from Waaco to Zulu, saying, "He's big and black, hence his new name. He was purchased from Jan Maathuis in Holland."

Zulu was sired by Resident out of Laurina. In 1990, the ten-year-old gelding won prize money in 17 Grands Prix. He was at the top of the American Grandprix Association's Horse of the Year list for most of 1990, finishing second by earning over $65,000 in prize money. He placed fifth in the AHSA National Open Jumper standings.

California rider Hap Hansen has shown Zulu since 1987. In a recent interview for *Horses Magazine*, Quirk asked Hansen about the horse's early performances. Hansen remarked, "He was spooky and a little bit nervous, but once he'd been around a preliminary course, I had the feeling that he had all the jump and all the courage it takes to jump the biggest jumps."

Describing Zulu's personality, Hansen said, "He's very friendly. Loves people. Loves horses. He likes everything. He's got the power and scope to jump any course."

He noted that Zulu thrives on jumping. The horse is quick to respond and needs 10-15 minutes to relax before a workout. "To watch him, you aren't going to think that that big black horse with that big head is a very sensitive horse...But you get on him and you find out he's a lot more sensitive than you imagined he would be."

Zulu has a reputation for neighing when he enters the jumping arena. Hansen and Quirk speculated about the reasons, with Hansen suggesting the horse was "talkative" out of concern. Quirk said, "I'm not sure he's really scared any more with his whinny. I have a feeling he realizes that people like it."

Zulu and Hap Hansen. Photo by Tish Quirk.

ship. In dressage, a horse must attain a certain number of scores before it can progress to the next level and eventually qualify for championship shows.

Dutch shows attract a large number of knowledgeable spectators. The audience participates enthusiastically. Searle described, "They make a big to-do, chanting and whooping when their favored horses do well. They have their own ideas on whether a horse is judged correctly or not, and they make remarks about the judging.

"Shows are terribly important to the breeders. No matter what the show, whether it's a dressage or general show, there's a great interrelationship between the breeders and the riders or drivers. The breeders are there to see how their horse is doing. And whenever they announce a horse, they never announce its name without mentioning the sire's name, and often the dam's sire's name, too."

Horses are named alphabetically, according to each year's designated initial. Dutch breeders use all letters except Q, X, and Y. The Dutch describe horses by the sire and dam's sire. For example, the stallion Beau le Mexico, (Le Mexico—Leander).

Breeders use artificial insemination widely, and the KWPN also accepts foals born through embryo transfer. The stallion, mare, and foal must be blood-typed when a foal is conceived through these methods.

Dutch Bloodlines

Dutch breeders have combined a variety of bloodlines from various European societies. Searle described their approach: "As the Dutch say, you can reproduce ability, but not the talent itself. You cannot breed performance—you can breed the ability to perform."

Examples of stallions which pass on such ability are Nimmerdor, Lucky Boy, and G Ramiro Z—all products from other breeding areas. Nimmerdor *preferent* came to the Nether-

lands from the Holsteiner breed. He stood a year in Schleswig-Holstein before being sold to the Netherlands. After proving himself in international competitions, he became one of the leading producers of jumpers in Holland. Two of his sons are Ahorn and Zadok.

Lucky Boy xx *preferent* was a grandson of Nearco. Four of his sons competed in the 1984 Olympics. An extremely popular sire, he sired over 1000 offspring, including the jumpers Calypso, The Freak, and Medrano.

Another Holsteiner, Ramiro is a currently influential stallion. Sired by Raimond (Ramzes), he is also a popular sire in the Westfalen breeding area.

Because Schleswig-Holstein is so close to Holland, many Holsteiners have contributed to the Dutch sport horse. Three foundation Holsteiner sires were Amor *preferent*, Farn *keur*, and Farn's son, Joost *preferent*.

Abgar xx *keur* sired many jumping horses, competing at the Grand Prix level. Two of his offspring competed in the 1988 Olympics.

Other prominent sires include Le Mexico *keur* (Selle Français), Ladykiller xx, Furioso II (Oldenburg), Ibrahim (Selle Français), Duc de Normandie *preferent* (Selle Francais) and Inschallah x (Oldenburg).

Like the Germans, the Dutch found that many of their best horses were sold abroad. In affiliation with the Dutch Equestrian Federation, the Nederlands Olympiade Paard (NOP) was formed in 1985 to prevent the foreign sale of world-class Dutch horses. This foundation helps owners subsidize the cost of preparing horses for the Dutch team, and it also purchases talented prospects. NOP horses feature the prefix "Olympic. " The Ministry of Agriculture does contribute some funding to NOP.

North America has become a major market for Dutch horses. In 1983, NA/WPN was founded as a branch. It is the 13th (and only foreign) department.

CHAPTER 11
The Danish Warmblood

For centuries, Denmark was famous for breeding horses. Today's warmbloods, however, have developed primarily from imported, not native, stock.

Denmark's famous Frederiksborg horses took their names from a royal stud near Copenhagen. Founded in 1562 by King Frederick II (1559-1588), the Frederiksborg stud provided work and army horses for three centuries. Horses descended from Andalusian and Neapolitan stock were used as school horses for European nobility.

The Frederiksborg horses were popular across Europe for their elegant yet sturdy conformation. Most were chestnut in color. They made Denmark an important horse-breeding nation in the 17th and 18th centuries, providing stallions to improve breeds at various state studs. When other studs no longer needed foundation stock from Denmark, the royal stud was disbanded in 1839 and closed in 1862.

After World War II, a group of private breeders determined to market a new breed, the Dansk Varmblod (Danish Warmblood). They organized societies in the 1960s, which joined together in 1962. U. S. breeder Peter Kjellerup said, "The Oldenburg, Frederiksborg, and Holsteiner had three different associations in

Denmark. All got fused into the Danish Warmblood, and the whole policy was changed. Today you find the Danish Warmblood, and [in the pedigree] you see all kinds of horses."

Without any state support, breeders imported foundation stock from Germany, Sweden, and England. Starting with the Frederiksborg and Oldenburg, Danish breeders added first Thoroughbreds and then Hannoverian, Holsteiner, Anglo-Norman, Trakehner, and Swedish Warmblood.

The Danish Warmblood Association reported, "It quickly proved a great advantage that the breeders did not have to feel bound by tradition, but were free to consider only the suitability of the individual horse in relation to the wishes and requirements of the modern rider. Only exterior requirements counted, and through a very critical selection of stallions and mares, the Danish Warmblood Society managed to establish a uniform and well-qualified breed in the course of only 3-4 horse generations. Following the old saying, 'A good horse has no race,' the Danish riding horse breeders have been able to utilize their knowledge of the rider's requirements of the horse."

Most of Denmark's small farms raise livestock, mainly cattle and pigs. The owner-farm-

The Danish horse Windsor competes in Grand Prix dressage, ridden by Ellin Dixon Miller.

ers must attend agricultural school, and they strive to improve their breeding strains. The government enforces quality and scrupulously monitors and inspects the farmers' livestock.

By the 1980s, Denmark had established its reputation for producing world-class horses. Breeders concentrated on gathering the best breeding stock from around the world. Kjellerup reported, "They're trying to find good sport horses, and they still look to improve them. They bought one American Thoroughbred stallion, and the breeding association is looking to find another one over here."

Danish Warmbloods are known primarily as dressage horses. Marzog won the Olympic silver medal in dressage in 1984 and was Euro-

pean Champion, 1983. This bay gelding won the 1986 individual World Championship.

Competing for Germany, Muscadeur was fifth individually at the 1984 Olympics. Aleks was on the 1984 Olympic bronze-medal team (Switzerland). Matador II was silver medalist at the 1990 World Championships, and won the 1991 World Cup (Finland).

In the U.S., the dressage horses Enterprise, Monsieur, Windsor, and Rugby are Danish Warmbloods. The three-day event champion, Monaco, was European champion in 1979 and won the gold medal at the 1980 Olympics.

The Danish horse is indistinguishable from other breeds. Individuals reflect their ancestry. Some, like Marzog, are lighter and more refined due to the Trakehner and Thoroughbred influence. Like other sport horses, the Danish Warmblood has sturdy, dense bone. The breed shows its coach horse background in its well-sprung ribs.

The bloodlines reflect a continued influence of Holsteiner and Trakehner stallions, such as Ibikus and Marlon. Danish breeding stock has yet to establish its own lines.

The Danish Warmblood Association maintains the registry. Kjellerup explained that the Association's structure resembles the German Verbands. "There are some differences. The Danish Warmblood is a more democratic association. Judges are voted in, and they have an educational system for judges."

The Association continues to restrict its activities to Denmark. The Danes decided to concentrate efforts on the business of horses in Denmark—to promote the local horse industry rather than a worldwide breed. The Danish Warmblood has not established a North American branch, as the Danish decided not to visit this continent to inspect, approve, and brand. They will issue registration papers for foals sired by an approved Danish stallion out of an approved Danish mare.

Rugby

A 16.2 bay gelding, Rugby was sired by Schwalbenfurst out of Anita. His owner Douglas Mankovich said, "My horse is a branded Danish Warmblood, but when you look at the pedigree, he's 3/4 Holsteiner." Mankovich imported the horse as a dressage prospect.

"It took a lot of looking, and not settling for what's just okay," recalled Mankovich. "After many years, I have found a horse that has made history." In 1989, Rugby was the USDF Horse of the Year in First and Second Levels, and also first in the Freestyle for First Level. In 1990, the horse again took three Horse of the Year honors: Second Level Freestyle, Third Level, and Third Level Freestyle. Mankovich said, "No other horse has ever done that. It's very representative of the Danish breed."

"It's his temperament, his desire to please, his tractability, and trainability. It's the quality of his movements and most importantly, his consistency in showing. He isn't one that will go in and do a really super test one day, and a mediocre test the next day. He just goes in and puts in the tests every time."

Mankovich noted that in 1989, Rugby's median scores were above 70 percent. In 1990, his median was 68.5 percent over a dozen shows, with a 74.5 percent median in freestyles.

"I've had a lot of horses, but with this horse the chemistry's just right. I can count on him. I can push him, and he will carry and he will perform. I know what to expect from him, and he knows what to expect from me. I am so comfortable with him, and he with me, that it's an ideal competitive partnership."

CHAPTER 12
The Belgian Warmblood

Like its neighbors, Belgium has bred horses through the centuries. Relying on an agricultural economy, it produced a substantial number of horses. Belgian farmers also brought in stock from neighboring countries, and many of its riding horses were imported through the 20th century.

The Belgian Half-Blood Society, originating in 1920, contributed to the national breed of sport horse. Most stallions came from France, with some German and Dutch imports. By 1935, about 40,000 foals of all breeds were born annually.

In 1937, the priest Canon André De Mey founded the Rural Cavalry in Boezinge (in the province of west Flanders). He intended this organization to bring together country youth in equestrian pursuits.

At the first riding tournament in 1938, entrants performed on both heavy and light horses. All horses were results of crosses between Thoroughbred or trotter stallions and heavier mares, and the Rural Cavalry aimed to breed a proper riding horse type—an agricultural riding horse—for its members.

After World War II, breeders refined the Belgian Warmblood with Gelderlander, Norman, and Hannoverian lines. In 1953, au-

thorities inspected the first stallions, and the Minister of Agriculture approved the founding of a studbook. In 1954, the studbook registered 27 foals.

The market for agricultural riding horses decreased in the post-war decade, but supporters presented public demonstrations of the animals' worth. Using 82 horses, they intended to describe the type and organize draft tests, dres-

Wouter, a Belgian Warmblood, competed in the three-day event at the 1990 World Equestrian Games.

Big Ben

This two-time World Cup winner has won many Grands Prix. He has also triumphed in the world's richest event, the du Maurier at Spruce Meadows, Calgary.

Foaled in 1976, Big Ben was sired by Etretat, a Thoroughbred from France, out of a half-Thoroughbred dam. He was bred by J. van Hooydonkk. The horse went to Holland for schooling at the age of four. In 1983, Dutch agent Emiel Hendrix sold the horse for owner Bert Romp, to Canadian rider Ian Millar.

The 17.3 hand gelding first represented Canada in the 1984 Olympics. He placed second in the World Cup Final in 1986 and won the individual and team gold medals at the 1987 Pan American Games. In 1987, Millar syndicated the horse, now owned by Canadian Show Jumpers Unlimited, Inc. Big Ben won the World Cup finals in both 1988 and 1989. As of early 1990, he had won over $750,000 in prize money.

The lanky chestnut is a light mover despite his size. An exceptional athlete, he can handle both tight indoor courses and the longer galloping courses outdoors. His flexible length of stride allows him to extend or collect to meet any type of obstacle.

Big Ben has an independent temperament. Millar described him as a "curious" horse, who notices sights in and around the ring during competition. He also has a great athlete's will to win, the desire to jump clean.

In 1990, the horse underwent surgery for colic. He recovered in time for the World Championships, but did not compete because Millar was sidelined due to an injury. Less than a year later, Big Ben suffered an impaction in the colon, and a second operation successfully relieved the colic.

sage, pleasure riding, and jumping.

Today's *Belgisch Warmbloedpaard* (BWP, or the Belgian Warmblood Breeding Association) was founded in 1955 as a private society, the National Breeding Association of Agricultural-Riding Horses. That year demonstrations in five Flemish provinces included 368 horses.

Competitions replaced the demonstrations in 1958, and the government officially recognized the association as a separate breed in 1960. In 1970 the association changed its name to BWP to reflect the horse's use in sport.

In its first 34 years, the BWP registered over 57,000 horses, including 538 stallions. In 1989, there were more than 5000 members, owning 20,000 horses. Belgian Warmbloods now comprise over half of the country's horses. Over 2100 foals were born in 1988.

Belgium continues to import Hannoverian stallions for its breeding program. In the past 35 years, this country has purchased close to 60 stallions through the Verband—more than any other nation.

The association's goal is to produce excellent

riding horses. The BWP holds an annual auction in December at Mechelen. Oud-Heverlee is the site of inspections and shows.

Belgium now markets its equine athletes in the global market, with most of its performers showing for other nations, like Canada's Big Ben. Belgian horses which remain in their homeland include Darco, who finished 13th in the 1989 FEI World Cup and 6th in the 1990 World Championships. Saygon won the bronze medal at the European Military championships. In the U.S., the jumper Brussels is a Belgian Warmblood.

The BWP has six districts in Belgium. Like the KWPN, the BWP has started a North American Department. Koen Overstijns founded this subsidiary, the Belgian Warmblood Breeding Association, to promote and recognize the horse in North America.

CHAPTER 13
The Swedish Warmblood

Sweden has a long tradition of breeding horses. Its royal stud, Flyinge, was established in 1661. As early as the 12th century, Flyinge served as a fortress and breeding center for Danish cavalry.

King Charles X ordered the founding of the royal stud in 1658, intending to produce cavalry horses by crossing Oriental, Spanish, and Friesian stock with native mares. An earlier stud, at the King's summer castle at Strömsholm, also produced riding horses.

Breeding continued at Flyinge, with the fortunes of war affecting the population of breeding stock. The Crown Prince Adolf Fredrik enhanced the breeding program in 1747, adding a supply of stallions from his estate in Holstein.

Now in its fourth century, Flyinge has bred riding horses continuously. In the early 19th century, the stud attracted international interest due to rider and veterinary surgeon Adam Ehrengranat. He brought students to Flyinge to study riding, breeding, and veterinary science, and he also contributed to the development of the modern riding horse in Sweden.

Organized horse breeding under government legislation dates from 1814. In 1874, the government began regulating the breeding program and published the breed's first stud book.

By the end of the 19th century, the breeding program had produced the Swedish Warmblood as a unique remount, both for riding and driving. Military authorities chose Swedish horses for their endurance, temperament, and athletic prowess during all seasons of Sweden's weather. Swedish horses won Olympic medals at the first equestrian Games, in 1912, with three horses taking all three individual medals in dressage.

The breed's open studbook started in 1918. The government continued improving the breed by importing Trakehner, Thoroughbred, Arabian, and Hannoverian stallions. By 1956, the state stood over 50 warmblood stallions. These horses added size to the cavalry horse, which was smaller than today's sport horse.

Sweden's military riders studied at the school in Strömsholm, established in 1868. Riding and training Swedish horses, they made Sweden one of the world's foremost equestrian nations. Young officers studied all segments of horsemanship in addition to riding. The cavalry recruited 3000 three-year-old warmbloods each year, to be trained at ages four and five.

With its well-trained military riders, Sweden has won more Olympic gold medals than any

Two Swedish riders perform a pas de deux at the 1990 World Equestrian Games.

other country. Their horses have excelled in all four classic sports, especially in dressage. Swedish horses have taken medals in this discipline in all Games through the 1976 Olympics—either for Sweden, Switzerland, or West Germany. A Swedish horse won the individual gold medal in the three-day event in the 1952 and 1956 Games. At the 1978 World Championships, 15 Swedish Warmbloods competed in dressage. Twenty percent of the dressage horses in the 1988 Olympics were of Swedish breeding.

Sweden's breeding successes have attracted buyers seeking quality prospects. Foreign buyers have purchased many of its best horses. The Swedish stallion Herzog sired Marzog, the Danish dressage champion. The stallion Piaff went to Germany, to win the individual gold medals in dressage at the 1968 (team gold) and 1972 (individual gold) Olympics. At the 1990 World Championships, a team of Swedish Warmbloods won the gold medal in combined driving.

With the decline of cavalry in the 1940s, the government decided to abandon the breeding

of horses. The stud at Strömsholm closed after the second World War. In 1983, the Swedish Equestrian Breeding and Sports Foundation Flyinge assumed the operation of the stud.

The Swedish Warmblood Association began in 1928. It supervises the breed through setting up rules for registration and promoting the breed in competition. The government established the Swedish Riding Association in 1948, to preserve and promote the Swedish halfbred. This association now promotes riding and the teaching of riding instructors who instruct young students.

Swedish Warmblood Characteristics

The Swedish Warmblood is an elegant horse, standing from 16 to 17 hands. It has a deep body and long lines, appearing lighter and less substantial than some other warmbloods. Horses have expressive heads, with intelligent eyes set far apart. The neck is long and muscular.

Bred as an athlete, the Swedish horse has shorter legs than the Thoroughbred, especially in the cannon bones. Its conformation gives it springy, rhythmic gaits. The breed is known for its purity of gaits and its exceptional, long-strided trot.

Known for its rideability and intelligence, the horse's temperament makes it an outstanding dressage horse. Its disposition is courageous yet tractable. Presently, Swedish horses are used primarily for jumping and dressage competitions.

Some riders have characterized the horse as "hot," compared to the German breeds. They believe the Trakehner influence has affected the Swedish Warmblood's sensitive temperament, and they claim the breed is not as reliable as the quieter German and Dutch horses.

Breeder Peter Lert said he has never found the horse to be hot. "The horses are a little smaller and have a Thoroughbred infusion, but so do other breeds now. It was maybe true a few years ago, compared to larger warmbloods. It's the individual horse. Maybe certain lines are hotter, but people say my stallion's horses are the easiest ones they've worked with."

Linda Zang has imported over 120 Swedish horses, and she considers the breed "sensitive, not hot. When I first went over there, the bloodlines of the horse I bought [Fellow Traveller] were considered very hot, and the horses considered difficult. I think it's because of my training with American Thoroughbreds, that I responded to this horse with light aids.

"There are some heavy ones and some dull ones. It depends on your technique of riding. If you're hard, a sensitive horse can't take it. All breeds have horses that aren't stable in their minds, but Americans can train and get along with sensitive horses."

The Swedish Warmblood is slow to mature. Swedish horsemen realize this fact and allow young horses time to develop without stress. Trainers start young horses at three, with serious schooling starting at four years of age.

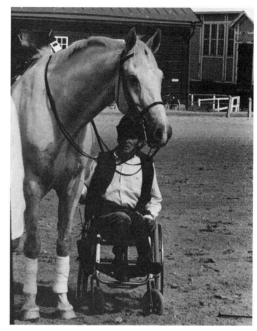

Sweden's Sven Holm is a world champion in riding for the disabled. He stables his attractive gray at Strömsholm.

Swedish Warmblood Breeding

Unlike horses of other countries, the Swedish horse has not undergone drastic changes in recent decades. For the past century, breeders have consolidated the type, aiming to breed specifically for riding horses. The change from military to sport horse was not a drastic transformation.

"The history of the Swedish horse is very much from developing to supply the military with usable horses," said Lert. "In other countries, horses worked as combination ride and drive horses, or ride and work. For hundreds of years, the emphasis was a medium size horse for the cavalry."

Swedish authorities describe the breeding goal as a "multipurpose riding horse, competitive in several disciplines; for dressage, show-

jumping, eventing, and driving. Of great importance is the temperament of the horse as well as health and durability."

In Sweden, there are about 7000 broodmares and 150 stallions. The National Breeding and Equestrian Center at Flyinge owns about 50 of the stallions, with the rest privately owned. Twenty of the stallions standing in Sweden are Thoroughbreds.

Although the Swedish Warmblood Association handles registration, the government continues to license stallions. According to Swedish law, only approved stallions may stand at public service.

Zang noted, "The Swedes spent so much time developing the breed. The one thing that really helped was being under the guidance of

The Swedish stallion Juvel (Flamingo—Utrillo) competes in dressage in the U.S. Gwen Blake riding.

the Swedish government. They're very tight on their stallions. They look at the mares and decide where to place the stallion to improve the mares—to produce a fine quality of sport horse."

As in most other countries, farmers own the majority of broodmares. They aim to produce sport horses with an emphasis on scientific husbandry through a strict selection program.

Swedish Warmblood Bloodlines

The breed combines horses of different backgrounds—Hannoverian, Thoroughbred, and Trakehner—introduced in the early 20th century. Of East Prussian sires at Flyinge, Attino sired dressage horses, and Heristal sired 25 stallions.

Three sires have established the most popu-

lar contemporary lines of performance horses. The offspring of Drabant have excelled in dressage, show jumping, and eventing. One of the most important stallions of the breed, he sired 9 approved sons and 96 broodmares. Some successful sons are Vagabond, Brabant, Brisad, and Urbino.

Urbino sired Flamingo, who was on the Swedish team that won the bronze medal in dressage at the 1984 Olympics. A popular sire, Flamingo's son Juvel is a winning dressage horse in the U. S.

Gaspari is one of the world's most successful sires of dressage horses. He sired 11 sons and 96 broodmares. His son Piaff won two silver medals at the 1970 and 1974 World Championships, in addition to the gold medal at the 1972 Olympics.

Other Gaspari sons include the dressage horses Emir, Gassendi, Elektron, and Herkules. These stallions have established themselves as world-class performers and sires. Another son, Imperator, excelled in show jumping. Contemporary dressage stars of the Gaspari line include Gaugin de Lully and Laylock.

The third prominent sire is Jovial. This stallion sired champions in all disciplines. His son at Flyinge, Ceylon, also sires both performance horses and broodmares. Ajax won the team bronze medal in dressage in 1972.

Lansiär was a foundation sire of the breed. This stallion was the top sire of horses scored by conformation, 1973-1982.

Utrillo is a contemporary sire, a son of the Hannoverian, Erno. He has sired hundreds of winning performers, and his sons Chagall, Maraton and Kaliber also stand at Flyinge. A grandson of Chagall is the sire Napoleon. The U.S. dressage stallions Zorn and Prego are Utrillo grandsons.

Other sires include Nepal, who sired the highly rated stallions Hertigen and Fantam II. Pontus, by Abbé, represents Swedish and

Oskar II

Owner Susan Haupt describes this stallion as "very special from the very beginning. He's always been a gentleman—never studdish, no vices, hauls like a dream, and never a spook. His manners are second to none."

Linda Zang imported Oskar II as a yearling in 1984. Bred by Lars Dyrendahl, the horse was sired by Urbino out of O'dette by O'den. The 16.2 hand gray received his CRB from the Swedish Warmblood Association in 1987.

Renowned horsemen Andrew de Szinay and Willi Schultheis have both praised Oskar II as an promising dressage prospect. Trained by Uwe and Betsy Steiner, Oskar II has excelled in shows since his debut in 1987. In 1990, he showed from Fourth level through Intermediare I, placing high on the Florida circuit. In 1991, he continued to show at Prix St. Georges and Intermediare I.

"Oskar has a great mind and talent for dressage," said Haupt, of Cedar Rapids, Iowa. "He knows all the Grand Prix movements. It is quite remarkable to have a Swedish horse at this young age do so well at FEI. He hasn't been rushed—he's just talented, and the training has been correct."

Trakehner lines. This stallion has very old breeding and produces elegant offspring. Ganesco also sires excellent performers, such as the dressage horse Encore.

The bloodlines at Flyinge also include recent imports from the Continent. Young stallions represent sires such as Bolero, Zeus, Wendekreis, and Ramiro. Sweden itself exports about 200 horses annually.

Sweden is broadening its market by aiming at all disciplines. Almost 95 percent of competition horses show in jumping.

Zang observed how this trend affects the breed's traditional strengths: "They're trying very hard to produce horses that jump. I see it every time I go over there. I hope they don't lose the movement, what the Germans call 'the Swedish *Schwung*.'"

PART 2

European Quality Control

European horses have succeeded because of selective breeding and a system of inspections. Authorities scrutinize each individual to ascertain its identity and grade its quality. Formal inspections occur at specified ages, with more in-depth procedures for potential breeding stock. Breeds group animals into various sections of their studbooks.

Throughout all breeding areas, the type remains consistent. Dr. Roland Ramsauer of the International Sporthorse Registry noted, "If you put together the best mares or riding horses from every breed, I guarantee you that you will find no difference among the different breeds and the associations—only if you have good eyes and can see the brand sign on the left hip. All over the world, the intention is to breed the same Thoroughbredy sport horse type, with a good character, good movements, and good rideability. The brand sign has nothing to do with the quality of the horse. It is only a trademark for the geographic breeding area where the horse is born."

One book cannot cover details of all registries. The descriptions of registries' activities in Part II will focus on particular breeds, specifically the Hannoverian, as examples.

CHAPTER 14
Studbook Registrations

The Hannoverian has established its breed through strict selection procedures through the generations. Its process, duplicated by many warmblood registries, includes the foal's branding, the studbook inspection of young mares, and the licensing and performance testing of superior stallion candidates.

The foal inspection is preliminary to the later selections. The association's representatives accept the warmblood foal by verifying its parentage and branding it with the appropriate trademark.

At this time, the owner of a foal in Germany also decides the horse's future. Approximately 22,000 warmblood foals are born in Germany each year. Of these, owners or riders register 13,000 with the German Equestrian Federation (FN) as riding horses. A *Turnierpferd* (competition horse) is eligible for upper-level competitions. Four thousand mares are future breeders, and the remaining 5000 animals will be pleasure horses.

The selection process begins before conception. First, the mare must be registered in one of the sections of the Studbook. In the Hannoverian breed, the studbook includes:

1. *Hauptstutbuch* (Main Studbook)

2. *Stutbuch* (Studbook 1, sometimes called Foalbook)

3. *Vorbuch-1* (Pre-Studbook I)

4. *Vorbuch-2* (Pre-Studbook II)

Main Studbook. The mare's pedigree must prove four generations of recognized ancestry through her sire, dam's sire, and dam's grandsire and great-grandsire. The stallion can be of the breed's "approved population," or registered with a breed society recognized by the Verband. The mare's dam must be entered in either the Main

European associations traditionally require thatt a handler show the mare with the foal at liberty.

Studbook or Studbook. A Main Studbook mare has the designation "H" as the first character of her registration number.

Studbook. The pedigree proves three generations, and the mare's dam must be in either the Main Studbook, Studbook, or Pre-Studbook I.

Pre-Studbook (Appendix) I. This includes a warmblood mare with a pedigree from a breed society recognized by the FN.

Pre-Studbook (Appendix) II. A mare of a warmblood type, with no recognized pedigree, may enter this section.

The Pre-Studbooks keep the registry open. Mares may enter these categories, and future generations sired by Hannoverian stallions may eventually advance to the Main Studbook—if they earn the required scores at the studbook inspections.

The breeder, an active member of the Verband and a resident of Niedersachsen, receives a *Deckshein* (breeding certificate), with the mare's information pre-printed by the Verband's computer. When he breeds the mare, the stallion manager processes the *Deckshein.*

Early the following year, the Verband sends the mare owner an *Abfohlmeldung* (Notification of Foaling). The breeder completes this foal certificate when the foal is born. This form is the basis for registration.

In the late summer and fall, the directors of the breeding stations visit breeders' sites throughout Niedersachsen to brand foals at six months of age. The *Fohlenbrand* signifies that the society has accepted the foal of registered parents. It does not represent the foal's quality.

The representative brands the foal on the left hip with the society's trademark. The foal receives the same brand its dam has on the left side of her neck, which she received when she was accepted into a section of the studbook.

Before its birth, the foal received a reference number. Across Germany, nine figures com-

pose the horse's life number. Example:

31 22 130 88

The first two numbers are the Verband's reference number. All Hannoverians receive the numbers 31. Horses of other regional breeds receive appropriate numbers for the breeding area which registers them:

Schleswig-Holstein	21
Westfalia	41
Oldenburg	33
Rheinland-Pfalz-Saar	52-53
Baden-Württemburg	71-73
Bayern	81
Rheinland	43
Hesse	61-62

With the Hannoverian and Holsteiner, the breeder resides in the breeding area. The owner of a Hannoverian born in Bavaria would apply for Bavarian registry. A horse does not have to have the same reference numbers as its parents, and its brand sign only means that both parents are in the same registry or an accepted registry. Dr. Ramsauer described a situation: "If you have a mare with the Hannoverian brand sign, when she is presented as a three-year-old she can qualify for the Main Mare Book. If you move to Oldenburg, near the border with Westfalia, you can transfer her to the Oldenburg Main Mare Book and use a state stud stallion from Warendorf. Then you have three choices to get a brand on this horse. The Hannoverian accepts the national stud stallion of Warendorf. The Oldenburg also accepts the stallion, so the breeder can have the Hannoverian, Westfalen, or Oldenburger brand sign." (The breeder of a Hannoverian must reside in the state of Niedersachsen).

The second set of numbers represents the breeding station where the mare was covered. The next three unique numbers are the serial numbers of the covering at that station. The number 130 represents the 130th mare bred that year at that station. The final two numbers are the last two digits of the foal's year of birth, here 1988.

German breed societies recently began branding foals with identification numbers, to assure correct entries at horse shows. Currently, each breed may choose to place numbers on the neck or hip. This system helps identify horses in cases where papers are not available. A brand number can be compared with a photograph of the horse.

The Hannoverian uses a series of three digits, excerpted from the horse's life number. They use the sixth, seventh, and last numbers, and they brand this series on the foal's neck.

After the inspection and branding, the owner submits the *Abfohlmeldung* to the Verband. The society then issues the *Abstammungsnachweis*, or pedigree paper. The society issues this only in the year of the foal's birth. Also known as "pink" papers, this pedigree and proof of ownership identifies the horse and includes a four-generation pedigree, brand and dates of branding, and if the owner has registered the horse in a studbook or as a competition horse.

Holsteiner. Some German breeds inspect and evaluate foals, combining this with the branding. In the Holsteiner breed, foals are scored at the inspection, or the material selection. They receive two marks using the international scoring system:

10   excellent
9   very good
8   good
7   fairly good
6   satisfactory
5   sufficient
4   insufficient
3   poor
2   bad
1   unacceptable

(3-1 are rarely used).

A Holsteiner foal which receives at least 7 on type and movement, for a total minimum score of 14, receives a merit award. Foals which score 15 or above receive the premium award.

Shown running free at the dam's side, foals perform on the triangle, a triangular-shaped track. This three-sided course is used to show horses in-hand by many European breed associations and in European shows.

According to Canadian Trakehner breeder Gerhard Schickedanz, the course originated in Germany around 1852. It was designed for judges to stand in one place and easily watch the horse's way of going from front, sides, and back. Schickedanz said the first site was probably the main stud at Trakehnen.

A sampling of other associations' registration/evaluations:

Trakehner. Verband officials evaluate foals on type, conformation, way of going, and development. The Verband records these marks and

The Holsteiner Verband and American Holsteiner Horse Association evaluate weanling foals at their approvals. Officials watch foals canter at liberty.

Branding the foal signifies its acceptance by the breed society. The official uses a brand with a metal stamp. The stamp is heated in a fire or with an oxygen acetylene torch until the metal is red hot. With a handler holding the foal, the official will quickly stamp the iron on the haunch.

uses them to evaluate genetic performance of the stallion.

French. Government regulations specify the registration process for all French breeds, according to a 1966 law and a 1976 breeding code that affirms each animal's identity, registration, and offspring and performances.

Each stallion has a serving card, listing each mare bred. The mare's owner receives a *certificat de Saillie*, or breeding certificate. The owner also submits to the Haras Nationaux (HN) a result of breeding, the *Declaration du résultat de la Saillie*.

After the foal's birth and before its weaning, HN authorities confirm the foal's identity by

completing a "Drawing up of the particulars." This graphic description of the animal notes its sex, color, markings, whorls, and any other marks or anomalies.

The HN issues two documents to accompany the horse through its life. The *carte d'immatriculation*, or registration card, lists its name and number. The *document d'accompagnement* (accompanying document) is a detailed identification of pedigree and precise description. It serves as a passport, health memo, genealogy, and list of breeding information.

The Ministry of Agriculture enters the horse's registration into the appropriate studbook. The Ministry also inscribes the horse's parents, descendants, and brothers and sisters, for future references relating to breeding values.

Swedish. All foals must be registered in order to enter shows and competitions. Foals are registered as Swedish Warmblood if sired by a licensed Swedish stallion out of a mare of these breeds: Swedish, Thoroughbred, Anglo-Arabian, Hannoverian, Oldenburg, Trakehner, Westfalen, Holsteiner, Danish Warmblood, Dutch Warmblood, Wielkopolska, or Selle Français. The breeder must submit a breeding certificate to the Swedish Warmblood Association after the foal is born.

Foal Evaluation

Even experts find it difficult to judge a young horse's quality. Hermann Friedlaender said, "Foals grow in such uneven ways. They grow in spurts. You cannot tell a foal that looks good one month, and not so good the next month. When you look at a foal, you form your own opinion."

Louis Thompson, Jr., President of the American Hanoverian Society, said, "In one month in the summertime, a colt born early in the year could look awkward. A younger foal, born later, may look good. It's not a fair judgment."

Some authorities consider milestones of three days, three weeks, three months, and three years. Most agree that it is very difficult to judge horses in the yearling to two-year-old range.

"We think breeders should present foals at the mother's side, not a yearling or two-year-old," explained Dr. Ramsauer. "The yearling grows from one side to the other. We have a slogan in Germany: you should look for a horse when it's three days and three years old, and don't look in the meantime, because he's always growing from one side to the other."

Dutch trainer Willie Arts noted, "You have to know how the horse moves, how the horse has to be built, how the horse grows, so you can tell at a young age. When he is maybe a little bit less, you can see it will be all there when he's three or four years old."

Generally the newborn foal is easiest to judge. The foal will show its potential. Visible are the contours of the body—the slope of the shoulder and croup. The joints should look well-formed, but the expert realizes that angles can change as the foal grows. Overall, the horseman looks for quality of expression and a harmonious appearance.

The foal also shows its natural movement even at a few weeks of age. A foal should move like it has "springs in its feet." European judges prefer to see the foal move at liberty, alongside its dam. "Weanling foals should always be judged in an area where they can move quite freely, with the dam in hand," said Ramsauer. "Only in this manner may the foal's gait be properly seen."

Prospective buyers also evaluate foals in Europe's breeding areas. Dr. Jochen Wilkens of the Hannoverian Verband noted how breeders in Niedersachsen market foals to those from other German states: "From Westfalia and Southern Germany, when buyers come to Hannover, they pay more than they pay in their own area. They say, 'I will go once, because I want to have a good offspring in my herd. So I pick up a real good one.'" He noted that out-of-state shoppers could pay from DM 8-10,000 for filly foals, sold to local breeders for around DM 5000.

Selling foals does affect the breed, as Wilkens said that breeders might choose to sell prospective State's Premium mares as foals. He noted how these transactions affect the overall quality of horses in certain regions within the breeding area. "A lot of foals go to other countries and other German breeding areas. The breeder can say, 'I will keep my second foal, not the best one. The best one is for sale.'" The better foals that leave the Hannoverian breeding area bring profit to the breeder while enhancing the development of another regional or national breed.

CHAPTER 15

Studbook Inspections and Gradings

E uropean breed associations ensure the quality of breeding stock through inspections, gradings, and approvals of young mares and stallions. For mares, the selection process helps breeders determine which horses to breed. They recognize that they cannot produce excellent offspring from a mare with obvious faults.

Again, the Hannoverian illustrates a typical procedure. Authorities evaluate potential broodmares at studbook inspections and in mare shows. The studbook inspection is a formal evaluation, in which a commission meticulously examines each mare and accepts her into the appropriate portion of the studbook.

The commission consists of three authorities: the *Landstallmeister* of Celle (or his deputy), the Verband's breeding manager (or his deputy), and a breeder who serves on the Verband's board. These inspections occur in April and May, at 40 to 45 locations throughout the breeding area, associated with the stallion stations.

The mare must meet specific requirements, including pedigree, conformation, and move-

ment, before the society accepts her in the studbook. She must be at least three years old. The Verband does recognize mares of other warmblood societies. "The pedigree shows if the horse is eligible or not for inspection. We approve the breed society and its pedigree," explained Ludwig Christmann. Recognized societies include Thoroughbred, Arabian, Anglo-Arabian, Selle Français, Westfalen, Holsteiner, and Oldenburg.

The commission compares the pedigree with the horse, to establish the mare's identity. They verify markings and the numbers branded on the mare's neck. (Markings could have changed if the foal was registered as a chestnut). They also measure and record the mare's height.

Usually the breeder shows the mare, presenting her to the commission for conformation and movement judging. In 1990, the Verband included free-jumping. Christmann said, "We added free-jumping to the normal studbook inspections at stations that had good jumping blood. The mares free-jumped up to four feet to show their style and potential."

In the Hannoverian breeding area, almost all

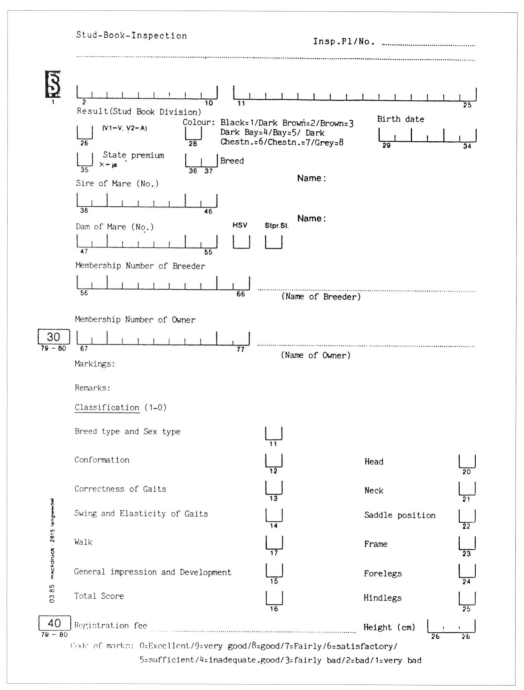

Hannoverian judges grade mares using this form at the studbook inspection.

mares enter the *Hauptstutbuch*. Besides the pedigree requirements, they must achieve a minimum score of 6 on conformation, with no individual score under 5.

Christmann explained that factors other than arithmetic affect the final score. If a mare shows serious faults, the commission agrees to adjust the math by rounding off numbers. For example, a mare could achieve an average of 5.5 on conformation, and the commission would determine to make this a 5 or a 6, depending on the animal's strengths or weaknesses. In this manner, authorities apply standards and can modify judgment according to the individual.

A *Stutbuch* (Foalbook) mare must have a score of 5 on conformation, with no individual score less than 4. There are very few Foalbook mares.

The inspection differs from a show. It is a procedure, not a competition among mares. Mares receive neck brands to verify that they have been inspected and approved (licensed) for breeding. Some Americans describe such a mare as "double-branded."

Hannoverian Mare Shows

The mare show (*Stutenschau*) has been an important tradition since the mid-19th century. Breeding clubs present these events through June and July. Each mare may compete in one mare show in the breeding area. About 2400 mares enter one of four classes: Two-year-old (eligible for *Hauptstutbuch*, but not yet inspected), three-year-old *Hauptstutbuch*, four-year-old, and five- and six-year-olds who have already given birth to at least one foal. Each show also includes family classes: a dam with two daughters, or a dam with two foals which are full sisters. This class should show improvement between the older and younger generations.

The competition serves as a showcase for the local breeders. A commission of three officials judges each show, enlisted from a rotating group

At the studbook inspection and mare show, each handler stands his or her mare in the open position so the commission can judge all four legs. The horse's legs nearest the judges are straight, and the offside legs are spaced with the foreleg slightly back and hind leg slightly forward. This three-year-old (Abajo xx—Akrobat) won her State's Premium in 1990.

of approximately 10 officials and breeders.

At the show, breeders and spectators can judge the progress of the breed. The mares shown demonstrate the production of the stallions at the surrounding stallion stations, and the quality of the local mare stock. (A popular stallion's get can dominate a show, with dozens of his daughters competing). Shows are well-attended, with some attracting hundreds of knowledgeable spectators.

Breeders show their two-year-olds for the first time, often in classes with as many as 35 fillies. Here breeders see how their animals, the results of their breeding choices, compete with others of their age group and similar breeding. The show serves as an education for breeders, with authorities grading their stock and guiding their future breeding decisions.

Each show follows a set procedure. A cata-

A German handler allows his mare to move at a relaxed walk. The horse pushes with the hindquarters to stride well under herself. She appears mannerly yet expressive as she moves with energy and loose muscles.

log lists each mare in each class, ordered sequentially from the two-year-old through the six-year-old class.

Each horse first shows individually. The handler (often the mare's breeder) leads the mare into the ring, allowing the mare to walk freely forward so she presents a pleasing first impression. When they reach the triangle's apex, he turns her so her near side faces the commission.

The handler poses the horse in the open position. The horse stands still and stretches its neck forward with an alert yet responsive expression. Judges briefly scan the mare, for 30-60 seconds. The head judge nods to the handler and asks, *"Bitte"* (Please), signalling the handler to lead the horse onto the triangle at a trot.

Upon the handler's signal, the horse readily moves into a trot, clockwise around the triangle's perimeter. It trots freely, unrestricted by the handler.

The handler matches strides with the horse, keeping his right shoulder even with the horse's left shoulder. As they complete the first leg of the triangle, the handler signals the horse to collect and both turn in unison to the right.

On the far leg, which gives judges the side view of the trot, the horse extends its gait to show its length of stride and suspension. The pair round the second corner and complete the course to halt before the commission. German handlers often rely on voice cues to slow the horse, typically a trill. A soft "Brrr" tells the horse to slow down; a commanding "Brrrup!" tells the horse to halt. At the halt, the handler stands the mare so her off side faces the judges. After another brief look, they dismiss the horse.

The expert judges quickly determine preliminary scores for the mare. In the individual presentation, they judge general impression and the trot. Next they will study the class as a group to make the final assessment.

All mares return to the ring, in class order, to circle the triangle at a walk. The commission, standing in the center of the triangle, discuss placings of the class. (If the class is large, the commission judges half the class at a time).

They will rank each mare, from the best to the worst, by watching all horses walk around the ring. Each judge has applied individual criteria, but as a group they often adjust placings upon viewing the entire class. Dr. Wilkens said, "We make the placement on the ring. Then we compare."

Dr. Ramsauer noted, "When judging a horse, we find different opinions mostly deriving from differences in taste. Apart from taste, there are some clearcut rules by which to judge conformation. There is no disagreement among the experts about these criteria."

After a few moments, they begin to instruct specific handlers to cross the middle of the triangle to change places. The ringing order begins to form, as the better mares advance to the head of the line.

The class ends when the head judge signals the first-place mare to halt at the triangle's apex.

The Crucial Moments

The simple act of leading a horse assumes major importance in a breed inspection or mare show. The officials' evaluation can make the difference in a horse's worth and future career. Judges score only what they see, and the horse that fails to show its qualities could receive lower scores than it deserves.

"The task of the handler is to show the mare in all her possibilities," said Dr. Wilkens of the Hannoverian Verband. The Verband's Ludwig Christmann agreed, saying, "Our main aim is the horse's movement. If you have type and not movement, it doesn't help. It's very important to school the people so they can show the horse. You should show a Hannoverian like you do a Welsh cob."

German breeders recognize the importance of presenting a mare at her best. At mare shows, some breeders engage professional handlers.

The professional's expertise results in a superior presentation. Dr. Wilkens said, "At the national mare show, often you must change the handler. You have the best in a national show. The owner gives the mare to the handler before the show so he can learn how to handle her."

At the prestigious national and European events, mares represent their regions and countries. Handlers communicate regional pride by wearing appropriate colors of clothing:

Hannoverian	Yellow shirt, white trousers
Holsteiner	Red shirt, white trousers
Trakehner	White shirt, black trousers
Oldenburg	Red shirt, blue trousers
Dutch	White shirt, white trousers, red tie

The announcer begins to read a brief critique of each mare, from first to last place.

Descriptions are straightforward, yet tempered with modifying adjectives. Judges rarely rave about a superior animal or condemn a lesser one. Positive comments include: "Very good," "Good," "Very nice," "Satisfactory." Negative remarks: "A little bit ___," "A bit weak," "Not very much," "Very light," "Not so good," "Could be bigger," or "Limited."

Judges give three awards for quality: 1A, first, and second prizes. The superior horses receive 1A, and most of the others receive the first prize. The second prize is rarely given, usually to younger mares.

The results help breeders to cull mares. Trakhener breeder Guenter Bertelmann noted, "The judge shows the mistakes. If a breeding combination didn't work out, to see what stallion would fit the mare. Or, sometimes it's a hard decision, to use her as a sport horse and not any more as a broodmare."

U.S. Trakehner breeder Judy Yancey encourages the horse to move with long strides. The horse remains beside her shoulder as it reaches its head and neck forward in a natural, relaxed position.

The results of the two-year-old class preview which horses are candidates for the coveted *Staatsprämie* (State's Premium) award. Three-year-olds compete for this honor, awarded to Hannoverian mares only in Niedersachsen. It encourages breeders to produce and retain outstanding breeding stock. The State's Premium mare (abbreviated St. Pr. St.) is a potential dam of stallion candidates and should benefit the breed by remaining in the Hannoverian breeding area.

Hannoverian authorities realize the importance of the two-year-old class. Dr. Wilkens recalled an outstanding two-year-old, with excellent conformation and a very good trot. Yet on the circle, she did not show a good walk. "We looked at her again and again—perhaps the walk will come. This year we didn't give her a 1A, because the walk didn't come. Perhaps when she is under a rider next year she becomes

better. But next year it will be a bigger problem—we will have to come to a decision if she's a State's Premium or is she not."

The high point of each mare show is the three-year-old class. Candidates for the *Staatsprämie* must receive a 1A prize and be out of *Hauptstutbuch* mares. Each breeder must agree to fulfill the following requirements:

The mare must have been bred.

The mare must pass a performance test under saddle.

The mare must produce at least one foal within three years.

The mare's owner signs a contract to keep the mare for three years, and to breed her each year. He will report the births of colts to the *Landstallmeister*, offering them for sale to the state stud. He will show the mare at mare shows for three years, at ages four, five, and six. (If a mare is ill and cannot attend, the owner must present a veterinarian's certificate. If she is lame the day of the show, the owner presents her only at the walk). During the period of commitment, he will not sell the mare without the consent of the Chamber of Agriculture. (Recently some mare owners have chosen to refuse the award due to its obligations).

The state pays the monetary award, approximately the amount of a state stallion's fee, after the mare passes the performance test. However, the birth of the first foal certifies the State's Premium honor. "The title is given, because it's on the foal's pedigree," explained Christmann. "When the first foal is born, that could release the obligation."

The show is a social occasion for the local breeders. Breeders share a comaraderie, although they consider the occasion serious. U. S. dressage trainer Jan Ebeling explained, "The contact between people interested in breeding is much stronger than what we have in the United States. They see each other often, a lot more often—I think because Europe is so much smaller. They used to have shows where they took the cows and the pigs, and they took the horses, too. Everybody wanted to have the best horse. The people really got an education in breeding, no matter what animal—cattle, pigs, or horses."

Exhibitors show courtesy in the show ring, with handlers often greeting the commission with *"Guten Morgen."* The show usually breaks for refreshments after the three-year-old class. After the show, breeders often meet at a local restaurant for a banquet.

Holsteiner

Like the Hannoverian, the Holsteiner Verband emphasizes the two- and three-year-old mares. The Verband, not the state, awards premiums, a practice duplicated by the Oldenburg and Trakehner Verbands.

The best three-year-olds win a State's Premium award. They are registered in the *Hauptstammbuch* as *Pramien*. At local mare shows, Verband officials invite the best young mares to compete at the elite mare show in Elmshorn.

The total of a Holsteiner's scores is described as a *bonit*, or *bonitierung*. The approval committee scores mares in-hand, on the triangle, and at liberty on seven factors: type, topline, depth of body, front legs, hind legs, correctness of gaits, and brilliance and impulsion. The scoring system is:

10	perfect
9	excellent
8	very good
7	good
6	sufficient
5	marginal
4	insufficient
3	poor
2	bad
1	unacceptable

Officials inspect three-year-old mares for entry into one of the studbooks' three sections,

similar to the Hannoverian's. To enter the Studbook, the mare must score a total of 37 to 41 points on the seven factors. Main Mare Book mares must achieve at least 42 and have at least three generations of Holsteiner breeding on the dam's side. A mare scoring 48 or more is a Premium mare, with five generations. Her papers are noted, "HSP." She must be bred the year she wins the Premium and pass a performance test—her scores are added to her registration papers.

Trakehner

The Verband inspects mares at three years of age and scores them on Trakehner type, conformation, movement (regularity/impul-

St. Pr. St. Batani (Bolero—Grande) was champion at the Freiburg (Germany) mare show in 1990, as a six-year-old. She shows an excellent walk and respects her handler by remaining at arm's length.

A German handler has folded the reins and holds them in his right hand, ready to use his left hand to signal the horse. His assistant follows with a whip.

Trotting on the triangle, the handler keeps the reins loose and never pulls on the mare's mouth. He allows her to move straight forward. To encourage her to trot out, another handler follows her with a whip.

sion), and general impression. The evaluation marks, or *Bewertung*, are added to the registration papers, along with measurements of height, heart girth, and cannon bone. The mare gets white papers (*Zuchtblatt*).

The Verband approves mares for either its Main Stud Book or Stud Book. Only the best mares enter its Main Studbook. They receive a neck brand in addition to a hip brand. Those of less quality or smaller than 158 cm enter the Studbook. Exceptional mares can qualify for a State's Premium award. As an example of the breed's restrictions, the stallion Hartung covered 800 mares in his career and 40 daughters were approved.

French

The French select breeding stock by performance, pedigree, and conformation. The HN sponsors shows for young horses and broodmares. Horses compete in shows in hand and under saddle.

These shows help market young horses, and breeders compete to win cash premiums from the state. The government actively encourages breeding quality stock.

Saddle horses of Selle Français, Arabian, and Anglo-Arab breeds compete in classes for fillies and *hongres*, or geldings, (grouped by age) and mares with or without foals. One- to three-year-old colts compete in their own classes.

Show classes include conformation and gait to test three-year-olds, and *Épreuve de modele, allures, et dressage* (Testing conformation and dressage). Horses are separated by three height categories and by breed and sex (stallions or mares and geldings). They receive scores that place them into one of three levels: first, second, or third *série*.

Dutch

The KWPN inspects three-year-old mares for official admission into the studbook. About 93

Recent Political Implications

Due to the impact of the European Community, German societies now allow a mare to be re-evaluated. If her score did not qualify her for the *Hauptstutbuch*, a Studbook mare can be re-inspected.

The reunification of Germany brings horses from East to West. According to the Hannoverian Verband's Ludwig Christmann, the DDR's central studbook (the five states) was divided into district offices. The state owned most of the 8000 mares and stallions of warmblood and Thoroughbred lines.

Of Hannoverian horses with East German papers, Hermann Friedlaender noted, "It depends on the manner in which the registry has been kept. If breeding can be authenticated, it should make no difference if a horse is from West or East. If the horse is good, they won't turn them away. Quality is always appreciated."

In 1990, the Trakehner Verband accepted 300 purebred mares and 26 stallions from the former DDR. These horses, bred by the government since 1945, proved their purity through authenticated pedigrees.

Breeder Guenter Bertelmann found it ironic that the Trakehner, which does not have any state-owned horses, received these horses as a gift from a government. "Those Trakehners were owned by the former East German government, and now they should be owned by the province of Saxony or Brandenburg. At least the Trakehner Verband has new, very good Main Studbook mares. And new stallions bring in new bloodlines, and new blood combinations."

Dr. Eberhard Senckenberg of the Trakehner Verband said, "They're totally incorporated. They got some stallions from Poland and Russia, to keep the breed running." He noted a difference in type with these horses. "Maybe they haven't had some very typy ones. They haven't had the chance to compete like we have. Their bloodlines weren't lost, but they are rare in the breed."

percent qualify. Mares also enter mare shows in the Netherlands' 12 departments. Winners advance to each department's central show, and those winners compete at the national mare show.

The KWPN jury ranks mares and awards premiums of first, second, and third. Judges recognize certain bloodlines, and a horse's pedigree can influence its score. Elizabeth Searle noted, "If they know a bloodline is suspect for a certain fault, when they select a mare, they are not going to be favorably disposed to a horse heavy in that particular line. If it's absolutely outstanding in its conformation and movement, they will not be as severe."

Beginning as three-year-olds, Studbook mares can qualify for predicates to indicate superior quality. First is the *stermerrie*, or star.

Robin Koenig runs in harmony with a Trakehner stallion candidate, wearing running shoes so he can match strides with the horse. He holds the reins lightly, without inhibiting the young horse's trot.

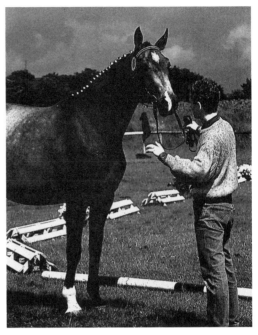

European handlers usually hold one rein in each hand while standing the horse. They hold their hands farther apart than the width of the horse's muzzle to encourage the horse to remain straight.

A three-year-old Hannoverian, full sister to the state stallion Weltmeyer, wins the State's Premium at Freiburg, Germany. Her handler raises his left hand to signal her to collect for the second turn on the triangle.

Thirty percent receive the First premium and the star predicate for conformation and movement in hand.

Next is the *keurmerrie*, or *keur*. The mare must be at least four years old. From 8 to 10 percent of mares qualify for this predicate after showing in hand and under saddle. Judges also evaluate the mare's breeding value by inspecting at least one foal she has produced.

Danish

Denmark's seven regions each host local shows for mares and foals. At four years of age, mares are judged to receive approval.

Peter Kjellerup explained the strict regulations that govern the breed, and the high aver-

A Russian Import

The second World War caused thousands of horses from the West to "emigrate" to Russia. Russia absorbed horses of the best German bloodlines, and equestrians rarely see the descendants of prized breeding stock lost in the war.

A Russian stallion of Hannoverian ancestry recently arrived in the town of Galisteo, New Mexico, when Sally Graburn, a judge and trainer at Goose Downs Farm, bought Dambrats. This nine-year-old grandson of Duellant is out of a Latvian mare. The horse was imported to Canada with a group of Russian horses intended for driver Tim Wright. (The horses were exchanged for bulls the Russians wanted).

At 16 hands, Dambrats ("Brett") wasn't tall enough for Wright's team, so Graburn was able to buy him. She enthusiastically described the black stallion: "He does first and second level dressage—he has good extensions. He jumps like you can't believe—he cracks his back over a fence and really tucks his hocks."

Involved with driving and combined training, Graburn is unsure which discipline she'll pursue with this stallion—dressage, eventing, or combined driving. She believes that warmbloods do well in eventing. "This horse could go preliminary. Warmbloods don't have the speed for advanced, but you still need the warmblood for the bone and the mind. Thoroughbred crosses are good for the speed."

age quality. "All mares have to be registered [approved] before they are bred and foals can be registered. But you see the Danish horses at the top of all sports all over the world. We have a higher percentage of success rate. A little country like Denmark has to look at the quality side to compete."

Mares can be approved as young as four years old. Most are approved at four to six years, or as old as eight or ten. In this small country, the judges recognize the horses by seeing them show from foalhood.

Swedish

Authorities pass suitable breeding stock according to conformation and gaits. U.S. breeder Peter Lert said, "In the Swedish breeding program, more attention has been paid to the mares. The mares are all graded very carefully, and they evaluate the mares more than is done in Germany."

Officials score two, three-, and four-year-old mares on five factors: type; head, neck, and body; legs; walk; and trot. They use a 0-10 point system for each score, with a maximum score of 50.

Mares are graded into three classes: I (38-39), II (35-37), and III (30-34). A mare aged three or four can receive approval if she scores at least 30, with no trait lower than 5 points. At special shows in the spring, exhibitors present about 500 three-year-old mares for grading. About 30 percent receive Class I. Of these, approximately 90 achieve at least 40 points and the Diploma.

This honor signifies that the mare has superior potential as a broodmare.

The same standards apply to broodmares aged four and older, which have produced at least one foal by a stallion from the approved population. Mares are evaluated to enter the studbook, with about 10 percent qualifying. Officials grade broodmares for conformation, performance, temperament, and offspring.

These mares also show under saddle at walk, trot, and canter.

Broodmares qualify for one of two performance grades, B or AB. The AB mare already has a Diploma or has qualified through a Riding Quality test for four-year-olds, or through a superior record in sport. Mares can also receive A and Elite gradings through performance of their offspring.

CHAPTER 16
Selection by Conformation and Gaits

E uropean authorities judge horses by their conformation, movement, and performance qualities. By objectively comparing a horse to an ideal, they can select superior individuals.

Dr. Ramsauer said, "The evaluation of horses has to follow certain rules and regulations, based on long tradition and experience. The conformation should guarantee not only beauty and elegance for human eyes, but also a high standard of performance and quality for riding."

"A breeding horse must be a potentially good sport horse," said Gert van der Veen at a Sport Horse Seminar sponsored by the United States Dressage Federation. "But not all sport horses are good breeding horses. Only the best are good enough for breeding."

The Hannoverian Verband's Ludwig Christmann added, "A good broodmare must be a good riding horse, and on top of this, she must have some more qualities—more correct on the legs and look more feminine."

When evaluating a riding horse, the judge looks for a functional sport horse. He has to consider whether a fault—judged by the de-

gree of angulation—will reduce the horse's efficiency. A performance horse can overcome imperfections of conformation and movement by its desire to perform under saddle or in harness.

The renowned German horseman Hans Joachim Köhler considered judging, "a most difficult job! One at which we passionately work...always striving to improve. Georg Graf von Lehndorff, the eminent German horseman, once said, 'Most of us are not *Pferdekenner* [horsemen] but rather *Fehlerkenner*, meaning we could not recognize a good horse if we saw one, but we can find all its faults.'"

"One should not be overly critical of faults," explained Dr. Roland Ramsauer. "Observe them in the context of the complete horse and decide whether the item in question is one that will make the animal difficult to ride or shorten its useful working life. Judge faults accordingly."

Although many factors affect the horse's success with a rider or driver, conformation remains the first selection tool. "On the basis of conformation, you can predict a horse's performance capability," said van der Veen.

The judging of horses' conformation is a

The judges evaluate the horse as a whole, calculating strengths and the effect of its faults. They realize that a horse's character, what Gemans call its "interior" qualities, can compensate for any physical limitations.

science—and an art. In scoring the parts, the judge must always consider the whole. A horse could receive good scores on individual components, but its parts lack the essential harmony.

General Impression

The horseman looks at the entire animal to see if it presents a picture of balance. Christmann said, "Everything you look at should be connected with the horse's suitability as a riding horse. We don't want to look for conformation for itself. The horse must be constructed like a riding horse, and move like a riding horse."

Selection standards:

• Middleweight horse is the most popular contemporary type.
• No one feature appears too prominent.
• Large shoulders and powerful hindquarters match in depth, length, and strength.
• Horse stabilizes its weight over all four legs.
• Deep heart girth longer than the horse's height.
• Height matches overall build.
• In a broodmare, the capacity and strength to carry a foal to term.
• Depth of body in proportion to the length of leg.
• Strong, streamlined connections in all parts.

The Head

After evaluating the general impression, most horsemen examine the head. Its beauty does not affect its performance, but the head affects the horse's balance and rideability.

Selection standards:

• Size relates to the rest of the horse's body.
• Wide forehead, with bones close to the surface and veins apparent.
• Kind expression with friendly eyes.
• Ears properly set and alert.
• Jaws sized to fit the proportions of the head, with space between them for flexibility in head position.
• Long, supple poll so the horse can lift its head (about one hand's length).
• Clean throatlatch with a fine gullet allows the horse to flex at the poll comfortably.
  Van der Veen mentioned the importance of the atlas (see illustration): "It articulates and

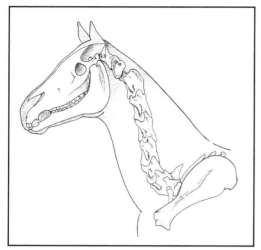

Ideally the atlas and occipital bone are at the same level. The atlas is the highest of the neck's seven vertebrae, and it has a different shape from the six axis bones. The occipital bone, which connects the head and neck, influences the horse's carriage of head and neck.

The horse's jaw matches the proportions of its head—not so large that it inhibits the bending of head and neck.

needs good muscle. It must be long enough for the neck to bend into position." The atlas should look flat on top, forming a straight line parallel to the ground.

The Neck

An impressive head and neck enhance the sport horse's appearance. The horse appears light in front, and easier to elevate in its movement.

Selection standards:
- "Medium long" on its topline.
- Well-muscled at the crest.
- Straight on its underline.
- Small toward the head.
- Connects smoothly to the chest, wither, and shoulder.

"If the neck sits too low on the chest, you have problems getting the horse upright," said Christmann. "You want a horse that looks like it's going a little bit uphill. You want the horse to look higher in front when it moves. So the neck is very important to balance out the horse. Too low, it gives the impression that the horse digs in the ground."

Wither and Shoulder

A substantial wither holds the saddle in place, while the diagonal shoulder acts like a spring. The horse can elevate in front. The dressage horse reaches forward with its forelegs; the jumper lifts its forehand in the take-off.

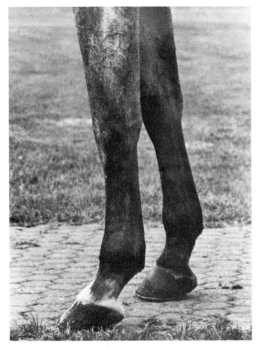

On an ideal foreleg, the judge should be able to imagine a straight line down the middle of the leg. The knee should be flat and broad in front. This horse lacks the desirable flat and evenly wide cannon bones, and it also has short pasterns.

Selection standards:

- Pronounced, long, widely set wither.
- High wither combined with a high-set neck so the horse elevates.
- Wither reaches well into the back to form a correct saddle position.
- Wither's highest part a few cm higher than the highest part of croup to enhance the uphill feeling. This conformation frees the forehand for the horse to raise itself to jump or piaffe.
- Wither muscled at its sides.
- Long, sloping shoulders for free, forward movement.

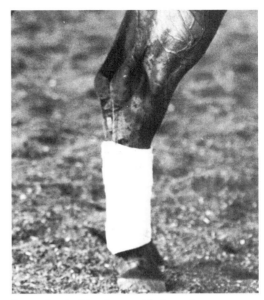

Large hocks blend smoothly into short cannons on this equine athlete. Feet should be proportioned to the size of the legs.

- Shoulder laid back to form a 90° angle with the upper arm (the humerus).
- Well-defined shoulder with strong muscles describing its structure apart from the neck.

Van der Veen chose length over slope. "Length gives reach. I prefer a long and straight shoulder to a short, sloping one."

The Foreleg

The front limbs carry the weight of horse and rider. "The foundation should be clearly straight and strong, to leave enough room for the tendons," said Ramsauer. "It is quite important to find a complete and correct foundation. The more the legs are like the ideal, the more you have a chance to keep your horse sound in the legs."

Van der Veen pointed out the distinction between legs' construction and stance. He described construction as the bones' shape, and stance as the angles bones create in relation to one another.

Selection standards:

- Legs constructed with dry, clearly-marked joints and tendons.
- Substantial bone, appropriate to the size of the horse (measured by the circumference of cannon bones).
- Clean joints with no excess tissue or softness.
- Stance of foreleg placed under the horse, centered under the shoulder to support the forehand and back.
- Forearm (radius) long, broad, and well-muscled.
- At the elbow, a hand's width between the elbow and body.
- Big, long, and flat knee, set straight over the cannon bone.
- From the side, cannon bones flat and evenly wide, measuring shorter than the forearms.
- Fetlock joint lean and clearly-marked, connected to strong pasterns to support weight.
- Pastern long, sloping at 45°.
- Feet proportioned to the size of the legs, wide and oval in shape.
- Hoof angles in line with the slope of the pastern.

Leg deviations affect the strength of support and can cause interfering. A defect can unbalance the horse and cause painful joints, leading to lameness. Judges severely penalize leg problems that appear on two- or three-year-olds, which have not yet begun training.

The Frame

The horse can have a medium or large frame, which usually includes back, loins, and croup. "A cooperative back is the center of the horse," said van der Veen. "The horse without such a back looks stiff. It lacks in elasticity, and power

An impressive head and neck enhance the sport horse, making it look light in front and easier to elevate in its movement. Length of leg can vary, compared to body depth. Some authorities prefer legs equal to the heart girth; others feel the legs should be slightly longer. Dutch Warmblood Udon, ridden by Steffen Peters.

cannot flow over the relaxed back to the forehand."

"The kidney area is very important for a riding horse," explained Christmann. "It is the connection of the hind end with the rest of the body. The power of the hind end should be carried to the front, and any disconnection here will always have an effect on the movement."

Selection standards:

- Large frame connects a big shoulder and croup.
- Back appears strong and firm, yet supple so it can swing.
- Back's shape resembles a square more than a rectangle.
- Smooth topline forms a slight downward curve, without a dip at the wither.

The sport horse has functional angles. The shoulder is laid back to form a 90° angle with the upper arm (the humerus). This open angle allows the horse to lift its shoulder. Ideal hind leg angles are 90° in hip and stifle and 130° in hock.

• Wide, deep trunk with well-sprung ribs.
• Loins broad, substantial, and well-padded to form a smooth, unbroken connection between the back and the croup.
• Elastic loins help the hind legs to reach forward toward the middle of the horse's body.
• Croup's long muscles and strong bones provide the energy for natural impulsion.
• Long and wide hips, muscled on the top and along the point of the buttock to the gaskin.
• From the rear, croup appears oval in shape with high hipbones and substantial muscles.
• From the side, croup shows a moderate slope.

The Hind Leg

Van der Veen described the lever system of the hindquarter's stance, centered under the hindquarters to support weight. "The stifle must lie far forward. It must lie almost perpendicular under the hip socket. This improves the length of stride, drive, elasticity, power, and flexion of the hindquarter."

He added that hindquarter weaknesses can cause problems with the horse's mouth and back. "The rider tries to get the horse to use its hind legs, and the horse resists. It is handicapped by its conformation and can't get its hind legs under its body. The rider works more vigorously and the horse resists more. A horse that can bring its hindquarters under its body is less reluctant and easier to ride."

Christmann instructed, "Look at how the hind leg is connected to the body. If the hind end is disconnected, the horse stands out behind. The horse won't really come under the center of its body, and the effect is the hind end shovelling out, not propelling forward."

Selection standards:
• Long, broad, well-muscled stifle and gaskin, matching in proportion.
• Hock long, broad, and strongly affixed to the leg.
• Hock blends smoothly into the cannon.
• Bone below the hock is flat, to support the joint.

Judging the Gaits

Conformation suggests athletic ability, but the judge studies the horse's locomotion to see how efficiently it covers ground. Dr. Ramsauer described five criteria: "In trying to get a clear feeling about the quality of the sport horse, we judge the movement in its three basic gaits, its conformation, and its general impression. These five points make up the overall quality of the horse, and in my opinion, they are of absolutely equal importance."

Natural, balanced movement makes a riding horse easier to train. The rider does not have to remedy mechanical defects by training the horse

Judging Young Horses

European judges do not usually evaluate horses between the ages of six months and two years. In some breeds, authorities may give opinions, but they do not formally judge horses under the age of two years.

The young horse should not look like a mature animal. To have room to grow, it might look "imperfect" as a yearling, or even as a two-year-old.

Van der Veen offered comments about young horses: "The young horse has a longer leg than body depth. That will change. The body depth will grow, as you want a deep body compared to length of leg. A two-year-old should be almost a one-to-one proportion [of foreleg length to body depth].

"A young horse will have lower withers. You can look for length, but not the height. Withers will grow in height with the age.

"The neck should be a good length, but it will not be as muscled. The muscling on the neck's topline will be improved with maturity. The length stays the same in relation to the other parts.

"The shoulder slope will stay the same. The length will increase. The croup should have a good shape and muscle—the top of the croup will fill out as the horse grows."

to engage its hindquarters and elevate its forehand. Ludwig Christmann explained, "First a riding horse must move. A horse is not of any use if it looks nice when it stands, but not when it moves."

At all gaits, judges look for powerful, forward movement. The horse springs with elasticity and natural impulsion. Despite its size, it moves with a fluid lightness and agility. It elevates its forehand proudly and lifts its spine to use its back. The horse is supple—it swings its back, loins, and hips, "like Marilyn Monroe."

The Walk

Judges consider the walk very important, feeling that it predicts the quality of trot and canter. Judges emphasize and reward good walks. In a dressage clinic, Hilda Gurney said, "The first gait you look at, the most difficult gait to fix and the easiest gait to ruin, is the walk."

European judges observe the horse from both sides, from the front, and from behind. Hannoverian judges evaluate leg deviations from the front and rear views in the correctness of gait score. Christmann noted, "Correctness means if the leg turns in or out, of the straightness of the legs in motion. You see a tendency to wing only when the horse moves."

Selection standards:

• Regular, pure, four-beat walk with no period of suspension.

• Horse uses back loosely for a big reach.

• Soft, swinging back for elastic movement.

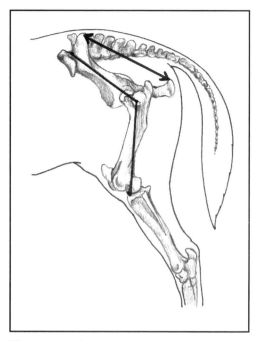

The croup's length gives forward thrust. Its length comes from the distance between the hip and the point of the buttock. From the rear, the croup should appear oval in shape with substantial muscles to propel the hindquarters forward.

At a rhythmical walk, this horse's legs form a "V" to indicate a regular gait. The hind foot reaches forward toward the forefoot as the horse strides well under itself. All parts of the body move with "lubricated" joints.

- Light, free step.
- All joints bend and flex.
- Hind foot oversteps front foot at least one hoofprint.
- Freedom of shoulder allows horse to reach forward.
- Angle of hindquarter allows horse to stride well under itself.

The Trot

Beginning to trot, the horse first engages its hindquarters, shifting its weight to free its fore-hand. Van der Veen explained, "Look for a vigorous strikeoff and flexibility when the foot hits the ground. Does the horse move in the right way at the first step, immediately in a good body position? You need good balance and sequence of hoofbeats at first. Immediate balance indicates a good mover, and that the horse will be balanced in training under a rider. If he can grow big at the trot in the first step, he can grow into a dressage horse if he has the character and temperament."

Footing influences the quality of the trot. In Germany, horsemen trot their animals on a hard surface to evaluate a horse's true way of going.

Selection standards:

- Regular, two-beat rhythm.
- Effortless, energetic steps.
- Light, bouncing, buoyant strides with suspension.
- Shoulder reaches up and over to swing forward and push off in long strides.
- Horse swings hind leg forward under its body.
- Horse points its hoofs to where it steps.
- Movement of front legs matches movement of hind legs—cannons stretch forward to form parallel angles.

Contemporary authorities prefer a reaching,

round movement, with more elevation of knee and hock and articulated joints. However, the "big" trot and "fancy" front end can affect the gait's regularity. "Purity of gait is more important than length of stride," advised van der Veen.

The Canter

In some associations' inspections, horses canter at liberty so officials can judge the gait. Others wait until a performance test to judge the canter under saddle. Van der Veen noted, "Usually a horse with a good walk and trot will have a good canter."

When the horse changes into the canter, it should shift its weight to the hindquarters for the strikeoff. To canter and gallop in any discipline, it must work off its hindquarters.

Selection standards:

• Horse displays natural impulsion.
• Canter shows a fluid rhythm of three distinct beats and a clear moment of suspension.
• Horse freely "sweeps" in flowing, athletic strides.
• Horse maintains balance and agility around turns.
• Topline remains quiet as horse lowers its hindquarters.

Free-Jumping

Jumping fences at liberty is part of most associations' stallion approvals, to demonstrate the horse's natural talent over fences. Officials usually start horses over a series of low fences, measuring an average 30 cm. A handler trots the horse into the lane, and groundsmen crack whips to encourage the horse forward. Officials raise the height of verticals and height and spread of oxers, sometimes to a height of four feet, six inches.

In a correct trot, the cannon bones of opposite legs reach forward to form parallel angles as they touch the ground simultaneously. The horse's hoofs point toward the ground.

The dressage horse shows pure gaits naturally, with a reaching and round movement. It swings its hindleg forward under the body.

The equine athlete displays presence and self-carriage as it moves with fluid gaits. The Hannoverian state stallion Wanderer and his handler show the moment of suspension at the trot.

Temperament and conformation affect the horse's ability to perform. This mare resists trotting forward and her hind legs do not reach under the center of her body.

The quality of the bascule over a fence can also indicate the horse's ability to collect, as in the piaffe. The horse "humps" its back to stretch the topline and lower the croup. Its belly muscles contract.

"They look for power and elasticity," said Trakehner breeder Henry Schurink. "They don't want a horse that jumps straight up. Look for the arc, the lifting of the front legs."

Van der Veen explained, "A jumper needs a relaxed back over fences. The muscles are not taut, but they bow over the jump. The horse that doesn't use its back is unsure and unpleasant over fences."

Selection standards:

- Horse boldly and willingly meets each fence.
- Horse canters smoothly in the approach, collecting or extending itself before takeoff.
- Horse calculates length of stride to take off at a comfortable distance.
- Leaping over the obstacle, horse displays its scope so the jump looks like a long, effortless stride.
- Jumper's technique demonstrates a classic, round bascule.
- Horse easily lifts its forearms high while thrusting actively from its hind legs.
- Horse lands in stride after clearing the fence.

The Judges' Final Scores

Each individual judge arrives at an overall score for each horse. With a commission, members must come to a mutually agreeable conclusion.

Dr. Wilkens of the Hannoverian Verband explained how the members of the commission reach agreements in mare shows. Two good gaits mark the best mares, which score 1A. A problem arises when a good mare lacks one gait, or her marks don't quite reach the score required for 1A. "Sometimes we have different opinions. You may put a mare's conformation

What Discipline?

Willie Arts explained that three pure gaits form the basis for all disciplines. "The trot is less important for a good jumping horse. Usually if it moves well, it will jump well. But for dressage and eventing, it's all three—if you miss one, you are wasting your time."

Any sport horse must move in a relaxed manner, shown in the position of ears and poll. Its energy travels straight through its body to the bit. It engages its hindquarters and lowers its croup while bending the stifle, hock, and fetlock.

Douglas Mankovich explained how stallions can become categorized toward producing sport horse offspring. "Every stallion has a predisposition—some of the freedom of the shoulder, use of the hocks, engagement of the hindquarters naturally when they are turned out, to produce more dressage or produce more jumping. Some have a predisposition for the bascule, the form over a fence."

A dressage horse must be a natural athlete, suited for the demands of the discipline. "The dressage horse has to have it all," said Lilo Fore. "It has to be everything—the movement, the mind, the total athletic ability."

Horses bred from jumping lines may lack the quality of walk seen in dressage lines, yet a supple, free stride can indicate a powerful jump. Jumpers do need balanced gaits to excel over fences. Qualities that indicate jumping potential include an oblique shoulder, strong frame, supple loin, powerful thigh, and strong hocks. The shoulders move freely so they can lift the fore-hand over the fence. The strong loin produces a round bascule.

In eventing, the horse must be correct, sound, and durable. An event horse has bone and substance, and a deep heart girth for cardiovascular efficiency. It gallops with free, sweeping strides. Again, a long, swinging walk can indicate a quality gallop.

The driving horse must be supple, fit, and obedient. It should have a long, sloped shoulder for pulling power. It shows a ground-covering walk and trot, with the ability to extend or collect easily. Its movement resembles the dressage horse—light in the forehand, engaged with the hindquarters.

Driving horses must be able to maneuver through hazards and pull the vehicle, driver, and passengers through deep footing. Ellen Epstein guides a pair of Dutch warmbloods through a water hazard.

a 9, her trot 8 or 9, but the walk could be a question...It must come together. Every point must be on a level which is a minimum."

The judges determine how to weigh characteristics, comparing them to arrive at a result. They consider the horse's age, sex, and physical changes resulting from its schooling.

Christmann described, "When judging, you adjust and compensate the degrees of faults and strengths. It's important to develop a system when judging. You see a lot of horses in a short time."

CHAPTER 17
Stallion Licensing

With most breeds, the approval of young stallions occurs at a traditional licensing event. Selection is strict, with only licensed stallions allowed to sire foals eligible for the studbook.

Because a stallion can sire 150-250 foals a year, authorities choose only a few young stallions to represent the breed. European associations realize that the breed requires a certain ratio of stallions to mares, and the sires they register compose only about one percent of the breed's population.

Hannoverian Stallion Licensing

The German method, using the Hannoverian as an example, begins with the stallion receiving a license to breed. Representatives sift through candidates in a rigorous selection process.

The stallion breeders or *Aufzüchters* (raisers) have selected candidates, and the state of Niedersachsen raises its own colts at Hunnesrück. Owners select only the best two-year-olds to go through the process, which includes the licensing, a performance test, and a progeny test. A potential stallion must have at least four generations of approved ancestors on its dam's side. It does not have to be foaled out of a State's Premium mare.

Choosing a stallion prospect involves chance. Dr. Jochen Wilkens of the Verband noted the difficulty of judging foals. "They change so much. I can't say, 'It's a stallion prospect.' Dr. Bade buys 40 stallion foals each year—2 to 5 come in the breed after the performance test."

Hermann Friedlaender said, "They wait till the horse is 2 or 2 years old. If the breeder sees this horse will never make a stallion, he has it altered earlier, because it's easier to raise a gelding than a colt. Of about 4500 colts born each year, of those at best 90 will stay entire."

Trakehner breeder Judy Yancey defined raising a stallion as a gamble. "I know it sounds very romantic, but less than one percent of a colt crop is ever approved for breeding purposes. Raising a stallion is fraught with peril."

The young stallions are raised outside in groups, so they can exercise naturally. Before the first inspection, the stallion manager will increase the colts' rations and teach them to longe for controlled exercise. With free-jumping a part of most associations' testing, young stallions will learn to handle small jumps.

The handler introduces the colt to a snaffle bit and longes it with bridle and surcingle, with side reins. The handler aims to get the horse rounded and fit, so it will move in balance.

When colts are two years old, the Verband conducts a pre-selection of the candidates. The

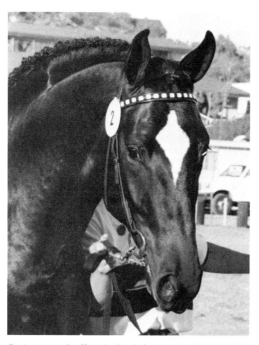

Raisers and officials look for young horses that show a distinct stallion presence. Trakehner stallion candidate Puszta's Diamant displays the desirable "controlled fire" at the 1990 stallion certification of the American Trakehner Association.

gree influences a stallion's chances for approval. Ludwig Christmann explained, "We make our selection according to standards we want to keep. All stallions must fulfill requirements, but we make exceptions."

Older types may not place as well by conformation and movement, but often these horses represent proven performance lines. Not as attractive as the modern sport horse, these animals have historically contributed to the breed's success in international competition.

Handlers present their perfectly groomed candidates first in a veterinary inspection. Although veterinarians already screened stallions on the farms, a team judges soundness and rejects candidates who fail to meet their strict standards. Officials also measure the stallions' height.

The commission of five authorities first inspects stallions for conformation and gaits. They watch horses trot on a hard surface to judge the correctness of gait. Colts must display a masculine presence. (One factor is the size of their testicles. Like cattle breeders, many horsemen claim a positive relationship between testicular size and sperm production). On all points, stallions must score an average of at least seven to pass. The marks are not made public.

Next the commission examines stallions in hand. They use the same criteria as in the mare shows to grade conformation and gaits. They also judge the colts' canter and jumping ability at liberty. The free-jumping test occurs on the second day.

After the second inspection, the president of the commission announces results in a parade of all horses. Spectators eagerly await the pronouncements on each horse. As a colt walks before the commission, the president announces, "Licensed," or "Not Licensed." Some horses are judged, "Not licensed at this time," meaning they are still in contention.

The State Stud has the right to purchase 10 of

commission visits farms to sort through approximately 500 colts, or about 10 percent of male foals born in that year. They choose approximately 100 to attend the stallion licensing. This public event is a pass-fail examination, with horses usually receiving a single opportunity. The rejects are targeted as riding horses, with almost all gelded.

In the Hannoverian breed, officials examine colts at the late October four-day *Hengstkörung* in Verden, at the Verband's headquarters. They look for both individual excellence and a stallion's possible contribution to the breed.

Besides conformation and movement, pedi-

the licensed colts. Before the final public announcement of successful candidates, the *Landstallmeister* has chosen the "First Lot," those newly licensed stallions that the state will buy.

"For a breeder, the greatest honor is to get a foal into the State Stud," explained U. S. breeder, Dr. Richard von Buedingen. "It's a prize, a point of pride. It's the prestige of producing a quality animal."

On the third inspection, officials announce final results for all stallions and note which animals Celle has selected. The *Landstallmeister* also offers to buy 10 additional stallions for Celle in the stallion market. In 1990, 62 of 105 colts became *gekört*, or licensed. These stallions receive a neck brand which designates their status as breeding animals.

The Hannoverian commission licenses the majority, more than needed in the state and private studs, primarily to sell horses in the stallion market. Buyers from other German state studs and foreign countries eagerly purchase quality stallion prospects. Buyers purchase the newly licensed stallions through the Verband. They negotiate with the commission, who controls the sale of the horses. In these transactions, the state determines the disposition of the breed.

The stallion market is the final event of the *Hengstkörung*. An auction begins with a parade of the new state stallions, from which officials choose a Champion and a Reserve.

Politics and economics have traditionally affected the stallion licensing. Horsemen who wished to determine the sale of their colts, or maintain ownership after licensing, can choose to present their horses in other *Körungs* with less stringent controls. Sellers could gain a substantially greater profit by marketing stallions to private buyers rather than the state.

The state paid DM 35,000-50,000 per horse in 1990. Of 57 licensed stallions available, 52 private sale horses sold. The highest sold for DM 100,000, and seven more went for DM 70,000. In 1990's

auction, licensed stallions sold for an average of DM 16,261. The top price was DM 28,000. Unlicensed stallions sold for an average DM 16,100; the highest price was DM 26,000.

The purchaser and raiser may sign a contract to agree on partial payment at this time. The buyer will pay the remainder only if the stallion passes the performance test.

Other German breeding areas follow the Hannoverian model. A breeder could brand a Hannoverian colt as an Oldenburg, and present it for licensing at the Oldenburg *Körung*. Westfalen and Holsteiner stallions have gone to Holland's stallion examination.

Recently, a supplemental stallion inspection, the *Nachkörung*, has been held in December. In case a colt missed the original date due to illness or injury, the owner could bring it to this event a month later. The Verband has also added another *Körung* in May.

The licensed stallions, the best of those presented, advance to the next phase of testing. A performance test, described in the next chapter, scores their abilities as riding horses.

Holsteiner

The Holsteiner Verband inspects stallion candidates in the German city of Neumünster. Dr. Thomas Nissen described the process: "The *Aufzüchters* report their stallions to my office. I travel throughout Schleswig-Holstein and look at every stallion aged 1 years. We are very cautious, but we tell the *Aufzüchter* if the stallion has a chance to come to Neumünster."

"We see the stallions again in August of their two-year-old year, and say if it's good enough to come to Neumünster. We look at 60 or 70 to invite. The breeder can bring a stallion at a later date to Elmshorn." (Elmshorn is an alternative site for horses not invited to Neumünster).

Nissen explained that in 1989, of 1200 colts foaled in 1987, the Verband eventually selected

18 at Neumünster. These went on to the performance test, and the Verband eventually acquired 14 of these. (Some belonged to the Verband before the approval).

"We pay DM 40,000, a set price for an approved stallion," said Nissen. "The Verband has a contract and can buy any stallion that comes to the approvals. If the horse wins the approvals and the performance test, the breeder and raiser get a higher price. A stallion that wins at the performance test, his price goes up to DM 60,000."

Like other German societies, the Holsteiner Verband has developed a system to retain the superior stallion candidates. By avoiding "stallion raids," the restrictions benefit the breed and the Verband's mare owners. Nissen explained, "The Verband does it for the breeders. When we sold stallions by an auction, foreign buyers would pay $100,000 to $300,000. We need the best stallions in our breed. Sometimes we can let good stallions go, but not every year.

"The breeder can't look over the whole breed. He sees only the money he could get. He could sell a stallion at a high price, but he accepts the necessity of benefiting the breed as a whole."

Holsteiner stallions do not have to be foaled from State's Premium mares, although Nissen noted that the Verband tries to get stallions out of these mares. The State's Premium mare does receive preference in breeding to the best Holsteiner sires.

Trakehner

The Trakehner Verband's inspection also uses Neumünster as its site. In May, a committee travels for two weeks to pre-judge two-year-olds throughout Germany. One member is the Verband's breeding director.

Stallion candidates must be out of Main Studbook mares. U. S. breeder Henry Schurink described the process: "They have received the applications, and they see if it's worthwhile to let each horse come. They say, 'This one you might as well keep at home. That one we will take.' When they come to Neumünster, they already have in their heads an idea of what's coming."

Schurink added that the committee chooses over 100 young stallions, even though they realize only 10 to 15 percent will receive approval. "They could have been more critical when they looked at the breeders'. Or, between May and November, a horse could change a lot." He noted that a colt can change greatly in as short a time as three months, either for the better or worse.

Neumünster hosts the *Körung* as a gala event. The number of stallions enhances the program, making for an extravagant show. Over three days, candidates progress through five phases:

1. Measuring and veterinary inspection. The committee compares the horse with its registration certificate, verifying its color and markings. An official measures each candidate to confirm that it meets minimum size requirements: 160 cm in height, 183 cm in heart girth, and 19 cm cannon bone circumference. He uses a measuring stick at the highest point of the withers, a tape around the girth just behind the withers, and a short tape placed below the knee at the narrowest part of the cannon bone.

Size is a factor. Authorities frown on colts being too tall, realizing that a too-large horse can be less athletic than an average-sized one. Dr. Schilke recommended that the colt, at 2 years, should stand from 162 to 166 cm.

The veterinary inspection checks the horse for physical flaws which could disqualify it as a breeding horse. The pre-selection removed horses with obvious weaknesses, but this inspection verifies that each young stallion meets minimum health and soundness requirements.

2. Presentation in-hand. A handler presents the horse to the committee, on a hard surface. As in the Hannoverian breed, the horse first stands, near-side to the committee in the open position. The handler then leads the horse in a straight line away from and back toward the inspectors at the walk, and again at the trot. The inspection concludes with the horse standing again, with its offside presented to the committee.

3. Presentation on the triangle. In the arena, the handler again presents the horse, with the committee standing in the middle of the triangle. The horse stands for inspection, then walks one lap and trots the next. It again stands, before the committee dismisses it for the next candidate.

4. Free-jumping and presentation at liberty. Each candidate performs over a line of four vertical fences and oxers, set up along the arena wall. Groundsmen guide the horse into the jumping lane, raising the heights of the fences after each pass. To judge the quality of the trot and canter, horses run at liberty.

5. Judging of finalists. The announcer calls the numbers of finalists, who circle the ring at the walk. After deliberation, the committee selects five premium stallions, a champion, and a reserve champion.

The Trakehner stallion approval fills a 6000-seat stadium. With the Trakehner a worldwide breed, spectators represent dozens of nations. At the 1990 approval, 116 stallions from 24 nations entered the competition. With 99 actually showing, the committee chose only 15 as approved. These represented Germany, Switzerland, Hungary, the Netherlands, and Denmark.

Once the approved stallion leaves the arena, it immediately receives a neck brand identifying it. Trakehner stallions may breed after approval, but they must complete the performance test at 3 years of age to receive complete approval.

At a public auction, individuals bid for the newly licensed stallions. Breeder Guenter

The stallion's trainer may work the horse in a surcingle fitted with side reins. This appliance teaches the horse to collect while moving forward with impulsion. Willie Arts demonstrated how to school in long lines, with a Dutch horse.

Bertelmann said, "It's a free market. You never know who will jump in and want to get a horse. The average price [1990] was DM 70,900. Three buyers fought until the last moment for the highest priced stallion—DM 230,000."

France

A national commission selects three-year-old stallions, based on the horses' conformation. In 1988, officials also began testing these horses on free-jumping. At the age of four, stallions are tested on their temperament and jumping performance.

Dutch

The KWPN conducts a yearly stallion examination of three-year-olds, with some four-year-olds that missed the previous year or want to try again. Breeders may present candidates in a six-

Henry Schurink measures a Trakehner stallion candidate.

day event in February, the largest stallion approval in Europe with as many as 15,000 spectators.

In 1990, owners presented 700 entries at three locations: Arnhem, Zuidlaren, and Utrecht. The stallions represented all three types of Dutch horses, with most of the riding horse type.

Authorities brand the three-year-old stallions at the event. Horses are shown on the triangle at the walk and trot. The jury selects about 250 for the "second ring," a term that indicates the stallion has made the first cut.

From the second ring, the jury picks about 125 for the "third ring." About 50 of these make the final cut, selected to enter the KWPN's 100-day testing.

"They are so careful with the stallions," explained Elizabeth Searle. "Their favorite saying is, 'The best isn't good enough.'"

She noted certain faults that immediately disqualify a candidate. "They will not accept parrot mouth or curbs. They weigh heavily—they will accept under certain conditions, if everything else is superb—standing under or sickle hocks, because those usually produce

curbs. They don't necessarily throw the horse out—if that is the only fault, everything else is good, and the bloodlines don't tend on either side to produce that.

"They really know their lines, and they see thousands of horses. If everything else is spectacular, then they know whether that particular line produces that fault, or whether it just happened."

Danish

Danish stallions, like mares, must pass strict selections. Peter Kjellerup explained, "They look at 150 2 year old colts. Then they go to 40 for the big breeding show at 3 years of age. Five or six, or a maximum of 10, go on to the Danish 100-Day test, and three or four are finally approved."

Swedish

Like the Danish, Swedish stallions are tested in a central location. An approved stallion must be foaled from a sire and dam registered in the official studbook. The mare must have a four-generation pedigree of registered breeding stock.

The Swedish government inspects colts every year, between the ages of one and four. At age three, colts are judged by their conformation and gaits. If a horse meets the standard and passes a veterinary examination with satisfactory X-rays, it may enter the stallion performance test.

How will 1992 affect the way associations approve stallions?

Until 1990, Germany's animal breeding law stipulated that only a licensed stallion could breed mares. A licensed stallion had a validated pedigree, its sire and dam had proved their performance abilities, and the horse had passed an examination by an official licensing committee. This law was revised on January 1, 1990, according to new European Economic Community regulations.

New regulations eliminate the state *Körung*. The European Community no longer allows government control of breed registries, and the state will no longer participate in deciding which stallions may breed. However, in most countries, the government will continue to support the horse industry, holding performance tests and contributing funds to breed societies.

Throughout the European Community, new agricultural policies worry farmers who strive to produce quality. They fear that relaxing rules and allowing imports will reduce the overall quality of their products.

Registries must accept horses which are registered with a pedigree from any other European Community breed society. According to the free trade regulations, any association is obligated to accept any registered stallion or mare with the minimum requirement of a two-generation pedigree. For example, a Selle Français, Dutch Warmblood, or Holsteiner stallion may enter the Hannoverian or Westfalen studbook.

The careful selection of stallions has fostered the success of European warmbloods. Controlling the ratio of stallions to mares has made it possible for breeders to determine a sire's genetic performance.

Hermann Friedlaender considered this "a very unfortunate period. Instead of comparing everything to the highest common denominator, we are pulling it down to the lowest common denominator. We are completely disregarding the selective breeding, which was developed at great cost and sacrifices over hundreds of years. So it will have a bad, deteriorating effect."

German breed associations have created different categories of their studbooks, following guidelines of the FN, the *Zuchtverbandsordnung*,

Most associations require stallion candidates to jump fences at liberty, usually through a chute over two or more post and rail obstacles. A Dutch stallion jumps a triple bar at a California keuring.

(ZVO). The Studbook I category will continue to register mares and stallions which fulfill the association's traditional requirements. The association retains its system of approvals.

The Studbook II category will register horses which qualify according to the new European breeding rules. The offspring of Stallion Book II sires will qualify only for the Studbook II.

"Stallion licensing is no longer part of the government, and the stallion does not have to be licensed," explained Christmann. "The Verband and all other German organizations will keep licensing, although breeders can still use the unlicensed stallion for breeding. The unlicensed stallion's progeny will get only a birth certificate, no pink papers. They won't be allowed to be branded, they can't take part in the breeding program, and they won't be considered as a Hannoverian. Only licensed and tested stallions will be part of the breeding program."

Christmann did note a positive aspect of the

new regulations: an unlicensed stallion could be presented a second time. Or, the horse could receive its license as a mature horse, proving its excellence through competition.

"It will make very little difference to the Hannoverian breeding," said Friedlaender. "The government dictates one book, and one is the breeding association's. They will maintain it. Look at what has been built up over hundreds of years, at great monetary sacrifices—just to throw it out does not seem reasonable. As far as the Hannoverian is concerned, the impact will be very small."

Trakehner breeders, concerned with controlling their "pure" breed, also established separate studbooks for horses of Trakehner ancestry. These horses will receive white papers and a half-antler brand. The double antler brand and pink papers will be reserved for only offspring of parents registered in the previous studbooks.

European viewpoints about 1992—voiced in 1990

Dr. Eberhard Senckenberg, Trakehner Verband: "Our breeders will keep on *Körung*. It will not be a state-approved *Körung*, but the Verband. The 100-day testing will continue, still set by law as the *Körung* was formerly. The animal breeding law has not affected the 100-day test.

"We now have to register a non-approved stallion. He goes into another department of the studbook."

Dr. Roland Ramsauer, International Sporthorse Registry: "The borders will be open for horse breeding. A French stallion can come to Germany. A German stallion can come to the Netherlands. If a breeder in France wants a German stallion, he can. The government can't say it's not allowed. The government won't protect its own breed, and the association has to issue papers for horses from other countries.

"A French stallion will be able to get Hannoverian papers. I know at the moment the Hannoverian Verband doesn't agree on that, but I guarantee you that they have to issue the papers. That's the reason they have the different books for the stallions. I think that's a discrimination, because there's not reason because of the breed. Quality would be a reason."

From the North American viewpoint—1990/1991

Trakehner breeder Robin Koenig: "They'll have to be more lenient. They might say, 'Not approved at this time,' and look at the horse again after 100 days. They'll approve more and give horses more time." Of the Hannoverian stallions, he felt it would take years to separate the licensing from the government. "It's part of the military. They have been told the government knows best."

Trakehner breeder Guenter Bertelmann: "There is a change, but it will be in the end a positive change for the breed. Some difficult things are going on, but if the breed associations watch their breeds, there is no damage.

"The breeding leaders and officers of the state studs will stay the same. Overall, the breed associations are very strong and well-organized."

Breeder and trainer, Dietrich Felgendreher: "In general, not too much will change. The knowledgeable and traditional horse breeders will stick to their guns. They will keep to their programs. There will be some difficult situations, which will take a number of years to sort out. Breeding warmbloods will stay the same. It's so embedded, the way of doing things—approving stallions, producing good broodmare bands.

"State studs cannot officially be connected with the government any more. Breeders will still go to state stallions. Private stallions, and there are many valuable ones, will be patronized just as much, if not more.

"If they want to stay with the times, they'll have to change some things. It's been very difficult to change things up at the top. Things might change for the better."

Trainer Guenter Seidel: "I actually think it's not going to make a lot of difference. You still have the same horse—a good horse if it's a good one. People are overrating anyway the approvals. It's not necessarily true that if the horse is approved it has to be a spectacular horse. A horse that's approved might be good for breeding, but not necessarily excellent as a sport horse."

Trainer Uli Schmitz: "1992 opens up a lot more. Now it'll be one rule for the whole European economy. It will probably end up with every breeding association will keep their own book, but they have to accept stallions from other breeds. I think it will come to more the European warmblood horse. They'll still have their own breeding associations, but they'll open up a lot more."

Trainer Jan Ebeling: "I think it will be the same if the state is not involved that much any more in the approvals. No matter what you do, people will always say there's politics. If a state-owned stallion wins, there's, 'Well, the government owns it so it's sure to win.' If a private stallion wins the testing, then it's going to be the same thing—'Of course he won—he's owned by the breeders.' I think it's good when the government is involved. They have a lot of funding from the government."

Importer Hans Schardt: "It is a very difficult question for me. I am a sport horse person—I have to say it will be for the sport horse aspect, good. It will be less who the federation likes, and more what did you perform.

"In reality, it will be between France and Germany. For hundreds of years, Germany and France have bred good horses. How it ends up to keep the bloodlines clean, that will change a little. Combining the bloodlines, only the top stallions will breed in both countries to top mares. The problem is if a small breeder takes his favorite mare to a stallion that before wasn't permitted [licensed]. We'll have to see how it ends up in a couple of years."

CHAPTER 18
Performance and Progeny Testing

A fter a mare enters the studbook, or a stallion receives its license, breed societies apply two more important tests to verify the selection of superior animals. These include standard performance tests and the inspection of the horse's offspring.

In performance testing under controlled conditions, the sport horse proves its rideability, soundness, and temperament. Tests help breeders determine how their programs succeed in producing performance horses. They validate the selections made in mare shows and stallion approvals. (Note: In 1990, the Oldenburg Verband added an under-saddle test to its *Körung*. Stallion candidates at 2 years must show under saddle).

Performance tests began in the mid-19th century. Breeding areas tested young stallions, such as Trakehnen's evaluation of young stallions' rideability on the hunt field. In 1925, East Prussia established a permanent testing center at Zwion. Trakehnen's 2 year old stallions underwent close to a year of training and conditioning for a three-day cross-country test. During the training, authorities observed the

youngsters' willingness, health, and athletic ability; they could target the future stud careers of the potential sires.

The final test eliminated horses which could not meet standards of galloping and jumping. Each day's hunt course challenged the horse with 10 jumping efforts. On the first and second days, the horse had to gallop 10 km, at a pace of four km per hour. The third day, the horse galloped 13 km, as well as a speed gallop of three km. Veterinary examinations reported the candidates' condition throughout the testing period.

Hannover established a similar testing program in 1927, at Westercelle. Trainers prepared stallions for a year, and the final test included five segments of riding, jumping, driving, and pulling.

East Prussia initiated a formal test for three-year-old mares after the first World War. Mares performed three gaits under saddle and pulled a heavy load for a specified distance. By 1936, the test was modified after models in Pommern and Mecklenburg. Mares had to be registered in the East Prussian Studbook and bred to foal the following year. The one-day test included plowing and pulling (both in pairs of mares), along with a riding test that included a galloping portion.

Contemporary Mare Testing

In most European countries, three- to four-year-old broodmares voluntarily enter performance testing. This gives the breed societies information on mares' potential as sport horses and their temperament. The KWPN's Gert van der Veen noted, "Fine temperament takes precedence over a perfect exterior. We can only learn about the horse's character and temperament if you work with the horse at what it performs. Testing mares in a central place helps compare results better."

In the mid-1980s, the Hannoverian Verband initiated a performance test for broodmares. Most of the breed's mares, including the superior State's Premium mares, were traditionally never ridden. This test, or *Zuchtstutenprüfung*, is meant to insure that the broodmares would pass on characteristics affecting rideability.

Of the 2400 mares inspected each year, about 500 go through two types of tests: field and station. Most mares have won the 1A award or State's Premium at mare shows and are three or four years old. The performance test information is added to the mare's pedigree, enhancing Studbook information and qualifying her to be the dam of stallion prospects.

"In the performance test, we look for the horse's natural ability, not how it is ridden," said Ludwig Christmann. "We look for the use of the back and neck. It's not a dressage test, but how the horse responds to the commands of the rider."

Field test. The mare receives three scores. Judges first give marks for the quality of walk, trot, and canter. They score each gait equally. The second score is for rideability. Here both the judge and

a test rider rate the mare's performance under saddle. The third score evaluates the mare's willingness to jump free and under saddle. (The latter section may be removed from the test). This segment gives judges information on the horse's behavior and response. Christmann noted, "We look for potential as a jumper—a round back, willingness, and the use of the legs over the fence."

The final score is the average of the three subscores. A State's Premium mare must achieve at least 7 in one subscore to fulfill the award's requirements.

Station Test. The Verband holds seven courses, each three weeks long for 25 mares. This more exhaustive test involves four subscores. The trainer scores the mare's interior qualities, including her temperament, character, and willingness to perform. The actual test covers gaits, rideability, and jumping (free and under saddle). Trainer and test rider score the mare, and her overall score reflects her performance in training and the final test.

Christmann sees the test as an incentive to those breeders whose mares did not win the State's Premium at the mare show. "If a mare scores 7.5 in the test, she can be shown again to compete for the State's Premium title. We invite those mares to come, and some have earned the Premium through that."

The test does cost the breeder, however, as it takes about two months training at DM 1000 to prepare the mare for the simple tests. Sponsorship has encouraged breeders to enter the test, and the results will enhance pedigrees for the marketing of future offspring. The breed magazine prints names of horses scoring 7 and better.

Christmann added, "We are trying new things, with the performance test combined with the mare shows and studbook inspection. We aim for all three disciplines...we are still in development—the way to select performance horses is not yet perfect. Our way to select the stallions is very good."

Holsteiner. The Verband started the first such mares' performance test in Germany in 1982. Dr. Thomas Nissen developed this program, which he noted has been duplicated by the Westfalen, Oldenburg, Trakehner, and Bayern societies.

"At three years old, the mare is tested for 14 days. We started with 1 months, four weeks, three weeks, and then two weeks. We made an evaluation after every week and found you can get information after two weeks. The better mares get better, and you get no other information if the test is at four or six weeks. We don't want it too expensive for our breeders."

The Verband selects about 130 mares a year to test at Elmshorn, and 50 to 80 others participate in field tests. At the field tests, the breeder brings the mare to a central location for a one-day test in free-jumping, movement, and riding ability.

Nissen explained that the owner prepares the horse at home. "The rider has a great influence on the mare. You get more correct and precise information at the station [Elmshorn] test. The problem is that you can't do three or four hundred mares at the station—you need a lot of capacity."

Dutch. The KWPN tests mares' rideability in its I.B.O.P. (loosely translated, "performance horse") test. Here the rider saddles and bridles the mare in front of the jury. The horse and rider then perform a program ride and a jumping test. The program ride shows the jury the horse's gaits and willingness. Although it reads like a dressage test, the rider should aim to present the horse with impulsion, or "ridden well forward."

The horse jumps a course of four obstacles twice, consisting of a wall, vertical post and rail, oxer, and triple bar. Obstacles must meet standard requirements of height and width. If the horse refuses three times, the jury dismisses it from the test.

Riders at Adelheidsdorf school the state stallions during the 11-month training period.

The jury scores each mare on six factors: Quality of walk, quality of trot, quality of canter, submission and self-carriage, character and temperament, and style of jumping. They use the international scale of 0 to 10, with coefficients to make a possible perfect score of 110. Mares' total scores place them in one of four classifications: AA—90-110 points, with no one score lower than 8; A—88-90 points, with the character score not lower than 7; B—77-88 points, with the character score not lower than 6; and C—66-77 points, with the character score not lower than 5. To qualify for the *Keur* predicate, the mare must receive an AA, A, or B. A "C" mare may retake the test again in order to try for a higher score.

The score becomes a part of the mare's record. In Holland, horsemen would describe an AA mare with a score of 97 as "97 IBOP."

At a *Keuring* in the United States, Rolf Brinkman praised such an AA mare. "110 is perfect. But you understand, a 10 is something that is very rare. Five horses in ten years have achieved a 10, but not all the points can be. The highest point on any category today was 9—judges can always find something."

He said that each score is a consensus, with all members of the jury agreeing. "We will talk and talk to resolve a disagreement. We try to explain when one gives an 8, and one a 9."

The Dutch are reportedly investigating a central training program to obtain more information on mares as producers. They also encourage breeders to have mares' legs X-rayed.

Stallion Testing—Germany

A performance test is the second step for the approval of a young stallion. Most European societies require that each animal pass a test.

Germany conducts 100-day tests at testing stations, a three-month training period which culminates in a two-day test. Niedersachsen began this program in 1962, as an alternative for its privately owned stallions and a way to test stallions from other German warmblood associations.

Since 1974, German law required that every riding horse stallion intended for breeding had to pass the 100-day performance test at one of the approved German stations. The horse had to prove its suitability with its total points not more than 1.5 points below the average mark for the group.

The Hannoverian stallions which have been raised or purchased by the state undergo the more exhaustive *Hengstprüfungsanstalt des Niedersachsisch Landgestüts Celle*, an 11-month training and testing period. After licensing, approximately 40 young horses begin training at the testing center in Adelheidsdorf, near Celle.

The program follows a planned schedule of four periods. The first stage, from November through March, introduces the youngsters to the facility's routine, along with carefully schooling them in longeing and work under saddle. In

the second period, trainers work on driving, dressage, jumping, and galloping on the track. Young stallions also learn to pull a sled, then a cart. Horses work six days a week and rest on the seventh.

The third period prepares and conditions stallions for the final test. Horses work in groups of six or seven. In the riding hall, riders work horses under the direction of *Hauptsattellmeister* Manfred Lopp. They also school the stallions outside, in a dressage arena or on the cross-country course. On certain days, stallions complete a 1000-meter cross-country schooling.

Riders are state employees, both riding students and staff from the stallion stations. They maintain the facility in addition to grooming and schooling several groups of stallions each day.

Scoring follows a standard developed by the University of Goettingen. Horses receive scores through the training and during the final two days of testing. Authorities evaluate candidates within the testing group, not compared with horses across other groups. They judge horses on the curve, using an average standard of 100 points. To pass the test and enter the Verband's studbook, a stallion must score a minimum 90 points. A potential State Stallion must earn at least 100.

The system involves a complex mathematical formula. Various elements are assigned economical weights. Weights can be adjusted depending on the importance of the various elements.

Christmann described the stallion's final score as "a mosaic of varied opinions." Riders and the director contribute to pre-test scores, with the stallion's qualities evaluated continuously. The director's score accounts for 50 percent of the final training score.

During the final test, eight judges contribute their opinions. Three judges and three riders independently score each horse, with two more submitting marks for free-jumping.

"The test is a good instrument for selection," said Christmann. "It gives a good ability to judge the horse at an early stage." It includes scores for rideability, jumping ability over a course (*parcours*), free-jumping ability, quality of the three gaits within a time limit, completion of a cross-county course, and speed at a 1000-meter gallop.

Christmann discussed research which proved a correlation between a stallion's performance test results and its value as a sire. "A good stallion that performs also produces a horse that performs in sport. There is a strong correlation between the free-jumping score and the progeny's results in the sport." He noted less of a link between the *parcours* score and the progeny's results, saying that other factors (such as the rider) affect this mark.

Each segment of the testing produces a champion. The overall champion of the final test in November, the *Prüfungssieger*, achieves a special honor. His breeder receives an award, the Steinkopff-Preis. General scores are published in the breed magazine, and they also appear in the Verband's *Hengstbuch* (stallion register) as the HLP, or *Hengstleistungsprüfung* (stallion performance test).

Horses finish in Class I, II, or III. Those receiving more than 120 points are Class I stallions. Class II horses have scored 100 and 120, and Class III between 70 and 100.

From 12 to 15 of the young Hannoverian stallions enter the state stud. Those that fail to meet the tests' standards are sold at prices from DM 30,000 to 40,000. The state may choose to sell successful stallions, if the State Stud already has sufficient sires of the bloodline.

Privately owned three-year-old German stallions complete the *100-Tage-Test für Warmbluthengste* (100-day test) at Adelheidsdorf, Warendorf, Klosterhof Medingen, Marbach, or Münster-Handorf. (Warendorf runs another test for only its state stallions). Adelheidsdorf is the largest and

most famous, attracting 70 young stallions who represent the various breeding areas and the Trakehner. Münster-Handorf, the Westfalen Equestrian Center, tests 60 licensed stallions.

Stallions enter a 100-day program in August. At each site, all stallions, regardless of breed, are trained and tested under identical conditions. They compete on an equal basis.

Half the score depends on the horse's performance during the training period: temperament, character, constitution, food consumption, rideability, jumping talent, willingness to learn and to work, and ability to recover from stress of hard work. The test includes performance on the flat and over fences, and timed tests over a 1000-meter walk, 2000-meter trot, and 1000-meter gallop.

The training leader scores stallions during the training according to criteria for each factor.

Weltmeyer (World Cup I—Absatz) won his performance test at Adelheidsdorf.

Horses receive half their final score during the 100-days' training.

The final test, accounting for the other half of the final score, is judged by the training leader and three judges. Three test riders contribute to the horses' scores. These horses also receive placings of Class I, II, and III.

Holsteiner stallions began attending the first performance tests in Celle in 1961. Dr. Nissen of the Holsteiner Verband said, "The information is better when all stallions are in one place. The commission can follow the development of the stallions."

He added that the Holsteiners excel in the jumping portion, although an emphasis on rideability poses a problem. "In our stallions, riding ability is not as important at three years. They need a longer time."

The test does pressure the trainers to try to prepare each horse to pass. With a horse's future—and the owner's finances—at stake, trainers assume a heavy responsibility.

"They have 100 days, and it is their priority to have the stallion pass," explained dressage trainer and Hannoverian breeder Lilo Fore. "Some stallions need more time, and the trainers just don't have that time. It's a lot to ask—it's like a combined training event."

A licensed Hannoverian stallion can complete approval through competition in lieu of taking the performance test. He can earn five placings from first to third at FEI-level dressage or Grand Prix show-jumping competitions. Or, he can earn three placings from first to third in international-level three-day event competitions.

All tests aim to verify the horse's qualities beyond its potential for sport. The stallion proves it is trainable, along with its ability to remain sound and improve its movement through training.

U. S. breeder Dr. Richard von Buedingen explained how a horse's temperament and desire can influence its performance. "A horse has

athletics between its ears. An athlete thinks it's an athlete. It doesn't quit; it goes on. Something makes it different—not always the conformation or perfect build. Animals are competitors if they have the competitive spirit."

The new European Community requirements have affected the stallion performance testing. These regulations consider a passing score as 70, while German associations require 90 points to pass. Again, observers note the conflict in quality, and caution against creating greater confusion.

According to Dr. Roland Ramsauer, the Bavarians have decided to establish three sections in their stallion book. "In section 1, they put all stallions which have more than 48 points (in the *Körung*) and 120 points in the 100-day test. Section 3, they put all stallions which are not approved by the 100-day test. Section 2, they put all the others."

Stallion Testing—The Netherlands

The Dutch stallion test at Ermelo is also a standardized evaluation. Each of the 60 to 70 candidates must prove its quality after its initial selection. Owners pay part of the cost, with the KWPN and the Dutch government also contributing.

Authorities eliminate candidates on physical factors, that could not show up in the *Keuring*. (Judges at the *Keuring* do not touch the horses, especially lively, unbroke three-year-olds).

Elizabeth Searle explained, "A lot of things happen after they're selected. Those horses are X-rayed and examined thoroughly. Sometimes they're thrown out the first day. Another reason they go out is if the semen count isn't accepted."

Officials score horses on walk, character, trot, stable behavior, gallop, training report, rideability, dragging test, jumping, riding ability, free jumping, pulling ability, and cross country. (Traits evaluated have varied from year to year).

Rolf Brinkman said, "After five weeks, the judge sees how the horse is doing. He looks at the performance of the horse, not at its conformation. It's dismissed if it doesn't meet the standards, down to about 35 horses who go on to the end.

"The horses are training all day in the 100 days. The owner relinquishes the horse for the 100 days. At the end of the training the horse goes through a three-day test—then you see if it is enough or not enough."

Three-year-olds are started under saddle during the test. Searle noted that in the training, the riders aim to ride the stallions forward. Officials want to see the horse's movement under saddle, and its willingness to respond to the trainer's aids. "They look that the horse is trainable, that he comes halfway to the trainer, that he's not against things that are presented to him. That he's quiet, has no stable vices. They throw them right out of the testing—if their temperament during that 100 days does not come up to par, out!

"They do accept stallion behavior. All have certain stallion traits, and you handle them a little bit differently. They don't have to be docile cows, but they don't want any antagonistic attitude toward man."

Van der Veen said, "The heritability of character is more than 60 percent, so good character is important. You can easily overcome deficiencies in conformation, but not character."

Only about 15 stallions pass the Dutch 100-day test. The Dutch publish the individual scores for each evaluation factor. Unlike the Germans, the Dutch do not require that failed stallions must be gelded. The horse will not receive its approval, but it can breed the owner's mares. Most do become riding horses, with many purchased by foreign buyers.

Other Nations' Stallion Testing

The French select both mares and stallions through performance. Beginning at four years of age, horses compete against one another in the show jumping circuit. The *Cycle Classique* (Classic Cycle) assesses a horse's aptitude, with events restricted to mares, stallions, and geldings aged four, five, and six. Horses compete to enter the finals at Fontainebleau in the fall, demonstrating their ability in either jumping, cross-country, dressage, or combined training.

In jumping, horses qualify for the finals by performing faultless rounds over fences. The four-year-old finals are open to horses which have achieved at least 6 clear rounds out of 9, or 7 out of 12. In 1989, one-twentieth of the potential jumpers foaled in 1985 qualified—almost 400 horses.

To qualify for five-year-old finals, horses must achieve a certain number of clean rounds along with winning prize money. In 1989, jumpers had to post 8 to 10 clear rounds out of 20.

The breeder of the World Champion Quito de Baussy, Alain Navet, wrote of the qualities required of a stallion to improve the breed: "Its dam and sire must come from families having produced top class athletes. It must have proven its own show jumping capability either by its performance or by the quality of its offspring. It must have the mental and physical qualities for the standard model of a good sport horse."

Sweden, Denmark, and Belgium train young stallions, which then take several prescribed tests. Denmark operates its own 100-day test at Wilhelmsborg.

In Sweden, authorities inspect about 150 three-year-olds for conformation and soundness. They choose approximately 50 for performance testing.

Swedish stallions are tested at intervals of 3, 4, and 4 years of age. The horse must pass two tests before receiving a license to breed. This system allows a young stallion three opportunities, so the horse's evaluation is not confined to one event.

The rigorous tests last for a week at each six-month interval. "Breeding Programmes for Riding Horses and Thoroughbreds in Sweden" described, "The stallion tests are considering cross-country performance and endurance, gaits, jumping ability, temperament and rideability, conformation and soundness. All traits are scored on a scale with 1-10 points and after each test the scores are summed up into an index. About 30 percent of the stallions are finally appoved for breeding."

Rideability, gaits, and jumping under saddle are not included in the first test, at 3 years. Five-year-old stallions compete under saddle in a spring event. The competition is for the Number One Prospect in both dressage and show jumping.

The current Swedish tests began in 1977, and with requirements becoming stricter, the percentage of stallions approved for breeding has decreased. In 1987 and 1988, 20 of the 66 received approval. These receive a temporary breeding license, good for one year. Licensed stallions are graded into two classes by performance, B and AB. Of the stallions approved, only four or five receive licensing after the final performance test.

In 1989 the Flyinge stallion Amiral (Napoleon-Flamingo-Lansiär) placed first in the 4 year old stallion testing. He received an all-time high score of 40 points for gaits and rideability and a conformation score of 45.

Progeny Testing

Hannoverian. Stallions may breed 20 mares their first year, even before passing the performance test. If they fail the test, they lose breeding privileges. However, foals from the test breeding can be registered.

Authorities rate the stallion's heritability by several methods. They evaluate his **first foal crop**, bringing all foals together to gather an impression of his produce. However, they do consider the quality of the mares bred, realizing that an unknown stallion might not get the right type of mares in his first season.

A jumper sire is at a disadvantage, with foals being judged on movement. "This is limited information," said Ludwig Christmann. "A stallion might not produce good movers at that age. His second year, breeding would improve because breeders would pick mares that fit with him."

Douglas Mankovich noted, "When stallions start actually breeding, they soon are slotted: 'This one is jumping, especially when you cross him with this mare.'"

Mare shows. The Verband also sees stallions' produce at mare shows, beginning with the two-year-olds.

Performance Tests. Colts and fillies demonstrate their sires' strengths in passing on his athletic ability. In *Materialprüfung* (Material tests), young competition horses show in classes limited to their age group. The three- and four-year-olds walk, trot, canter, and halt to demonstrate gaits and character. These classes are important to demonstrate the stallion's production, testing young horses according to their stage of development.

FN Yearbook. Results of the classes are included in the *Jahrbuch Zucht der FN*. The German Equestrian Federation's annual publication lists offspring's accomplishments by discipline, including yearly and lifelong earnings. German associations also award cash prizes to breeders, the *Züchterprämien* (Breeders' premium).

Holsteiner. Stallions may breed after they receive approval. The Verband surveys a stallion's offspring through the cycle of inspections and shows, and wins reported in the FN Yearbook.

Volckmar

Volckmar excels in the dressage arena and as a Dutch sire. Foaled in 1979, he is by Abgar xx out of a mare of Gelderlander breeding.

This gray stallion stands 16.3 hands. He passed the Dutch 100-day test in 1982, receiving scores of 8.5 on his gallop and jumping, and 9's on his stable behavior and Training Report.

Volckmar is owned by D. G. Bar Ranch, Hanford, California. "Volckmar is a perfect example of the kind of warmblood for the American rider," explained his trainer, Willie Arts. "He has good size but he's sensitive, easy off the ground, and has a super character."

In 1990, he was 3rd in the USDF Intermediare II Horse of the Year, and 13th in Intermediare I. He is on the roster of nominated stallions for the International Jumper Futurity. His offspring in

Volckmar performs a pirouette.

Holland and the United States excel at both dressage and jumping, and he has produced Star mares.

Verband-owned stallions are removed from stud if their produce do not meet the breed's standard in conformation or performance.

France. The French apply scientific research to horse-breeding through indexes. Through a contract with the state, the *Institut National de la Recherche Agronomique* (INRA) has developed indexes since 1974. INRA uses SIRE to calculate the Best Linear Unbiased Predictor, or BLUP, to measure a horse's genetic potential for show jumping. This genetic index, which includes the individual horse's entire family, has been applied to 130,000 horses.

The horse's performance confirms its BLUP. Its competition results and offspring modify the BLUP through its life and beyond. The index provides useful information on the family and relationships between pedigree and aptitude. It can estimate the future genetic worth of a stallion or mare.

Another index, the BSO (*Saut d'obstacles*, or BLUP in show jumping), applies only to competitors. It is recalculated annually to reflect the performances by the individual horse or its relatives.

Other performance indexes identify an indi-

In the Dutch stallion testing, horses must prove their ability over fences.

vidual horse's quality through performance. The ISO notes awards won in show jumping, the ICC three-day eventing, and IDR dressage. Each index compares the horse to its peers in competition. With a median of 100, about 15 percent of winning horses score 120.

Breeders rely on the ISO for mare selection. For example, the Prince du Cy daughter, Urgande B, had an ISO of 124. Six of her foals, sired by three different stallions, scored from 114 to 169, with the champion Quito de Baussy (by Jalisco B) with the 169. His half-brother, Kilver Matal (by Silver Matal xx) has an ISO of 144. Such a record proves this mare as a consistent producer of jumping talent.

France, like Germany, gives monetary awards to breeders of outstanding sport horses. France awards *primes d'aptitude a la compétition équestre* (aptitude prizes) to mares specialized in the Olympic disciplines.

Dutch. The best Dutch mares receive the coveted *preferent* predicate. A mare receives this award through producing superior offspring. Only a few qualify for *prestatie*, through the winnings of the mare's foals in competitions.

A mare's progeny affect her status. Mares occasionally receive predicates posthumously, with offspring's achievements qualifying them for the *preferent* and *prestatie* honors.

Stallions must complete approval through the third phase, progeny testing. The KWPN evaluates the first foal crop, with the breeder selecting one-half the foals, and the association randomly choosing the other one-half. The breeder tries to present the best foals to demonstrate the stallion's quality.

The KWPN does rescind breeding rights. Considering the stallions' effect on the breed, it has withdrawn as many as 20 stallions in one year. U. S. breeder Tony de Groot said, "The breed keeps improving. Some older stallions aren't the same quality as some of the younger ones. With only so many mares, you keep up the quality of the stallion pool."

The stallion's owner can apply to have officials re-inspect the progeny. The process follows the same method of one-half breeder's choice, and one-half randomly selected by the KWPN.

The stallion index is based on the performance of offspring, compared to the average performance of all horses in sport. A stallion receives an index when its offspring have reached performance age.

Gert van der Veen noted, "The index is an honest comparison. It takes into account the training, sex, and riding of the offspring. In Holland every horse has [starts with] 100. If a stallion has an index of 120, that means his offspring are better. 140 is twice as good as average, and 160 is exceptional."

He mentioned the stallion Roemer, standing in the United States, who has an index of 197. In 1988, with almost 200 offspring competing in

European dressage competitions, Roemer was the leading Dutch dressage sire.

Sweden. Swedish breeders rely on diligently compiled records. They use a computerized database to estimate the breeding values of stallions, and the heritability of dressage and jumping abilities.

Riding Quality Tests of a stallion's four-year-old offspring help accelerate the testing of a sire's progeny. The tests, begun in 1973, include conformation, soundness, gaits, and jumping ability. By 1989, officials were testing some 700 four-year-olds at a dozen regional shows. The best horses of these shows compete in the spring as five-year-olds, for championships at the annual Swede Horse event at Flyinge.

Sweden uses the BLUP model, calculated for an average of 100. Of the top 20 stallions with a BLUP of 106 to 115, sires included Utrillo (himself and five sons) and Nepal (himself and two sons), along with the performer, Flamingo.

Swedish authorities also rank how stallions' offspring have succeeded in shows. Here they note the percentage of offspring that have placed in advanced classes and international competitions. The offspring's performance affects the stallion's grade of A or Elite. Only 5 to 10 percent of licensed stallions achieve the Elite honor, with 30 to 40 percent reaching A. If progeny fail to perform to a minimum standard, the stallion loses its license to breed.

CHAPTER 19

North American Breed Associations

W armblood horses have come to North America since fanciers imported coach horses in the 19th century. In the 1970s, a new "invasion" began, bringing competition and breeding horses to this continent.

Equestrians have introduced European horses without the breeds' regional or national structure. Imported jumpers, dressage horses, eventers, and driving horses compete on their own, separated from their European antecedents.

North American associations attempt to bring the standards of European horsemanship to the American market. Some associations duplicate European parent groups, while others are uniquely American. The continent's geography tends to decentralize breed associations. Without the allegiance to a nation or region, breed supporters may focus on individual concerns rather than the progress of the breed as a whole.

Critics question the integrity of American associations for European breeds and horses of warmblood origins. They cite them as too independent and lacking the discipline of their European predecessors. The lack of tradition and the free enterprise system can fragment a breed.

Yet independence gives associations an American flavor, and a willingness to experiment. Frank LaSalle of the North American Trakehner Association said, "I'm too much American. I don't like to be subservient to Europe in any way. We left Europe because we didn't like the controls."

North America's associations vary, although most exist to register animals and to preserve the history and integrity of the breed. Some promote competition through sponsoring awards. Those that register have to consider how to incorporate imported and domestic horses and their offspring. Most associations that register European horses lament the fact that many of the outstanding representatives excel in competition but are not registered in American studbooks. The number of unregistered horses—domestic and imported—makes it difficult for groups to report exact population figures.

To maintain validity, the North American organizations must clarify relations with their

European counterparts. In most cases, North American horses do not have equal status with their European cousins. LaSalle commented how Americans have spent money to acquire bloodstock from the Continent, yet American-born animals lack recognition. "I can see the warmblood associations in this country wanting to exploit the European breeders' expertise and to get the best stock—but not to tie themselves up in it so the Europeans have the advantage. We register theirs, but they don't register ours. Everything is a one-way trip across that pond. Even if we need their expertise, we don't have to give up our souls to get it, along with our money."

This chapter briefly describes 10 associations. Information on registries was current in 1990 publications.

American Hanoverian Society, Inc.

The AHS aims to duplicate the inspection, registration, and licensing of its German counterpart, and it involves Verband officials in the inspection and approval of breeding stock. AHS registers horses in an Official Studbook, which totalled over 3000 animals in 1990. The book includes three sections for mares and one for its Elite stallions. All are based on pedigree and selection.

AHS evaluates horses by six criteria: sex type and breed type, conformation, correctness of gaits, impulsion and elasticity, the walk, and overall impression and development as related to age. Judges assign scores using the 1-10 point system, and marks are averaged for a final score. AHS inspects all mares it registers.

President Louis Thompson, Jr., said, "We've had a very close working alliance with the Verband. We put significant changes in our breeding regulations. Our Pre-Studbook is equivalent to their Foalbook."

Like the Verband, AHS issues pink registra-tion papers for mares and stallions. If a mare or stallion is foaled of parents both registered in the German Studbook, the horse can be registered in both AHS and German Studbooks. A horse eligible for German registration must also be registered in AHS. An American horse with one parent in the German Studbook can qualify for AHS.

The Main Studbook includes Hannoverian mares registered in the German *Hauptstutbuch* and mares who qualify by pedigree and score an overall mark of 6 in the inspection. Mares from other German Main Studbooks and AHS-approved non-German European breed associations may enter the AHS book after receiving a 6 in the inspection. Studbook mares score not less than 5, with no score less than 4. There are now 507 mares in the Main Studbook, and 131 in the Studbook.

The Pre-Studbook accepts exceptional mares registered with the Jockey Club, Arabian Horse Registry, Anglo-Arabian, or warmblood mare from a recognized non-German European warmblood society (or its American equivalent). These horses receive white registration papers.

AHS limits Thoroughbred mares to its Pre-Studbook, although superior Pre-Studbook mares scoring a 7 or higher in the inspection and the performance test are eligible for the Studbook. Daughters of these mares by AHS stallions could advance to the Main Studbook.

All AHS-registered foals must be by AHS stallions out of mares inspected and registered by AHS. A foal by a Hannoverian stallion out of a Pre-Studbook mare is registered in the Pre-Studbook. If the foal is out of a non-AHS mare, it is eligible for a Certificate of Pedigree.

Foals by AHS stallions out of Main Studbook or Studbook mares receive a hip brand, with no scoring or premiums. Mares and stallions receive neck brands after being approved for breeding.

Main Studbook mares can earn Elite Mare status after passing a performance test. The mare must have received a score of 7 or higher on inspection. AHS adds the letter "E" to her registration number. To retain the designation, the mare must produce at least one foal that rates above a 5, within three years after the performance test. As of 1990, there were 28 Elite mares.

The performance test brings together German officials and American riding techniques. The German authorities look for horses to be ridden well forward. Ludwig Christmann explained the differences between the equestrian cultures: "In the U.S., riders rode horses as hunters, and they scored lower than the bold and forward horses did. Americans need to know what to look for in the performance test, and what and how it is scored."

Elite Stallions are registered in the Stallion Book. AHS accepts stallions approved by the Verband, and will not register one disapproved by the Verband. The Mare and Stallion Committee may deny registration to a stallion approved by the Verband, if they feel it does not meet the goals of the AHS breeding program.

Stallions born in North America must pass inspection, held at two U. S. sites. A Judging Commission of both AHS and Verband judges carefully examines candidates. They study horses running free and free-jumping, and then in-hand for conformation and gaits.

Young stallions that pass with an overall score of not less than 7 (and no mark less than 5) receive a provisional license. They can enter the stallion book as fully licensed Elite Stallions within one year, after passing the performance test or qualifying in sport. In sport, they must score 60 percent or better in five FEI level dressage tests at AHSA recognized shows. In 1990, AHS had 107 stallions.

Stallions must be blood-typed. Mares and foals involved in the transported semen program must also be blood-typed. AHS accepts foals conceived through transported and frozen semen and embryo transfer.

Each summer, a commission tours North American sites. In 1990, two Verband officials and three AHS members registered and branded over 200 foals and accepted 203 of 234 mares presented. Approximately half of the foals received dual registration with both associations.

Purebred Hanoverian Association of American Breeders and Owners, Inc. (PHA)

The PHA was formed to preserve bloodlines of Hannoverians which could trace their lineage to foundation stock in Germany. PHA maintains two separate registries, one Purebred and the other Part-Hanoverian. Horses qualify only according to bloodlines, and each registry includes a book for stallions, mares, or geldings. Stallions and mares can be certified as "G" (Germany-approved), "A" (American-approved), or "P" (approved through performance).

American Holsteiner Horse Association, Inc.

AHHA's Breeding Stock Approvals and registration duplicate those of the Holsteiner Verband. The association registers foals by AHHA-approved stallions out of approved mares. (Foals out of non-qualified mares can receive a Certificate of Pedigree).

Mares eligible for inspection must be of an approved population:

1. AHHA-registered

2. Jockey Club registered

3. European born and registered, by a European-approved sire

The North American Trakehner Association recently began branding horses with the "T" and crown.

4. American born and American or European registered warmblood, with a European-approved sire.

AHHA accepts applications from mares born in America and registered with ATA, AHS, ISR, SWA, or NA/KWPN. All breeding stock must be blood-typed.

At Breeding Stock Approvals, mares may receive the following approvals:
Main Mare Book Premium (scored 45 points or above)
Main Mare Book (scored 42-44 points)
Mare Book (scored 37-41 points)

Breeder Elizabeth McElvain noted how the Thoroughbred mares are scored the same as warmblood mares. "They have a separate class and are categorized as foundation mares. They don't go into the stud books—they are 'qualified' mares. Their foals may go into the stud book."

Mares may show again to try for a higher bonit. A mare scoring 41 points the first time might earn the 42 required to advance to the Main Mare Book.

Foals are inspected for two awards: Merit (12-14 points), or Premium (15 points or above). A foal conceived through embryo transfer must also be blood-typed. AHHA has about 300 foals eligible for registration each year.

AHHA inspects and licenses Holsteiner stallions, which must score a minimum of 45. A horse which does not achieve that score is ineligible to try again. In 1990, AHHA licensed its second American-born stallion, with 53 total approved Holsteiner stallions.

Stallions approved by AHHA can go through a 100-day test in North America or qualify through sport. The stallion must finish in the top 10 of a three-day-event, with at least a 55 percent dressage score.

The AHHA's Janice Scarbrough felt this requirement simple for a Holsteiner. "They're bold and will just whip around the course. Two stallions have completed this test, and they both won the event. It was like a playday to them. It does test their temperament to a certain extent, especially in the event atmosphere. The test will grow as we start to add more stallions. Now people are pleased to have a new stallion every year."

Mare and stallion approval scores are added to their registration papers. The scores will also appear in the pedigrees of offspring.

AHHA also evaluates sport horse geldings. Because few stallion candidates will be presented, these horses represent mature male offspring and allow breeders to evaluate their breeding programs.

AHHA maintains an excellent relationship with the German Verband, coordinating communication through a liaison officer in Schleswig-Holstein. McElvain explained, "They send members of their approval committee to stand on our approval committee. We send members of our committee to stand with their members as a learning situation, so we learn

How Americans Accept Associations´ Validity

With so many associations, equestrians are confused with which ones are the "real" ones. The growing industry has become fragmented among the groups.

Some associations impose European standards on American horses. Horses receive judgment from authorities. Can American horse owners accept the opinions of objective experts?

Willie Arts described the KWPN judges: "They don't hide anything. They're easy to talk to, and they explain. People can get disappointed that they actually heard the truth. But it's better to know you did something wrong, and you can change [your breeding]. I'd much rather change, through a learning experience."

Trakehner breeder Leo Whinery felt that breeding good riding horses requires discipline. "Through the years I've heard arguments that the American Trakehner Association is too strict and that the Germans are too strict. It reflects the discipline that's required when you have an approval system with horse breeding."

Elizabeth Searle commented on the NA/WPN's pre-selection of two-year-old stallion candidates: "I think most of the people appreciate it. They think it's an extremely fair and extremely careful situation, that it is not slanted in any way. It's trying to keep the level absolutely the same as it is in their country, without the 100-day testing. We have not had any complaints about how it's being done and the fact that they [the Dutch] are so fussy."

American equestrians can respect the approval or disapproval from a European—yet some tend to distrust each other's judgment, especially on a prized horse. The NATA's Frank LaSalle said, "It hinges on our honesty and our lack of politics. You have to discount who you are, where you come from, and the facility itself. Dedicate yourself to what you're looking at. Our goal is to try to see that each horse passes.

"Surprisingly, our first impression was that the U.S. people won't tolerate someone telling us what to do. We were apprehensive, but it hasn't been the case. The people whose horses do not pass are disappointed, but very few come back and complain."

La Salle added that to his knowledge, owners of rejected stallions have not objected "violently" or pressed lawsuits against associations in North America. "We thought that when the prices reached high levels, we'd really have problems—like a $250,000 horse that doesn't pass inspection." He explains to owners why the horse was not approved, citing from the inspection sheet. (Owners do not see the actual score sheet).

The ATA's Helen Gibble noted, "To have a stallion approved is not something you can expect. People here think every colt is a stallion prospect. They are terribly disappointed if it is not approved."

She commented that American breed-

more about how they judge their breeding stock."

She noted a major difference between the two organizations, shared by other North American associations: "They get all their stallion candidates together in one place. That is a huge drawback for us, that we never get to see them together."

American Trakehner Association

Adopting the German breeding aim, ATA also coordinates activities with its German counterpart. It registers and promotes the fullbred and part-Trakehner. Like the Verband, horses' names follow the dam line. ATA allows crosses with the Thoroughbred, Anglo-Arabian, and Arabian breeds. In ATA's studbooks, one section accepts partbreds sired by approved Trakehners and out of mares other than the three breeds listed above.

The Official Stud Book includes mares and stallions which are approved for breeding. The owner of a 2 year old purebred filly may apply for broodmare status. Owners of Anglo-Trakehner and Arab-Trakehner fillies—7/8, 15/16, and halfbreds whose dams have qualified in sport—may apply for transfer to the Official Stud Book from the Official Registry Book.

ATA conducts voluntary mare inspections, for mares three years or older, in or applying to the Official Stud Book. (Some ATA-registered partbreds are also eligible). Three members of the Stallion Inspection Committee judge mares on type, conformation, regularity/impulsion of gaits, and general impression. Voluntary inspection does not affect a mare's status, although ATA adds the four marks to the mare's registration papers.

Colts advance to the Official Stud Book through the Stallion Certification. (A stallion or mare approved by the Trakehner Verband is automatically accepted into the ATA Official Stud Book. If rejected in Germany, the stallion cannot apply). A North American-foaled colt must be at least two years old and meet the minimum measurements of 160 cm in height, 183 cm heart girth, and 19 cm cannon bone.

The Stallion Certification Commission, selected by ATA's Board of Trustees and including one member of the Verband, inspects colts annually at two sites, East and West. They evaluate each candidate in the same five phases as practiced in Germany, without free-jumping. Approximately 20 percent of colts presented receive approval.

The colt must complete a performance requirement within two years of approval. ATA requires stallions younger than six years to complete a USCTA or CEF sanctioned combined training event at Novice level (Pre-Training if CEF). A stallion six or older must complete an event at Training level or above.

Candidates are already registered in the Official Registry Book, which contains five divisions. (Horses are not inspected to enter this book). Two divisions accept purebreds, including American-foaled and imported horses which can prove their ancestry. The American-foaled horse must be sired by an approved Trakehner stallion and out of an approved, ATA-registered mare with at least a four-generation pedigree.

Two other divisions include Anglo-Trakehners (Trakehner stallion—Jockey Club or ATA-registered Anglo-Trakehner mare) and Arab-Trakehners (Trakehner stallion—Arabian mare, Anglo-Arab mare, or ATA-registered Arab-Trakehner mare). The Official Registry Book also accepts part-Trakehners. These horses are sired by approved Trakehner stallions (with a four-generation pedigree) and out of part-Trakehner mares or any mare other than a Trakehner, Thoroughbred, or Arabian. Imported Trakehners, previously registered with the Verband or an affiliated association, enter the Official Registry Book, if they have papers

How Americans Accept Associations' Validity (continued)

ers tend toward "barn-blindness," rating their horses better than they are. This narrow viewpoint makes it difficult to accept the decisions of the stallion inspection committee. "When a horse is not approved, the Europeans are just as disappointed. They complain, too."

Trakehner breeder Henry Schurink recalled the response of owners when ATA started its stallion inspections. "They said, 'You mean to tell me that these guys are going to tell me what I can do with my stallion?' Then if you don't approve one, a lot of them would put him at stud anyway. In Europe, they will not. He's not approved, they geld him. They're mad that day, but they accept the decision."

For North America to improve, associations are tightening their standards. La Salle noted how the NATA's 1989 inspections accepted 50 percent of mares and stallions. "In the beginning, we were on the lenient side in order to build up the numbers. Now we have a big enough herd to be more selective. Rejecting horses can stop people who have mediocre horses from applying for breeding status."

Hermann Friedlaender said that in the stallion testing, authorities look at candidates realistically. "Here we are trying to build up a breed. In Germany, it is established for a long, long time. It is not equal. Sometimes here we have to accept out of necessity something that might not pass in the old country. You have to get off the ground first, before you can fly."

Lilo Fore, a Hannoverian breeder who was born in Germany, feels that the asso-

ciations are trying to retain the integrity of the breeds. "I hope they will keep the same quality. I don't think it will help us here in this country to be too lenient—especially with breeding stock. But this country is so big, the associations will not be able to control breeding as much as they do in Europe."

As an example of American associations' quest for quality, previously AHS had a Pre-Registry category. This section registered foals with only one Hannoverian parent. President Thompson reported, "We now register only offspring from registered stallions and mares. We've increased our population 71 percent in the last three years—instead of losing, we've gained."

American breeders do accept the standards and apply them to their stock. Henry Schurink mentioned the ATA stallion approval: "When we started, people had no idea what it would take to have an approved stallion. Now in the stands, a lot of spectators figure out pretty much. Those who have presented once or twice a stallion know to leave one home, because the committee won't take him."

American associations have to determine if they will follow the European precedent of exchange. Will the registry maintain an open studbook, accepting horses from other breeds, and which will it accept? Europeans open their books to bring in other desirable bloodlines, in controlled doses. Yet the American tradition is the closed, "exclusive" studbook.

Douglas Mankovich noted that breeding should emphasis the sport horse rather than the trademark. "Are we breeding a

tracing each bloodline to the Verband's studbook.

The Official Appendix Book registers part-Trakehners and purebreds whose pedigrees do not meet the requirements of the Official Registry Book. These include a horse sired by an approved Trakehner stallion out of a purebred registered in the Official Registry Book, an Anglo-Trakehner sired by a Jockey Club stallion out of an Official Stud Book mare, an Arab-Trakehner sired by a purebred Arabian stallion, and a horse with a four-generation Trakehner pedigree on either sire's or dam's side. Imported horses registered in the Verband's *Stutbuch* and branded with the single moose antler brand are also eligible for the Official Appendix Book. They and their offspring may apply to transfer to the Official Stud Book if they meet breed standards.

Branding is optional. Members of a Branding Committee brand foals before weaning. If a horse carries the German brand of the double antler, ATA will not "double-brand" it. Approved stallions may receive a neck brand, if the owner desires. Part-Trakehners may receive a special brand.

ATA accepts foals conceived through artificial insemination, transported semen, and embryo transfer. Stallions must be blood-typed, and the association can request bloodtyping to verify parentage.

ATA differs somewhat from its German counterpart. Members feel that it should relate to American horsemanship. "Our association does have a little different focus," said Judy Yancey. "We don't follow every change that the Trakehner Verband goes through. We do try to be aware of trends and what they're doing, but we do operate independently. We tend to be even a bit more conservative, because we don't have the vast history behind us of changing the type."

North American Trakehner Association

The NATA preserves, registers, brands, and promotes the warmblood horse of Trakehner and East Prussian origin. Frank LaSalle noted how the association is independent of any European controls: "We are not bound by a closed stud book registry and are therefore able to seek out horses that may have advantageous influences on the breeding herd." NATA's Corporate Regulations state, "A horse shall be produced which shall be an 'improver' of all horse breeds for equine sport."

The six divisions of the Official General Registry Book admit horses according to Stud Book Trakehner Registry (SBTR)—offspring of horses registered in NATA's Official Stud Book, or horses whose bloodlines can be traced to East Prussian lines in the amount of 7/8 identified ancestors or 15/16 blood.

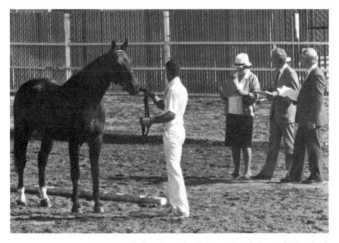

At a Dutch keuring, the international jury of Elizabeth Searle, Gert van der Veen, and Rolf Brinkman evaluate a mare.

Divisions include:

1   Fullbred

How Americans Accept Associations' Validity (continued)

sport horse, or are we breeding a brand for its rear end? My Belgian Warmblood stallion is a branded Hannoverian, but he's a licensed Belgian breeding stallion. They have certain bloodlines that they accept as their foundation stock. In the case of the Belgian, it's to produce the sport horse, not the breed. It's the difference we have in the American thinking, which is to produce a horse, like a pure Arabian. It's like breeding dogs vs. breeding sport animals."

(No Division 2)

3 Three-quarter (One SBTR and one SBTR grandparent)

4 Half (one SBTR parent)

5 Anglo-Trakehner (one SBTR and one Jockey Club parent)

6 Arab-Trakehner (One SBTR and one Arabian or Anglo-Arabian parent)

7 Three-eighth (At least 3/8 SBTR ancestry)

Imported Trakehners may apply to enter the Official General Registry Book. This book accepts stallions, mares, and geldings.

For stallions and mares only, the Official Stud Book registers horses after inspection. NATA's trained inspectors evaluate horses on pedigree, conformation, movement, gaits, temperament, and conformation to type. Because NATA aims to breed for performance, stallions must show under saddle on the flat and over small fences. The association recommends that presenters also ride mares. Inspectors award points for type, front legs, hind legs, shoulder, croup, head/neck, character, and movement in hand and under saddle.

Horses can advance from the Official General Registry Book. No horse may have white markings on the body above knees or hocks (other than the usual head markings). NATA can remove a horse from this book if its offspring do not meet the breed standards.

To obtain broodmare status, a mare must be 2 years old, stand a minimum of 15.2, obtain a veterinary report, and pass inspection by at least one person representing the Mare and Stallion Approval Committee. If she fails the inspection, the mare can be re-inspected once, at least six months later. Mares who pass receive a certificate, "Approved for Breeding."

LaSalle noted, "We have three shots at getting approval. If the first time the horse failed, the owner can retry. They can have the horse inspected again with different inspectors. Or they can pay a higher fee and name two people from the Mare and Stallion Approval Committee to sit with me and one other member I would select. We go back and inspect the horse again, and the majority would rule. We are so set in our mind that we want no politics, and we give every chance to let the horse pass."

A hardship clause allows a mare registered in Divisions 3, 4, 7 or the NATA Performance Horse Appendix Registry to qualify as "Advancement of Breed." These mares lack the pedigree requirements of Divisions 1, 5, and 6, but are accepted according to their quality and performance ability. The owner must submit the mare's written history to document her accomplishments as either a sport horse or broodmare. If the entire Mare and Stallion Approval Committee recommends the application, the mare receives an Approval for Breeding certificate.

Stallions must be three years old, stand 16 hands, and pass inspection. They receive temporary approval for a three year trial period, with a certificate, "Approved for Breeding." A stallion failing inspection may be re-inspected six months later.

The Mare and Stallion Approval Committee inspects offspring after the three years of breeding, for final approval or disapproval. An approved stallion is registered in the Official Stud Book, "For Productive Life."

An "Advancement of Breed" program allows a stallion in Divisions 3, 4, 7, or the Performance Horse Appendix Registry to apply for temporary approval. Regulations are the same as for mares.

The Performance Horse Appendix Registry recognizes superior sport horses that do not qualify for the other two books. To add horses which could improve the breed, horses qualify by an outstanding performance record and correct conformation of Trakehner type. They must possess an authenticated pedigree, registered in another association's studbook. A mare or stallion can progress to the Official Stud Book, following inspection.

NATA registers foals conceived through artificial insemination, including transported and frozen semen. Stallion, mare, and foal must be blood-typed, and the sire must be registered in the Official Stud Book.

NATA follows the practice of naming the foal after the dam's first initial. In 1990, officials began branding horses with the T and crown (Stud Book) and T (General Registry and younger horses).

Westfalen Warmblood Association of America

Unlike the previous associations, the WWAA does not register horses. This association exists to promote the breed, and to refer interested equestrians to German officials.

Only the *Westfälisches Pferdestammbuch* registers horses and issues papers. American owners may apply to register Westfalen and other sport horse mares. German officials visit the U.S. to inspect mares and foals, and to mark horses with the German brand.

Lucy Parker of the WWAA said, "The stallion owners would rather have the papers issued from Germany. If a horse is issued German papers and branded with the German brand, it seems equal in value to the horses over there."

Although Westfalen stallions are licensed and tested only in Germany, authorities did make an exception for the stallion Roemer. Parker commented, "He has a Westfalen brand, but was sold to Holland as a young horse. His get were so successful, that the Verband came here to approve him on the performance of his get. They will not again approve another stallion in the United States, because they can't reproduce the same circumstances as in Europe. They feel if it's a Westfalen horse, it should be approved in Westfalia."

WWAA serves as a clearing house for distributing information on the breed. Parker has gathered information on the six approved stallions in the U.S. in an electronic database.

Oldenburg

The Oldenburg Verband has a contract with the International Sporthorse Registry (ISR) to register mares in both mare books. Details are included later in this chapter, under the ISR.

100-Day Stallion Testing in U.S.

Two facilities conduct stallion testing for young breeding stallions: The AHS tests at November Hill, Virginia, and the ISR tests at Rancho Murietta, California.

Both programs duplicate the German process. Directed by horsemen who have conducted tests in Germany, the tests score stallions during the training period and in a performance test. Expert riders and judges evaluate the horses' rideability and athletic abilities. Both tests require a minimum number of participants, so the outcome demonstrates results similar to the German tests—some horses score at the top, some at the bottom, and the rest are in-between.

International Sporthorse Registry

The ISR program began in 1986. The results of its test are approved by the Oldenburg Verband, Trakehner Verband, and KWPN. In 1990, 16 stallions participated in the program.

The test is aimed at the three-year-old horse. Stallions older than three can participate, but officials deduct five points from the final score.

The training director scores each horse with the 1 to 10 scale, on the same factors as used in German testing: character, temperament, willingness to perform, physical ability to perform, jumping aptitude, rideability, and quality of basic gaits. The scoring system is approved by Germany's University of Goettingen, which supervises German testings. Two members of

the Oldenburg Verband must attend the final performance test, with seven phases:

1. Rideability. Three expert guest riders ride each horse to score its performance in a test resembling a training level dressage test.

2. Free-jumping. Two experts score the horse's technique and ability.

3. Stadium jumping. Three judges score each horse over a course of fences measuring from 100 to 110 cm.

4. Basic gaits. Three judges score the horse's gaits. Horses must move at specified speeds: Walk 300 m at 100 m per minute; trot 750 m at 250 m per minute; gallop 1000 m at 500 m per minute.

5. Cross-country. Over a 4000 m course of 10 obstacles, the horse must gallop 450 m per minute. Judges score the horse's galloping and jumping technique. They look for a courageous jumping style.

6. Hunt gallop. Immediately after the cross-country ride, the horse gallops at top speed for 1000 m. Officials judge the time and count the strides over a 100 m area. A fast time and long strides gives a high score.

7. Veterinary examination. When the horse completes the gallop, a veterinarian checks pulse and respiration to note recovery time. A horse that displays cardiovascular dysfunction will be removed.

Scores in each section are divided by number of judges, weighted, and totalled for the final score. The training director's assessment counts for 50 percent. The owner receives a copy of the test results.

German Hessen Foundation in America

This association is a subsidiary of the Hessen Verband. The Verband's breeding director has visited to approve mares and list them with the Verband.

Verband officials will inspect, grade, brand, and register foals sired by Hessen stallions from American warmblood and Thoroughbred mares. Horses will be equal in status to German counterparts.

The North American Selle Français Horse Association, Inc.

Formed in 1990, the NASFHA will register Selle Français, Anglo-Arab, and other French horses born in North America. France's *Haras Nationaux* and *Institut du Cheval* have authorized the NASFHA to continue French breeding. Horses foaled from 1980 to the present may entered the French Stud Book and receive French documentation. Previously, owners of French horses chose to enter their stock in other North American breed registries.

The association follows French guidelines to register Selle Français foals. A foal from a Selle Français sire and a warmblood mare can be registered as a Cheval de Selle. If a mare of another warmblood breed or unregistered Jockey Club mare passes inspection, she can receive approval as a Facteur Selle Français — her foals sired by a Selle Français stallion can be registered as Selle Français.

The NASFHA uses breeding and registration forms identical to their French counterparts, translated into English. However, a licensed veterinarian may complete the listing of identification markings in place of a representative of the *Haras Nationaux*. Horses will receive an identification form and will be listed in SIRE.

An inspection team toured North America in 1990. They approved French stallions, including 19 Selle Français, 3 Anglo-Arab, and 2 Facteur Selle Français. They judged stallions on genetic background, conformation, and performance ability (the horse's performance record or the team's onsite observations).

The NASFHA's Sheryl Akers noted, "Several of the stallions inspected did perform under saddle for the inspection team. Some, due to injuries suffered late in the season, were viewed via videotape for the performance portion of the inspection. Some of the stallions are older and have not been ridden for some time; these horses were not asked to perform under saddle.

"For those horses who were seen under saddle, the inspection team looked for good, fluid movement, 'covering a lot of ground,' with correct gaits and no obvious congenital skeletal problems which could be passed on to offspring. For the jumping horses, agility and style over the fences is an important aspect. For the dressage horses, graceful, well-executed movements, obedience, and proper carriage were considered."

In a technological first for North American associations, the NASFHA will establish the only online contact with its European counterpart. The association plans a direct link to SIRE computers. This will allow immediate data entry and retrieval of information on every French horse registered.

All Selle Français horses must be blood-typed to verify parentage. The association registers foals conceived through artificial insemination and embryo transfer.

KWPN—North American Department

The NA/WPN functions as the only foreign department of its parent. The KWPN registers and brands horses. "That has been a very big strength with the Dutch, that the papers come from Holland," explained Elizabeth Searle. "You

100-Day Stallion Testing in U.S. (continued)

To pass, a stallion must score 90 points. Horses are not judged on the curve, but all start the test with 100 points. If the horse fails, it can receive conditional approval to breed for two years. The quality of off-spring determines if the horse receives a permanent breeding license.

American Hanoverian Society

The AHS 100-Day Stallion Performance Test began in 1987. Open to any stallion approved by a recognized warmblood association, the program requires 10 participants. The test alternates every two years.

Young stallions receive basic training and discipline. November Hill's vice-president Yvonne Zuther noted that horses should have been handled and in good condition. They do not have to be shod.

Guidelines divide the test preparation into four segments. In the first three weeks of September, the horses are longed and introduced to free-jumping and work under saddle as a group. The horse adapts to its new environment and handlers.

In the second phase in October, the horse works on basic dressage, gymnastic jumping exercises at liberty, jumping cavaletti, and riding cross country. The third phase expands the work to familiarize the horse with responding to the rider's aids, more difficult gymnastics, more challenging fences, and conditioning cross country. After two months, stallions have been exposed to the elements of the performance test.

In November's final training phase, riders refine previous work to improve the horse's ability and physical fitness. Demands in all areas increase while maintaining the horse's soundness. Through the training, the training leader evaluates candidates on abilities and willingness to learn. His scores—50 percent of the stallion's total—are factored into the overall evaluation after the performance test.

The test's judges, representing both the AHS and the Hannoverian Verband, evaluate the stallions over the four days of the performance test. They rate horses on the same seven factors as the ISR test. Test riders also evaluate the stallions. A horse can be removed from the test for an unsatisfactory gait, during the basic gaits segment. If it scores a 2 or less for any gait, or for any point according to the training leader, it fails the test.

AHS requires a stallion to pass with a minimum score of 90. This score allows the horse to become an approved breeding stallion. The Hannoverian Verband also recognizes the stallion's performance. Other associations which accept results include the Westfalen and Rheinlander Verbands, KWPN, and ISR.

New to American horsemen, the stallion performance tests have generated interest and criticism. The program does offer the stallion owner the opportunity to have experts start a young horse. Many owners lack the expertise, facilities, or time to train a lively youngster. The test results—if the horse scores well—can also enhance the reputation of the horse, its sire, and its dam.

"It is the goal of every breed associa-

can take the horse back to Holland and that's it. Neither the Holsteiner nor the Hannoverian have that. If you took the horse back, it would have no standing over there."

The KWPN guides its "branch office" toward improving the breed, and it establishes regulations that the NA/WPN enforces. Horses' names follow the Dutch system of annual initials.

The NA/WPN stands out as a professional, well-managed organization. Its annual *Stallion Directory and Handbook* is the most comprehensive publication of any North American association. Like the Dutch, the officials of the NA/WPN have conducted an ongoing marketing campaign for their product.

Annual *Keurings* throughout the continent showcase the Dutch horse. These events combine studbook inspections, stallion licensing, and branding. A jury from Holland, including American judge Searle, judges horses presented. In 1990, the department conducted nine *Keurings* across the United States.

The NA/WPN follows the Dutch studbooks, with a complex system of admitting horses of Dutch, part-Dutch, and non-Dutch breeding. Horses and their offspring may advance in status, and mares and stallions can qualify for the same predicates as their Dutch counterparts.

Foals of Dutch stallions may be registered in the Foalbook or Auxiliary Foalbook. As foals, yearlings, and two-year-olds, each category competes in classes at *Keurings*. The jury applies the same standards as in Holland and awards Premiums of First (orange ribbon), Second (red ribbon), and Third (white ribbon). Premiums communicate the jury's opinion to the horse's breeder. First indicates a horse of good conformation and movement. Second notes a horse of lesser quality, and Third means that the horse may not be a sport horse or breeding prospect. With an emphasis on breeding, the

Second and Third premiums alert the breeder that the offspring could reflect a mismatch between stallion and mare.

The Auxiliary Foalbook includes all foals sired by Dutch stallions of Registered status out of Studbook mares. It also includes foals from these breedings: Licensed/Approved stallion out of Auxiliary Foalbook, Thoroughbred, or unregistered mare, and a warmblood stallion of the KWPN approved population out of an Auxiliary Foalbook mare.

The KWPN's approved population includes these European breeds: Selle Français, Oldenburg, Westfalen, Belgian, Trakehner, Swedish, Holsteiner, Hannoverian, and Danish Oldenburg (mares only). The KWPN must approve the pedigree of the individual horse before accepting it as qualified.

At three years of age, mares and geldings in the Auxiliary Foalbook may be inspected to enter the Auxiliary Studbook. A mare of sport horse type—registered or unregistered— may qualify through high quality and the quality of two offspring. The Auxiliary Studbook brings these animals into the breed to broaden the gene pool. They get a special brand on the left or right side of the neck.

Foals by Dutch stallions out of Auxiliary Studbook mares qualify for the Foalbook. The Foalbook also includes horses sired by a Dutch stallion out of a Foalbook, Studbook, or warmblood mare of an approved population.

Three-year-old Foalbook mares and geldings are inspected to enter the Studbook. Mares must stand 158 cm. Studbook horses receive the lion brand on the left haunch, and mares can compete for the predicates *star* and *keur*.

The NA/WPN also accepts qualified Jockey Club mares and stallions. An accredited Thoroughbred mare may produce foals registered in the Foalbook. She qualifies if she passes inspection and is at least three years old and a minimum of 158 cm. Mares in the ISR Main Mare

100-Day Stallion Testing in U.S. (continued)
tion to let only their best stallions become producers," said Yvonne Zuther. "The testing program will help to evaluate the performance ability and the willingness of each individual stallion."

Janice Scarbrough of the AHHA visited the ISR site in 1990. She had heard that when the stallions arrived, they were excited by the unfamiliar atmosphere and the sight of other stallions. "I was very impressed with the way the horses behaved and the way the riders rode them. About halfway through the training, they had stallions standing there perfectly quiet. They were all in the same barn, content and happy—very much gentlemen. I thought they did a good job of riding them.

"I had wondered if they'd be like the horses they run through the auctions in Germany—horses going almost in a fourth level frame in 30 days, but afraid of the bit. Those you have to start over after you buy them to correct the problems. But the riders seemed to take their time and school the stallions quietly."

Some breeders express a reluctance to relinquish control over their horse's training. If they want the horse to succeed as a riding horse, they do not want it started hurriedly with the goal of passing a test.

Dressage trainer and Hannoverian breeder Lilo Fore explained, "In this country it's so important to be able to show the stallion. It's very hard for me to let my horses go out of my hands, because I have a certain way I want them to go. I like horses with a soft mouth and balance and self-carriage."

She felt it important that horses be prepared before being sent to the test site. "A three-year-old could be ridden a little, maybe free-jumped and jumped over some little crossbars. Do it lightly, so they don't have to go there totally cold. Then the riders don't have to go through all this, when the stallion is prepared at home."

Some critics complain that stallions in the U.S. 100-day tests receive higher scores than they would in Germany. Friedlaender disagreed, saying, "I definitely do not find that. There are always one or two representatives of the Verband on the committee. They are very carefully listened to."

Book or receiving at least 42 points by the AHHA can receive accreditation without presentation. The Thoroughbred mare receives full accreditation with two accepted offspring. Performance of her offspring may earn her the predicates, *Preferent* and *Prestatie*.

North American Dutch stallions can be either Approved/Licensed or Registered. All stallions must be verified each year in order to register foals.

The 22 Registered stallions have only Foalbook registration. They have not passed through the strict Dutch approvals, either in the Netherlands or in North America. Beginning in 1991, their foals out of Studbook mares could enter only the Auxiliary Foalbook; all their other foals may receive only a Certificate of Pedigree.

In North America only, a Registered stallion at least three years old and standing a minimum of 160 cm may receive a provisional License. Inspected at a *Keuring*, the stallion undergoes a briefer evaluation than Holland's 100-Day Testing. He must qualify according to conformation, movement, and two performances of the I.B.O.P. test. Stallions also show in free-jumping.

The stallion's score must total at least First Premium. A horse could score highly in the I.B.O.P. test, yet not qualify due to lower scores in conformation or movement in hand. The jury eyes stallions very critically and licenses only 10 percent of the candidates. The Licensed stallion receives the same brand as Studbook mares and geldings. The day of the *Keuring*, the newly Licensed stallion must pass a drug test. He must also earn a satisfactory veterinary report based on radiographs and semen samples.

Preparing a stallion prospect for the inspection and riding test involves a substantial investment. In North America, a Stallion Prospect Evaluation screens two-year-old colts by conformation, movement, and X-rays. The evaluation can save the owner significant expense.

The dozen Licensed stallions had full breeding rights until 1992. By then they must have established a sport record in dressage, combined training, or show jumping. In 1992, the KWPN renewed the licenses of those stallions that met specific requirements. After three years, the association planned to evaluate the stallions' records according to the quality of progeny.

Elizabeth Searle predicted that progeny testing will become an important part of the *Keurings*. "They have to give the stallions enough chance, as there are not as many foals here. Here, they often breed stallions to mares of other breeds. But it will come up soon that the foals are evaluated." She noted that a stallion here could have 20 foals, not all eligible for the

Studbook, compared to a Dutch stallion with 100 foals.

Within this timetable, a Licensed stallion will either receive an upgrade to Approved, or return to Registered status. The 25 Approved stallions in North America have completed the 100-Day Testing in Holland and received at least a satisfactory report on their progeny. As in the Netherlands, the KWPN may withdraw the License or Approval depending on the stallion's production record.

To bring Thoroughbred stallions into the breed, the KWPN accredits Jockey Club-registered animals. A stallion must be at least three years old, stand 160 cm, and have established a record in either racing or sport. The owner presents the horse in hand at a *Keuring*. Foals from Foalbook or Studbook mares may enter the Foalbook, and foals of Auxiliary Studbook mares may enter the Auxiliary Foalbook. An unaccredited Thoroughbred stallion may sire Auxiliary Foalbook offspring out of Studbook mares only. (However, few owners present Thoroughbreds for accreditation as sport horse sires).

The office sends an application for foal registration to owners of mares listed on stallion service reports the previous season. Bloodtyping is required in specific cases, including those involving transported semen, embryo transfer, and late registration.

The *Keurings'* jury annually awards "Best of" honors in each class across all *Keuring* sites. In this way, the *Keurings* resemble Holland's regional shows. The NA/KWPN also publishes a stallion report of results of offspring presented in *Keurings*.

Belgian Warmblood Breeding Association

In *Keurings*, visiting Belgian officials have approved five stallions and plan to limit the number to 20. Stallions three years old or younger

Tallison

In 1990, the California-foaled stallion Tallison won the ISR testing over 15 other candidates, with a score of 133.72. A black four-year-old Hannoverian standing 16.3 hands, Tallison was sired by Taenzer by Trapper out of the Diamont mare, Duellyn. He is registered with ISR and the Oldenburg Verband, and owned by Brent and June Palmer of Silvershoe Farm, Utah.

June Palmer said, "We feel he won the 100-day testing because of his willingness to work and to give his trust to his rider, so that he did well in all phases of the competition. He is also naturally balanced, with light airy gaits, which also helped him excel over fences as well as in dressage. He is a more modern type, better suited to most riders. The old type heavy warmblood was great for the strong German riders, but no pleasure to ride."

Tallison. Photo courtesy Kyle Karnosh.

show in hand and in free-jumping. Those four and older show in hand, under saddle, and free-jumping. Riders present horses in a freestyle ride of 7 to 10 minutes, showing all gaits in both directions.

Foals by these sires out of quality registered mares are eligible for inspection, with rideability a key factor. Quality mares require proof of pedigree/registration and the ability to produce sport horse offspring. The mare must be at least three years old. At a *Keuring*, she shows in hand and under saddle. The mare may be of any registered breed, including Appaloosa or Quarter Horse.

An auxiliary studbook accepts approved mares without papers, whose foals by Belgian stallions are eligible for the regular studbook. Officials brand Belgian-sired foals. These must be presented at a *Keuring* at three years of age. Their quality affects the mare's status, and unacceptable offspring will remove her from the studbook.

Swedish Warmblood Association

The Swedish Warmblood Association serves North American breeders by approving and registering horses. Since 1983 Swedish authorities have toured this continent every two years.

A young Hannoverian stallion shows his style in free-jumping at an approval of the International Sporthorse Registry.

In 1990, they inspected horses at 13 sites in the U.S. and branded 129 horses. Kristina Paulsen, West Coast representative, estimates that there are less than 1000 Swedish horses in the U. S.

Swedish officials approve horses according to conformation, soundness, and performance. Mares are evaluated the same as in Sweden. Broodmares are registered in a special section of the Swedish Registry.

Fully approved stallions are those which were approved in Sweden and are registered in the Official Swedish Warmblood Studbook before export. Other stallions may qualify for a Certificate as Recommended for Breeding (CRB).

For the CRB, the stallion must be registered with the SWA. It must be at least three years old, have a four-generation pedigree recorded in the Studbook, and meet the same inspection

standards as in Sweden. A stallion must score at least 40 on the five conformation traits, with no mark below 7. The under saddle score must average 7, with no mark under 5. All stallions must be blood-typed and complete a three-day event within two years of receiving the CRB.

If sired by an approved or CRB stallion out of a registered mare, a foal is eligible for SWA registration. It must have a four-generation pedigree and be out of a mare of one of these breeds: Swedish Warmblood, Thoroughbred, Anglo-Arabian, Hannoverian, Oldenburg, Trakehner, Westfalen, Holsteiner, Danish Warmblood, Dutch Warmblood, Wielkopolska, or Selle Français. In some cases, a foal may qualify if out of a Swedish mare by a non-Swedish stallion of the above breeds.

The foal owner submits a Breeding Certificate to apply for registration. Foals and yearlings are branded if registered or eligible, and judged to be of good quality. A horse two years and older must score at least 30 points in conformation to qualify for branding.

SWA registers foals conceived through artificial insemination, but does not accept embryo transfer. Foals conceived through use of frozen semen must be blood-typed.

Crossbreds

In addition to preserving established breeds, North America has generated crossbred organizations. Unaffiliated with specific breeds, these groups maintain records for domestic stock, the offspring of warmbloods and American horses.

International Sporthorse Registry

Formed in 1984, the ISR is an open registry. It aims to duplicate the European system of an open studbook with uniform standards, modelled upon the Oldenburg's success of breeding warmblood to fullblood.

ISR's Breeding Director, Dr. Roland Ramsauer, said, "From the genetic view, it's the

Ibsen: An American-Born Trakehner Stallion

Foaled in Ohio in 1982, Ibsen was sired by the imported stallion, Graditz and out of the mare, Isadora, a granddaughter of Donauwind. His breeder was Christina Glass. At his approval, he stood 164 cm with a girth of 191.5 cm and cannon bone of 21 cm.

Ibsen is co-owned by Don and Linda Pederson of Las Vegas, New Mexico, and Nancy Chesney, of Larkspur, Colorado. The bay stallion currently shows in Fourth Level dressage and stands at stud at Pederson's Diamond L Trakehners.

Chesney said, "Ibsen showed a real knack for passage, and I knew I had a good chance that he would be a super horse. Then when I could get the piaffe, I had a much better idea. Then when the flying changes came, I knew I had an FEI competitor. Time will tell as to what caliber he will be."

In 1990, Chesney hauled Ibsen East to compete at the Dressage at Devon show. He tied for the high score award in Fourth Level at this prestigious show. In 1991 the horse and rider participated in the Reiner Klimke clinic in Los Angeles.

Ibsen is an American-bred Trakehner stallion, approved by the American Trakehner Association. Ridden by Nancy Chesney

"Ibby" has a dynamic personality. Alert and responsive, this stallion's expressive face and powerful movement make him an handsome competitor. He has stood at stud for three years, breeding Thoroughbred and Trakehner mares.

same, and in this country we do the same program from the mare's side. We are the first association to accept the Thoroughbred mares and involve them fully in our breeding program. We have good Thoroughbred mares here...the improvement in the movement comes from the warmblood stallions."

Ramsauer shares his knowledge with ISR members. He became involved with the ISR as a new project, after 18 years with the Oldenburg Verband. "America never bred a sport horse, and no sport horse registry in the U.S. has a breeding director," he explained.

ISR accepts all warmblood breeds described

The International Sporthorse Registry inspects and brands foals. A foal scoring 7.5 or higher gets a Premium award. Premium foal by the Oldenburg stallion, Grand Canyon, out of a Swedish Warmblood mare.

in this book, including Swiss, Austrian, Anglo-Arabs, and French trotters. Ramsauer noted, "Trotters can produce very good performance horses, such as Galoubet and Halla. We accept original [purebred] Arabians when they have a certain size. They should be between 15.2 and 15.3 hands."

ISR inspects the animals it registers. In 1990 alone, Ramsauer and the second ISR judge, Judy Williams, inspected and approved over 1000 horses.

Ramsauer said, "We are not just a registry on the table. We inspect every horse which comes in our registry. We have a certain overview of the quality of the mares, the foals, and the stallions."

He added that the ISR aids breeders. "We give advice in breeding clinics and personal advice on breeding successful sport horses. We

are trying to help them sell their horses, to establish a sales system in this country so you can breed successful sport horses."

ISR uses a standard score sheet, with marks from 1 to 10. The judge scores each horse on six conformation factors: head, neck, shoulder, frame, front legs, and hindquarters. The marks are totalled and then divided by 6 for a conformation score. The judge upgrades or downgrades the score subjectively.

Next the judge scores breed type and sex type, gaits, swing and elasticity, and overall impression. The total of these four marks is added to the conformation score, and that total is divided by 5 for a final score.

Mares with a minimum average score of 6 and at least a three-generation pedigree enter the Main Mare Book. With ISR's contract with the Oldenburg Verband, the mare's owner can apply to register her in a special department of that German Main Mare Book. (ISR and the Oldenburg Verband agree to accept each other's Main Mare Books). This mare's foal by an Oldenburger stallion can be registered and branded Oldenburger, if the sire is approved by both ISR and the Oldenburg Verband. A Main Mare Book mare with a score of 7 or higher receives a Premium award.

A mare scoring between 5 and 5.9, or with only a two-generation pedigree, enters the Mare Book. A Pre-Mare Book mare has only a one-generation pedigree, no proof of pedigree, or scores below 5.

ISR conducts Mare Performance Testing. Criteria include gaits at liberty and under saddle, rideability, free-jumping, and the horse's behavior and temperament during the test. The mare receives a certificate after scoring at least 6 points. Mares can also qualify through sport—dressage, jumping, or eventing.

ISR inspects and brands foals. Ramsauer said, "We created this new brand because in Germany the animal breeding law was cancelled. The responsibility now to make the rules and regulations was switched over to the associations."

ISR approves stallions, which are usually registered already with another European or American association. The ISR, not the Oldenburg Verband, also issues a Certified Breeding Permit to qualified stallions according to nine criteria: conformation, breed and sex type, walk in hand, trot in hand and free, canter free, correctness of gaits, free-jumping style and technique, free-jumping capability, and overall impression. The horse must have a four-generation pedigree and score at least 7. The Permit is good for one year, and the stallion receives a License after passing a performance test.

Ramsauer explained, "At the *Körung* for the young stallions in Oldenburg, we have four judges. The Oldenburg Verband said it's not fair to have only one Oldenburg judge in America—not fair to the breeders in Oldenburg to have it more difficult." The Verband generally agrees to accept American ISR stallions that pass the ISR's 100-day test (more than 90 points) or qualify through an outstanding record in dressage, jumping, or combined training. The breeding commission of each registry can disapprove a stallion licensed by the other.

American Warmblood Registry

Established in 1981, AWR functions as an umbrella registry. It registers horses which don't have a breed organization on this continent, along with horses of crossbreeding.

AWR's Sonja Lowenfish explained how proof of pedigree is the primary requirement. "We function like the Jockey Club. We treat the

registration form like a birth certificate. We don't pass judgment—we register all horses on an equal basis."

AWR has registered 37 stallions representing most breeds described in this book. The registry requires only proof of pedigree, or documentation for an unregistered horse. It accepts crosses with all color breeds, draft horses, and horses without registration papers. The sires of horses of color and draft breeds must be registered with AWR.

AWR requires horses to be blood-typed, and it was one of the first associations to accept embryo transfer.

American Warmblood Society, Inc.

This performance-based registry accepts horses of any breed or combination, excluding a fullblood Thoroughbred or Arabian or a draft breed. No proof of pedigree is required. U.S. owners may choose tentative or permanent registration. To qualify for the permanent category, the horse must be at least four years old and have qualified in dressage, show jumping, or dressage driving at AWS regional test sites or at recognized events.

As of 1990, 110 horses were registered. A computerized database records horses' test results. Mare owners can receive a list of stallions recognized by AWS, and match performance results of a stallion with the mare. AWS also promotes horses through sponsoring dressage awards. It will start to inspect horses for its breeding division, added to the performance registry. It will follow U. S. Dressage Federation specifications.

PART 3

Selection and Enjoyment

CHAPTER 20

How to Shop—Europe or Domestic?

I n today's sport horse market, the potential buyer can shop the source for European warmbloods or buy domestic horses descended from European stock. The next chapters will explore both options in light of the 1990s buying climate.

Buyers in the 1970s and 1980s chose to purchase animals from the old country. The warmblood breeds established name recognition, and marketing labelled European horses as world-class performers. By showing horses in Olympic stadiums, advertising communicated an image of the ultimate achievement in equestrian sport. Sellers developed sophisticated marketing programs to maximize their products.

With Americans aiming to bring Europe's best to North America, a trade deficit continues to exist. American authorities claim that U. S. equestrian sports will continue to rank below Europe, simply due to the Continent's superior horse breeding programs. Europeans have been willing to sell, but the strong nationalism works against equine exports. Incentives encourage farmers to retain ownership of top mares, and countries keep the top performers at home.

In today's global economy, all equestrian nations scour the Continent to discover talented equine athletes. Today North Americans compete against buyers from all continents, with Japan also developing into an eager customer.

Americans in Europe

Americans are influenced by the European mystique. They equate horses with sport cars, fine wine, and castles. The assumption is that a product with European origins must be of higher quality than domestic.

Americans consider European horses superior, due to their origin. With sport horses, the concept applies on an individual basis. Just like any other country, European nations have good horses, and lesser horses. A coveted brand does not always indicate an outstanding performer or progenitor.

The American equestrian in Europe enters an unfamiliar society. European horsemen form a close-knit network. Horses are a part of their culture and tradition, a matter of pride. Yet, Europeans tend to be provincial in their thinking, focused on horses of their particular region.

This Hannoverian shows the quality of sport horse that all buyers seek in Europe.

These horsemen are conservative. They are courteous and hospitable, but reserved in their enthusiasm. Many view foreigners with respect for the American riding style. Importer Hans Schardt commented, "In jumping, the American style is better than all Europeans. In jumping and three-day, they belong to the five best in the world."

However, European sellers can also consider themselves superior to the brash Yanks who shop on whirlwind tours. "I always say that America is the land of instant success," explained Henry Schurink, a Vermont horseman who was born in Holland. "Buy it, ride it tomorrow, and the day after tomorrow we've got to have a ribbon. Americans have a different look at life. They don't go by tradition or discipline— to me, the whole riding is discipline. Discipline of the rider and of the horse."

Willie Arts said, "You can't buy performance. You can't spend a fortune and get up to the top and stay up there. You have to work into that level, so you become really consistent and have a good feeling of everything that's going on in the horse."

Riding styles of the two continents also affect Americans' reputations. Robin Koenig expressed a concern that riders' limitations affect U. S. performances more than horses. "It will take more than money. Money won't buy training. You have to sit on horses to get education, to go through the steps to Grand Prix and learn why one horse doesn't make it."

Judy Yancey explained, "We're more used to riding Thoroughbred horses, and used to riding with lighter hands on a horse that's ready to go, and a lot of heart. Our technique is different— it's just our style."

Establishing Credentials

Those who plan to shop in Europe need to prove that they are serious equestrians. They should learn to view and evaluate horses as Europeans do. On foreign turf, they must open their minds to learn the European judging standards.

Americans should realize that when they go to Europe, some sellers will treat them like some Americans treat foreign buyers. The outsider might be a candidate for a lesser product simply out of ignorance.

Besieged by foreigners seeking to buy their horses, European sellers respond as would horsemen from any country. Some sellers are reputable and honest, dealing fairly with anyone. Others will take advantage of the tourist's enthusiasm and profit by selling horses weeded from their herds.

American buyers do have a reputation. For example, one dealer told an American importer, "That's a good horse, but Americans wouldn't buy it because it has a wire cut." Europeans also consider that Americans lack expertise in breeding. Instead of relying on bloodlines to predict a horse's performance, many American buyers don't care about an athlete's relations. Familiarity will help a buyer establish credentials.

Trainer Uli Schmitz advised, "Read about

the history, how the horses were developed. A lot of the European books are starting to get translated. The Europeans know that America is a big market, and they cater to Americans. All the auction catalogs are now in German and in English."

Although eager to deal, sellers can resent Americans who search for bargain prices. The "good deal" isn't practical in today's market, yet spending a lot for a horse doesn't guarantee satisfaction either.

Veterans of foreign buying trips recommend not to go alone, but to establish contacts before a tour and take along a knowledgeable advisor. An advisor can show a buyer around the country and direct her to reliable sellers. Importer Linda Zang recommended to ask a knowledgeable advisor for assistance. "Get with someone you can trust, to go with you, who knows how to deal European. Ask for more help—otherwise you might miss an opportunity of a good horse. With help, you're less likely to spend too much money."

Shoppers agree that trips are pleasant, with gracious Europeans showing excellent horses. "Going to Europe is fun, and it's also really dicey," commented breeder Anita Hunter. "You'd better know what you're doing, and have someone with you who's honest and who knows what they are doing."

Elizabeth Searle advised, "Have somebody put you in the right hands if you go abroad. Find someone who has gone and done some buying, because you can be had. Talk to people who go there all the time, who know where to go and who to talk to."

Advantages of European Shopping

Europe's compact geography groups a greater population of sport horses closer together than in America. Short distances between locations simplify shopping and present a wider selection of horses than available in North America.

By seeing the best—and the not so good—buyers learn that not every European horse is a great sport horse. They gain an education in learning to compare different types as they study many animals gathered at a show, auction, or stallion licensing.

"Go to Europe because you have a much bigger selection than here, especially trained horses," advised trainer Guenter Seidel. Trainer Steffen Peters added, "The quantity of good horses and riders is so high over there. If you see the stallions in Warendorf, you'd be amazed at the number and the quality. The competition in Europe is so much stronger, and the standards are so high."

Cost and Availability

The high standard makes desirable horses expensive. In past years, the fluctuating exchange rates have reduced the dollar's buying power. The dollar has dropped to half its former value in some countries. Because the dollar has lost its advantage, don't expect to find a bargain or to buy on a limited budget.

Importing costs and risks add to the chanciness. The buyer has to know where to go, and where not to go. Sophisticated sellers might take advantage of foreigners who don't speak the language, and who don't get all the information before they buy.

Authorities also explain that the market is drying up. Europeans themselves buy outstanding horses, and they will pay higher prices for them. Judy Yancey said, "The time to buy good horses in Europe is over. It's not worth it any more."

"The market has been really tapped," said dressage rider Kathy Adams. "It's hard to find good horses. They're paying from 200 to $400,000 for young, untrained horses! The quantity is there, but the quality—they know what they've got. It's real hard to buy their best

Willie the Great is an example of the modern type of Hannoverian sold through the top auctions. Ridden by Hilda Gurney.

horses. They've been in this business a long time."

Hunter trainer Frank Madden said, "Ten years ago you could go to Europe and buy top horses. In the last seven to ten years, we've educated the Europeans to spend their own money to keep their horses. Now it's more difficult to find the same kind of horses."

Dressage rider Marie Meyers noted how Europe and North America differ in valuing dressage horses. "We're getting a lot of U. S. horses being sold to Europe. It's a fallacy that the Americans have the money. The Europeans have the money and are buying the good horses. In the U.S., the dressage horse is not important enough. In Europe, dressage is very important. The big money will go to the dressage horses and the dressage riders—they will spend the money."

For a decade, Kentucky breeder Dietrich

Felgendreher has been importing young riding horses for resale. "With our knowledge, we could buy at reasonable prices and sell here at a reasonable profit. It's more difficult every year. I have to look hard and long to find. You have to have a good eye for a horse, expertise, and a bit of luck. In general, it gets a lot harder for the person who wants to go to Europe and buy a horse on a limited budget. If you have no limit, go, and pay a high price."

Linda Zang has imported horses from Sweden since 1980. "Horses cost more now anyway. It's harder now to buy a horse to sell and make what it cost you."

She has found that the changing marketplace makes it more difficult to find the horses she prefers for resale. "I could go see 200 or 300 horses and pull 20 I'd like to buy, and come home with 10. Now I see five and come home with two."

Trained horses are expensive in this country, too. If the buyer expects to spend a substantial amount ($25,000 or more), the European market offers more selection for the knowledgeable shopper.

The market does fluctuate due to supply and demand. In recent years, there has been a high demand for superior horses. Despite the economy, excellent horses will continue to sell. Henry Schurink said, "The horse business in Europe is booming, and here it is at a sort of standstill right now."

Foreign buyers will continue to shop the European horse market. Sellers recognize the allure of their product to foreigners, and they aim to attract buyers and maintain their sales leadership. They will expand their marketing strategies. Currently breeding areas promote the lighter horse, the animal that appeals to the majority of customers. Advertising campaigns in American equestrian publications promote the European image to buyers who equate the warmblood with luxury automobiles.

One source, who did not wish to be identified, remarked how the European Community regulations are already affecting European breeding and promotions. "We may find that we'll run into a heavy marketing effort by all the German breeds to the U. S., Canada, Australia, and Great Britain. If they are restricted on branding horses outside of Germany, the state studs are no longer fully government-subsidized, and the Verbands are on their own without subsidies, they'll have to make money. They are worried."

Sellers do want to make their reputations by exporting horses to other countries. Henry Schurink recalled, "I have been approached in Germany by breeders who say, 'I would really like that my horse goes to the U.S. Would you have a client for it?' That person is a smart businessman. He will say, 'I only want to sell you a couple of super horses. Perhaps you might come back next year with a friend who wants a couple too, or you might want to buy another one.' He's building up a name, so you would say, 'Go there—this guy has good horses.'"

Buying Opportunities

The American shopper in Europe can survey a range of opportunities. First, the buyer needs to find out where to go and who to contact, either as an advisor or as a seller.

Hans Schardt advised, "Don't try to be smarter than the person on the other side. Don't try to get the same deals. It's a different culture, a different attitude. It has much more to do with knowledge, attitude, and connections."

Those who plan a buying trip can research the opportunities by talking to former Europeans who reside in North America. They might decide to focus on one breed and join a breed association's tour group. On their own, they should establish a network for recommendations on sellers, and develop an itinerary.

Society. Many experts recommend starting with the breed societies, which exist to help breeders to sell their products. However, this does limit choices to the horses within a breeding area, and all areas produce quality animals.

Guenter Seidel suggested, "You could go by yourself if you know what you're looking at in a horse. It's better to have a contact person—call the Verbands, and you usually get help."

Elizabeth Searle recommended, "If you don't know who to talk to and don't know anybody, go to the KWPN. They will either help you themselves or put you in touch with somebody. They will not turn you over to a dealer of bad repute, because that would just work against them."

For the Holsteiner breed, Elizabeth McElvain said, "The Verband acts as agent. They will take you around and show you the horses, but they will direct you to where they want you to go and towards whomsoever has horses for sale. They will sell you the best horses they can—you have to trust them, but you don't have the freedom you have when buying horses in America."

Breed Auctions. Auctions of riding horses and breeding stock serve as showcases for the various breed societies. Promoted in attractive catalogs, these sales offer centralized opportunities to scan the current market and learn about particular bloodlines. The best, or elite, auctions offer excellent candidates to attract an international audience. In Germany, the famous competitors Deister, Simona, Amon, Ferdl, and Dollar Girl were all sold through auctions.

German auctions offer entertainment, a *Galaschau*. Extravagant displays of horses and horsemanship attract enthusiastic spectators. Some individuals offer guided tours to auctions, primarily as a pleasure trip.

At the elite auctions at sites like Verden, Vechta, and Münster, authorities have sifted through candidates to choose the best 10 to 25 percent of those nominated. For example, a sale of 60 to 120 horses reflects the best of 500 to 600 animals. Uli Schmitz explained, "The whole committee comes to the farm to inspect the horses offered by breeder or seller. They decide which horses go into the auction sale."

Horses arrive at the auction site well before the event. For instance, the candidates for one of the Hannoverian elite riding horse auctions arrive six weeks early. Here auction riders test each horse's fundamental training and characteristics, and assess the horses' athletic abilities. Head trainers supervise the training of horses in dressage and jumping categories. Horses also undergo a veterinary examination and X-rays.

Horses range from three to six years old. The breeder or raiser may sell a particular riding horse through the elite auction only once.

The training period allows potential buyers time to compare a variety of prospects. Before the sale, they can try out horses on the flat and over fences. Uli Schmitz, a former auction rider, said, "It takes riders about 14 days to get the horses going, and after that, you can go try horses out. All you have to do is go to the main trainer and tell him what you're looking for, and you'll get pretty good advice."

The elite riding horse auctions showcase horses at their best. A green prospect may move like a proven champion under a skilled auction rider. McElvain noted, "People go to Europe and say, 'The horses over there move so well.' They don't move any better than the horses here—it is just that they know how to show the movement."

About presenting horses in-hand, Schmitz recalled, "At the auction you have to be prepared to show 10-15 horses within two hours. You don't just show on the triangle—you run the whole arena."

The Hannoverian Verband also offers additional auctions in Verden. Elite Foal and Broodmare Auctions sell breeding prospects. In 1990,

foals averaged DM 7300, and broodmares were close to DM 16,000. The top 1990 foal sold for DM 28,000. A Yearling Auction sells horses at averages of DM 7000. Young prospects sell at Riding Horse Auctions, for lower prices than those selected for the prestigious elite auctions.

At the October, 1990 Elite Auction, 104 horses averaged DM 26,475. The top price was DM 200,000 —a record high for a son of Wenzel who was also the German Champion three-year-old riding horse.

With the weak dollar, few North Americans actually purchase and import horses at these sales. German buyers dominate these events. In 1990, most horses at the Verden fall auction went to buyers from Niedersachsen, Bayern, and Rheinland-Westfalia.

Other countries also host auctions. At a Dutch foal auction in 1990, foals sold for $2500 to 9000.

McElvain discouraged the novice from buying through an auction. "In Europe they have had horse auctions for millenia, so they know how to do it. They don't just show up the day of the auction, watch the horse do two free jumps, and say, 'I want that one.' They go up there seven or eight times, they watch the horse in training, they see people ride it, they have ridden the horse, and they know its soundness history. Everybody knows which ones are best, and they go for huge amounts of money.

"So for you to say, 'This one, I'll just bid on it and if it doesn't go for too much, I'll get it'— beware, because what you are going to get is what no one else wanted. And it is not just because it didn't have a pretty face."

Dressage trainer Michael Hedlund-Beining also warned of the hazards of this buying opportunity. He noted how a skilled rider can present a horse much better than it will perform in amateur hands. "It's not possible to get the good horse in a week, or going to the auction. Very often the horses that are not that far along, when a skilled rider is on the horse, they don't know what happens. The first two days they go real nice—the third and fourth day, or in two weeks, suddenly the real problems come out. It has to be a joint effort between the person who will ride the horse and the trainer who has the experience—what is the horse's capacity?"

The bidder must also be aware of the protocol affecting the sales of auction horses. Hans Schardt explained, "You have some good horses at Verden and Vechta. That doesn't mean it's true, what's offered for the horses. There is a certain standard price on each. The auctioneer will state the bid, and then it's open to the market to go higher. Sometimes bids are already in, and there are buybacks."

One American-based buyer (who did not wish to be identified) explained his buying approach: "I have gone to Europe for 17 years now, to the auctions every spring. I have bought over 100 horses at auctions for other people. I buy some horses before the auction. The horse goes through the auction, and I bid on it till I have the horse—but I get the horse for the price that I agreed on before."

Uli Schmitz noted that buyers tend to get caught up in the excitement of the event. "It's an expensive way to buy, and on the average you pay higher prices. For some people, it's competitive. 'I'll spend more money than this guy has. I'll show him what I have.'" He added that buying through an auction does reduce some risk. Veterinary examinations have screened through the horses, and the buyer would save time in travelling to several locations.

Agent. Many authorities recommend that foreign buyers purchase through an agent. The knowledgeable agent understands the marketplace and will guide customers through farms and dealers. He can also deal with a seller separately from the customer. The agreement is between Europeans, which can ease the transaction because the seller does not know the buyer's foreign status.

It also reduces the language barrier. Even with an interpreter, the inflection and idiom can influence the transaction. Virginia rider Pat Limage said, "I feel an opportunism. It's not necessarily scheming, but I walk on a farm, and the prices go up."

To avoid paying two commissions, a buyer can choose not to involve a North American trainer acting as an agent. However, a trainer could serve as a useful advisor for a future partnership with a new horse.

Elizabeth Searle described a Dutch agent, a farmer whose hobby is buying horses for clients. "He has an eye for a horse like few men have. He's very honest, and he knows about the bloodlines. About a yearling, he can say, 'Yes, this is an excellent one, but it isn't going to make the size.' He knows by what the horse had produced, and what that stallion with that mare had produced."

She praised the agent's honesty, and his goal to send satisfied clients home with horses that would make his reputation. "We would go to a place, and he'd say to us, 'Let me do the talking.' We would leave, and he'd say, 'He's asking too much. He'll call me tonight because I have said no.' Or on a high price, he'd agree, 'Yes, but this horse is worth that price.'"

Hans Schardt advised, "Go to an importer, who imports on a regular basis. It's knowing the market and knowing the people. To get the best price, buy from somebody who knows the country, who has a lot of selection. It's very difficult to get in touch with these people."

Dressage rider Karen Lencyk rides a Dutch stallion of the Ramiro line, purchased through the trainer and agent, Franz Rochowansky. Trusting his judgment, she bought the horse without travelling to Holland.

"He arranged that I see horses on film. I couldn't afford to go, but I trusted Rock after five years with him. I'd seen several of the Dutch horses he had imported. I liked two horses on the film, and he picked this one."

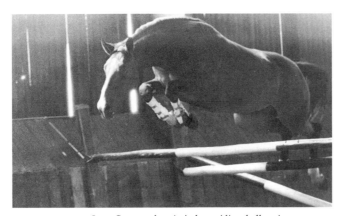

In a German farm's indoor riding hall, a jumper prospect displays its style over fences.

A buyer would want an agent who will not confuse her by offering too many animals. The customer needs to see numbers of horses in order to compare, but not so many that she can't recall specific horses. Seeing 100 horses on a large farm requires the buyer to catalog prospects on video or instant film.

Willie Arts said, "If you go to Europe for one or two weeks, you could see so many horses that after the first week you don't know what you saw! Especially if you want to buy something young, the horses are out in the pasture and you can't keep them apart in your mind."

Dealer. Prominent dealers offer a selection of many good prospects in one location. They sell quality performance horses. International riders like Ian Millar and Katie Prudent have purchased world-class jumpers such as Big Ben, Noren, and the Governor—all from dealers.

The typical dealer runs a professional operation. The facility usually features an indoor arena, where expert riders show well-groomed horses braided as if for a show. The formality of dealers' barns can intimidate buyers, who are expected to observe the presentation of prospects.

Like their American counterparts, dealers vary in their reputations. Some tend to show lesser-quality horses first, sizing up the customer's level of expertise. A rider would need to communicate her level of skill to the dealer and describe the horse she wants, so the dealer brings out appropriate horses.

Douglas Mankovich explained, "In Europe, normally the horses are shown turned out or longed to demonstrate the horse's natural gaits. Then if acceptable, they are ridden by the trainer or owner before the potential buyer gets on. It is considered acceptable and even preferable to state politely that the horse is not what you have in mind, before it is ridden. Thus the next horse can be shown without meaningless efforts being spent that waste both parties' time and patience."

At a dealer's, you will need to prove your horsemanship skills. Rider Dale Bormann described how the influx of foreign shoppers has made some sellers suspicious. She explained one experience: "They said, 'Oh, you're an American looking for horses. Good. Fine. Get up on this one.' It was green—it didn't steer. They had a giggle, because it's your reponsibility to get up on the horse, to be able to sit on the horse."

Canadian dressage rider Leslie Reid purchased two dressage horses from a major German dealer, who had 400 horses for sale. "It's not any different from horse dealing here. Professionals are the same. They don't know who you are, or how much you know."

Speaking from a dealer's perspective, Kathy Adams recommended to spend time looking at a range of horses. "A lot of people don't like to look. They just want to buy. Don't think, 'I'll go to Europe and buy something.' Don't send someone there to buy a horse for you. Try it yourself. You should seek advice, but I've seen so many people who just want to buy a horse."

She doesn't believe in showing every buyer every horse, wasting time for both dealer and customer. "I see their confidence level, and what they can cope with. I try to pick the most suitable horses that they would like."

Trainer's Barn. Unlike the United States, a trainer's barn is not usually a source for buying performance horses. Major trainers do not open their facilities to the public as sales barns. Visitors are accepted by invitation only, depending on the day's activities.

Americans who want to study riding and shop for horses can patronize barns catering to the serious foreign rider. Some facilities invite Americans to train with professionals.

Breeder. Young prospects are available on private farms, usually located through a breed association. European breeders treat horses as livestock on a farm, along with pigs, cattle, and sheep. They handle horses matter-of-factly, without pampering or sentimentalizing. Horses are not pets.

Young stock are not "finished," fat and shiny like their American counterparts. Farmers turn young horses out on pasture all summer, with no grain. In winter, the horses eat grass hay, with some oats. Farmers avoid feeding excess protein to warmblood horses.

Large farms may have as many as 80 horses. Steffen Peters recommended to visit smaller sites. "There are still plenty of breeders around, where you can get horses for decent prices. As soon as you go to larger farms or auctions, you spend a lot."

Visiting these farms, many Americans are surprised at the facilities and the way owners handle horses. As guests, shoppers should accept that horses are kept "rough." They can expect to trudge across fields to inspect horses, or walk through dark, ancient barns to see youngsters housed in groups in large stalls.

Can Americans Get the Best?

Yes, said Henry Schurink. "When you go to Europe, there are two kinds of people that want to deal with you. One says, 'Here is my chance to make some money,' so he starts on the bottom end of his herd and weeds them out. He might throw in a good one, if you pay enough. The other is a smart businessman, who sells horses for his own reputation.

"Those breeders and farmers there, they will sell you their wife if they can get enough for it! A lot of breeders, it's their living. They cannot afford to look at a $15,000, or $20,000 horse, a young horse, because they feel like we do here—he might drop dead tomorrow. 'I should take the money, because I have bills to pay.' You can buy the horse they won't sell—you keep wrestling and fiddling, and you suggest a figure that makes the difference."

A breeder who wants to promote his business realizes that selling quality enhances his reputation. He can retain quality stock and sell offspring.

Schurink mentioned a seller who breeds horses as a hobby, "He is very honest. He said, 'Why should I stick somebody with a horse? We lose money on it anyway. I want to do things right.'"

Those who buy a young horse as a breeding prospect will take the same risk as the Europeans do. Even the experts buy many stallion prospects and end up with only a few. Yet a foreigner can't expect to purchase a proven breeding stallion from a state stud. Generally, these sires are rarely for sale. If officials do decide to remove a stallion, the horse might be an unsuccessful breeder, or unpopular with mare owners. Laws may restrict the horse's sale to a citizen of the breeding area or nation, or prohibit its export.

"It's their game and we have to play by their rules," said breeder Judy Williams. "It is possible to buy [a prospect] if you want to spend the time over there, spend the money and take the risks."

CHAPTER 21

Locating and Importing the Suitable Warmblood

W hether a buyer seeks a horse with an advisor's help or on her own, she should first narrow the search. The right horse depends on the sport and goals the buyer will pursue.

"Expect to do a lot of looking," advised Douglas Mankovich. "Until you find a horse that blends with you and your approach and your temperament, you are searching for the wonderful answer and you haven't found it. The keyword is chemistry."

He added, "It's one thing to go to Europe to look. It's another thing to find."

The buyer might recognize this horse when she finds it, but during the search she needs to describe the horse to the sellers she meets. Her expectations will help the seller to present possible matches to try out.

Mankovich said, "People looking for a horse should realize that anyone endeavoring to do a good job in presenting a horse for sale puts considerable effort into the preparation of the horse. Normally the horse has a bath and is braided as if the animal were turned out for a show. It is the epitome of rudeness to expect someone to go through this tedious process, if the buyer in advance truly has no real expectation to acquire that horse."

Sellers mention instances of customers who fail to follow realistic expectations. Potential buyers may arrange to view horses of one age and training level—then when they arrive, they confess they wanted to look at older, better-trained horses. Such indecision inhibits the ability of the seller to match horse and rider.

The right horse will boost the rider's confidence and performance. A horse is an instrument, a partner in the chosen sport. To forge a successful partnership, the buyer should consider how the interrelated components of temperament, size, and movement complement her abilities.

"Temperament is the most important," said dressage rider Kathy Adams. "If you have an amateur, you don't need a spook. If you have a tense rider, you don't need a tense horse. If you have a lazy, nonathletic rider, let them have a little hotter horse."

Mankovich defined an equine athlete as having a sound temperament. Such a mind will help

Gifted is a large horse, best suited for a skilled rider like his owner, Carol Lavell.

both horse and rider handle the difficulties of their specific discipline. He explained, "As I have repeatedly told clients over the years, the only thing that counts is for you to enjoy your interaction with your horse. If every day is a battle of wills between horse and rider, then neither profits from the interaction and both become miserable. But if both develop a unison through understanding each others' unique qualities, then the experience is a positive one leading to success."

Trainer Willie Arts considers character vital. "The trainability of the horse is almost everything. The movement is important, but if you have a lot of movement and no trainability, you have nothing."

The horse and equestrian combination has to mesh in any sport, but especially in dressage. Many problems seen in the show ring trace to a basic incompatibility between rider and horse.

Size. In the past, American riders tended to buy animals that were too large for them. Elizabeth Searle cited rider-caused problems: "Women buy a warmblood, then complain it's not light and responsive. The women are too light and need to be exceptionally good riders, balanced and able to stay connected.

"Then the horse gets a reputation for being

heavy, when actually it's been desensitized by the rider who doesn't learn to ride correctly. The rider hauls back on the reins, and the horse loses its desire to go forward. The horse can feel the touch of a fly on its skin—there are no insensitive horses."

"Woman riders aren't strong," said Adams. "Riders shouldn't have to work so hard. The horse needs a little bit of hotness, a little spark. The heavier types were too dull, and we need 'blood.'"

A small rider on a large horse lacks effectiveness due to her leg position. Searle noted, "Think about what Baron von Blixen-Finecke said: 'When you go a certain direction, and you sit to the inside, your inside leg must be as steady as possible. It must give the feeling that it's hooked around the horse.'"

Judge Natalie Lamping emphasized the criticality of suiting horse to rider. She also advised against a small woman on a large warmblood, especially with the preponderance of Thoroughbred lines. "Hot and strong makes an impossible situation. Or, a horse could be a fantastic mover, and so big and wide and strong that the rider can't keep the horse connected and engaged enough. Sometimes the biggest mover isn't suitable for the average rider. If the horse is scopey, can the rider sit the movement?"

Movement. Both size and temperament influence how the horse and rider match in motion. Arts said, "If you have a good, trainable horse, the movement will come."

The big mover may not be comfortable to ride. Horses with round, reaching strides could jar the rider used to a flatter-moving horse. Also, a horse from a jumper line might have a strong back that many riders find difficult to sit.

Experts agree that the mismatched horse and rider can reduce the horse's athletic ability. Adams has seen the quality of young horses' gaits deteriorate due to bad riding. "You see beautiful movers, and they cripple themselves because the rider can't sit the horse. The rider hangs on the horse's mouth with no self-carriage—the horse gets very resistant and it starts to break down."

Especially in dressage, horse and rider should match for what Searle calls a "harmonious picture. Realize that every little lady isn't going to be able to ride a big horse and look good. It's an impression the judge gets. Harmony is a visual indicator. The judge can't ride the horse, so it has to look like harmony—not something that looks 'like a wart on a pickle,' as one of my instructors once said."

Examine the Horse's Credentials

When you have defined the type of horse you seek, study its genetic type. Become familiar with the major lines. As you see horses of various lines, you can compare your observations with others' opinions about a certain line's characteristics.

Pedigree can predict the horse's character, although individuals will vary. For example, in the Hannoverian lines, the stallion Ferdinand (F-line) was known for passing on confidence and courage to jumpers. Wenzel I, a winner of the stallion performance test, has the reputation for producing good movers with strong-willed personalities. Don Carlos, a jumper sire of the D-line, produces competitive, hot horses.

The G-line's Grande offspring are willing to work, with very good temperaments. Der Löwe xx produced dressage and event horses, also good performers but more challenging to ride.

Trainer Uli Schmitz said, "As Americans get more educated, they'll learn about bloodlines, too. It's especially important when you look at stallions. A lot of times in their performances, they can be super but temperamental horses. It can be misjudged sometimes—you can look only at the performance, not the horse itself and its bloodlines."

Beyond the fourth generation, the contribu-

tions of ancestors are minimal. Even a grandparent contributes 25 percent of an individual's genes, and a horse two generations beyond— one of 16 ancestors in that generation—contributes only 6 percent.

What intensifies the contribution of a famous ancestor is two or more crosses to that line. Horses with similar genetic structures strengthen the dominance of those characteristics.

Judge and Hannoverian breeder Lilo Fore commented, "Some lines and some breeds are more prone to be good movers. You have to pick what you want to do." However, American buyers should realize that their knowledge is limited compared to the European masters. A novice can't expect to master what experts have studied and debated for generations. Trainer Jan Ebeling cautioned, "Don't go out and buy bloodlines or look only for certain lines. You really won't know enough."

When buyers find horses that meet their goals, they should confirm that the horse matches its credentials. Registration papers should match a horse's color and markings. With changes mandated by the European Community, the Studbook II designation and differ-

The Dutch mare Zatelina performs willingly for her young rider.

The light-footed modern warmblood is often easier for a woman rider.

ent brand will distinguish horses accepted by the new regulations. New regulations will also restrict how breed associations brand horses. For example, after 1992 the Hannoverian and Oldenburg Verbands will brand horses only within their regions.

The horse´s papers and brand should match. A horse could be branded after its export to another country. Linda Zang noted that Swedish authorities attempt to brand horses of acceptable quality prior to exporting them. "However, many unbranded horses were exported to this country before this procedure was in place. Additionally, some horses are not branded now because new owners are reluctant to subject the horse to possible injury. All horses that remain in Sweden are never branded for any reason."

Purchasing through a society or society's auction validates the horse's background, as the society must uphold its reputation. In private transactions, misrepresentation has occured,

affecting American buyers.

Searle mentioned instances of buyers who purchased stallions that the Dutch association planned to remove from the studbook, or had been removed. "The seller would say, 'This is an approved stallion,' and show the buyer the book describing the horse. He didn't tell the buyer that the horse was removed."

Stallion buyers have also been told that a horse has not been presented for licensing, but the seller assures them it will pass. Buyers then present the horse, and it does not receive its license. Searle added, "Or that the stallion made the second ring in Holland, and it is sure to pass in the U.S. The trouble is that when the jury comes over here, they know those stallions that made the second ring. If it didn't make beyond the second ring there, it's not going to make beyond the second ring here." She noted that a young horse's maturity and improved movement could better its score.

Checking Soundness

American buyers expect to receive guarantees of soundness, which has caused conflicts with European sellers. In general, Europeans don't consider radiographs as essential as Americans do. Some sellers and breed societies do not see the need to X-ray young horses.

"We don't see leg problems as reasons that horses were removed from sport," said Ludwig Christmann of the Hannoverian Verband. "We don't have the problem in this breed of horses breaking down afterwards. X-rays of a 2 year old are so different. They would affect the selection process, because a horse could be 100 percent sound and a good mover—but the X-ray could remove it."

Young horses that are big movers might have questionable X-rays. Yet European horsemen do not see the joint problems that plague certain breeds in the United States.

"People who buy horses in Europe for resale here have to have X-rays that will pass in the

U.S.," said trainer Dorie Schmitz. "If you bring a horse over that won't pass an American vet check, it's very hard to resell it—and to convince an American that the Germans don't think it's important to have X-rays."

Uli Schmitz argued that X-rays can't guarantee soundness. "Even if it X-rays okay, it can have some other problems that don't show up on an X-ray. But if you want to go over there to bring horses over here, if you don't have X-rays, you don't have a chance."

Willie Arts said, "Americans want a guarantee for a lifetime, that there's no lameness and the horse will take them as far as possible." He noted that such expectations fail to account for unexpected influences—injury, riding technique, and training expertise.

In general, warmbloods do tend to show more navicular changes in X-rays than American riders see in Thoroughbreds. Elizabeth Searle said, "Lots of good horses have been turned down at five and six, and they have never taken a lame step at twelve and fifteen. If you do not have vets who are used to vetting out the warmbloods, you get excellent horses that get turned down."

She suggested soliciting a second opinion on a questionable animal. "We have two vets. One has done a lot of vetting on warmbloods. If we have the least bit of shakiness, we want both of them to vet. They're always in agreement, one way or the other."

Kathy Adams agreed on the validity of X-rays. "We've all had horses that X-ray very badly and are sound all their lives—or horses that X-ray beautifully and are lame." However, she did recommend to have a European horse X-rayed. The expense of the transport makes this check a logical one.

Importers recommend that if a horse is X-rayed prior to importation, the buyer should bring back the radiographs for interpretation by an American veterinarian. Results could be

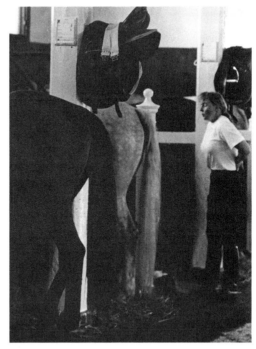

American buyers must politely accept European horse management. In a Swedish riding school, horses are stabled in tie stalls.

different from later X-rays made in this country.

American buyers have become used to relying on veterinarians' evaluations and soundness predictions. When buying a Thoroughbred off the track, X-rays serve a valuable purpose, and they are crucial with a substantial purchase price. With warmbloods, however, authorities wonder how the usual standards apply.

U. S. Holsteiner breeder Doris van Heeckeren said that in judging sport horses, "Americans aren't able to think for themselves. They are so dependent on the vet and want clean X-rays. I hope Americans open their eyes. For example, a bloodline in Germany has very straight legs. They are very good performance horses, and nobody cares. Those bloodlines, the Germans have seen for generations, and they can forgive that. But here they complain about the straight legs."

Adams noted, "You have to have a vet who has enough savvy and enough horsemanship to know when a horse is scared of something, when it's ticklish or extra sensitive. The horse could be sensitive to hard ground, and there are variables in the quality of X-rays. A good horseman makes more sense to me than a vet with all the credentials in the world, but without any practical experience."

Making the Decision

When deciding whether to purchase a specific horse, the wise buyer balances immediacy with prudence. The buyers should plan at least two weeks to look for a horse and test prospects over several rides.

Testing a riding horse in a European barn differs from the U.S. experience. The horsemen expect women riders to be reserved, not aggressive or argumentative. Under skilled professional riders, even horses of average quality can perform brilliantly. Even a difficult horse can look outstanding when guided by a strong rider.

Willie Arts explained how he tries for a combination between horse and rider, but riders often seek an impossible ideal. "You have people who have a kind of horse set in their minds. They see a horse go with somebody else and say, 'That's the kind of horse I want.' Then they don't realize how much it takes to ride a horse like that."

Dressage rider and breeder Dale Bormann described, "From what I see, most of the riders in Germany are very good riders. They ride big-moving horses, and they don't care if they get plowed, so that nobody protects them. If you're willing to go out and jump that big course of fences, they'll certainly let you do it and encourage you to do so."

Veterans of European shopping trips men-

tioned the pressure to make a decision. "When you see one you like, your first impression is usually your right impression," advised Kathy Adams. "So often the good ones go quickly, so you're forced to make a decision."

Trainer Katie Lindberg recalled, "They're used to people who drive over and buy, not foreigners. They want to deal and get it over with." She advised to take the time to watch the horse being tacked up to see its ground manners, and to ride the horse outdoors, not only in an indoor arena.

Completing the Transaction

Once the buyer makes the decision, next comes the paperwork. With an agent, this expert will handle the final agreement on the purchase price. Either buyer or agent will arrange for the transfer of funds.

European horses travel to North America by air transport. "Containerized" shipping simplifies the loading, flight, and offloading.

Horses are loaded into aluminum shipping containers, usually fitted with stalls three-abreast. The container is 8' wide and 10' long. Each stall measures about 28" wide, 84" high, and 80" long. The entire container fits into a widebody jet. Inside, the horses aren't bothered by the sights of air travel. An attendant enters a front compartment to check water and haynets. (KLM trains professional grooms to care for horses inflight and at airport holding facilities).

Horses enter the container on a ramp, which raises to form the rear. The secured container can allow horses to see out the front, or be completely enclosed. A rope net secures the entire container during shipment.

Bill Nichols of the Alex Nichols Agency noted, "Shipment of horses by air is so modernized. We have no problems so far as a rough trip. All horse traffic ships on a 747's main deck."

Primary carriers are KLM, Lufthansa, and

Air France. Amsterdam's Schiphol airport is the main hub of Europe's equine transport. Horses also ship from Frankfurt and Paris.

Horse traffic ships on two types of widebody jets—the combination passenger/cargo aircraft or a jet that carries only cargo. The latter aircraft can accommodate 36 pallet positions, for a maximum of 108 equine passengers. Such a plane can carry any type of freight, and shippers book space on scheduled flights.

Importing costs presently total from $4000 to $6000. A shipping agent will handle the ground and air transportation, payment of duties, VAT (Value-Added Tax), and veterinary tests. Agents on both sides of the Atlantic cooperate on arranging transport. A shipper can act as a broker, who handles all phases of the importation. The major airlines often refer buyers to these brokers.

Jann Hasenauer operates Jet Pets, the only private quarantine facility in the U. S., at the Los Angeles International Airport. She said, "Importing is very safe. Ten years ago it was more difficult. There are flights all the time.

"Get with a good importing/exporting agent for the best service and the best cost. He will find a co-load for you—it helps to share the cost with other people."

Nichols advised, "Get a quote in writing from the agent. When you're ready to ship, have all the necessary information—the horse's color, sex, and age, and exactly where it is located. We can arrange health certificates."

He added that buyers can help through preplanning. "The sooner we know the horse will be purchased, the smoother things can happen. Tell us a week ahead of time, and we can notify agents in Europe so they can arrange for a coload. Agents in the U. S. and Europe work together to get horses moved well."

For permanent entry into the U. S., the U. S. Department of Agriculture (USDA) Animal and Plant Health Inspection Service (APHIS) regu-

lations require that a horse must be accompanied by a health certificate from a veterinary officer of the country of origin. The certificate ascertains that the horse has resided in the country of origin at least 60 days before export and is free of communicable disease.

Horses must test negative for dourine, glanders, equine piroplasmosis, and equine infectious anemia. The importer must apply for an import permit from APHIS. In addition, the importer pays a reservation fee (at least $130) for the mandatory quarantine in a USDA-maintained facility.

Horses imported to the continental U.S. from Europe arrive at one of three ports of entry: Los Angeles, Miami, or Newburgh, New York. (Several land border ports can accept shipment of horses from Canada). Still in shipping containers, horses go directly from the aircraft to the quarantine facility.

Incoming horses are sprayed with an insecticide, which depends on the insects common to the country of origin. If foot-and-mouth disease is present in the country of origin, the horse also walks through a "pond" to clean its hooves. Port veterinarians, employed by APHIS, verify that horses are free from communicable disease and the diseases listed above. Veterinarians will release most horses from quarantine after three days; they can refuse entry to those not certified.

During quarantine, the importer provides attendants to care for the horses. The costs are high, with the first day the horse arrives at the station considered the first day of the quarantine period. Buyers should remove horses out of quarantine as soon as officials authorize release.

Horses imported to the U. S. from Canada must have a health certificate from every country visited within the preceding 60 days. They must test negative to the diseases listed above and obtain an import permit.

An imported gelding or a horse under breed-

When buying a young horse, the buyer should watch the horse canter. Holsteiner mare.

ing age is free to leave upon release. Breeding stock must undergo additional quarantine to verify they are free from the infectious disease, contagious equine metritis (CEM).

Mares and stallions can be chronic carriers of CEM. APHIS regulations require that imported horses over 731 days old test negative to this highly contagious bacterial venereal disease. CEM exists in the majority of European Community nations, including all countries represented in this book. (It has not been reported in Poland or Russia). Sport horses must meet the current APHIS regulations for permanent entry.

The following states maintain quarantine stations to test stallions for CEM: California, Colorado, Kentucky, Louisiana, Maryland, Montana, New York, North Carolina, Ohio, South Carolina, Tennessee, Virginia, and Wisconsin. All except North Carolina also maintain quarantine facilities for mares.

The APHIS modifies its regulations, but in general, veterinary officials in the country of origin conduct certain tests on mares and stallions before export. At the U. S. state-approved quarantine stations, veterinarians examine and treat stallions and mares to insure that a series

of specimens are cultured negative. Stallions presently test-breed two CEM-free mares, and officials culture the mares.

Because some mares can continue to carry the organism even after successful treatment with antibiotics, APHIS presently requires mares to undergo a clitoral sinusectomy to remove the clitoral sinuses. (Some veterinarians consider this a controversial practice). If the clitoral sinusectomy was not performed before export or was incomplete, the mare must have it done at either the School of Veterinary Medicine at Cornell University or the College of Veterinary Medicine, University of California, Davis.

When a pregnant mare foals, a veterinarian will collect a specimen from her and her foal. The treatments and laboratory tests make the average stay in quarantine about 10 weeks. Despite the care given to horses, some owners have had horses released with health or soundness problems.

To avoid the complicated and expensive quarantine, some owners purchase broodmares and board them in Europe to import only the foals. This also gives the breeder access to European sires.

Any imported horse must become acclimated gradually to its new home in a different continent. The horse might suffer stress from shipping and adjusting to unfamiliar care. Some horses, especially older ones, could take up to a year to adapt to a new climate, food, and handling.

Importing Experiences

About quarantine, Virginia rider Pat Limage said, "It's quick for a horse under two years, or a gelding. I bought a yearling stud, shipped him on Tuesday, and picked him up on Friday. You can choose your quarantine area so you can see and exercise the horse during quarantine."

New Mexico trainer Katie Lindberg imported a horse through an agent. For a client, she purchased a nine-year-old Hannoverian gelding sired by Wenzel. Her agent had selected a dozen horses that matched the client's needs, and Lindberg saw four horses on videotape. She arranged a trip to look at one specific horse. At a dealer's barn in Bremerhaven, she spent three days trying out the horse and having it vetted. (She ended up buying a different horse, not the one in the video).

She explained, "The agent handled the transaction. It was negotiated in marks, not dollars, so the price in dollars was calculated at the exchange rate in effect the day of the sale."

The horse was shipped to New York and spent three days in quarantine there. Lindberg recalled, "The horse was underweight and tired. The altitude here gets to them. It took two or three weeks to adjust, and two months to get its weight back up."

She felt the Europeans treated her with courtesy. "The rider and barn owner were very cordial. The rider that rode the horses first was exceptionally nice. This agent does a lot of business with the barn."

Reading a German *Abstammungsnachweis*

A horse registered by a German Verband will have a completed *Abstammungsnachweis*, similar to this example. Important areas:

Lebens-Nr Life registry number

Züchter Breeder, and breeder's address

Aus du Bedeckung der Stute out of dam

vom Hengst... By stallion *am* on (covering date)

ist nachfolgendes Fohlen gefallen The following foal was born

Geb. am Born on (date)

Geschlecht: Sex

Farbe Color

Abzeichen Markings

St.	Stern	Star
Fl.	Flocke	Small star
Bl.	Blasse	Stripe, blaze
Schn.	Schnippe	Snip
Utl.	Unterlippe	Lower lip
l.	links	Left
r.	rechte	Right
Vf.	Vorfuss	Front foot
Hf.	Hinterfuss	Hind foot
Vfsl	Vorderfessel	Front pastern
Hfsl.	Hinterfessel	Hind pastern
ohne	Abzeichen	No markings

Vater Father, sire

Mutter Mother, dam

Fohlenbrand Date of branding and name of official

Hannover

Leb-Nr.: **31 –** (1)
Deckstelle:

Aus der Bedeckung der Stute:

| | (2) vom Hengst: | am: (3) | vom Hengst: | am: | ist nachfolgendes Fohlen gefallen: (5) |

(4)

(7) Züchter:
Eigentümer /
Besitzer: (8) (9)

Geb am: (6) Geschlecht:

Farbe und
Abzeichen:

(10)

Vater: VV

Fohlenbrand (linker Hinterschenkel)

VM

(12) (linke Halsseite)
und Nummer
gebrannt:

Mutter: MV

MM

(11)
_____ _____
Datum   Brennbeauftragter
(Stutbucheintragung siehe Rückseite)

Vorstehende Angaben werden hiermit bestätigt:

Verden, den _____ (13)
(Zuchtleiter bzw. Beauftragter)

The **Abstammungsnachweis** contains the following information:

1. Life number and number of breeding station
2. Out of dam (name and life number)
3. By sire (name)
4. Covering date
5. The following foal was born (life number)
6. Date of birth
7. Sex
8. Breeder
9. Owner/Possessor
10. Colour and markings of the horse
11. Pedigree of the horse including names and numbers of at least 3 generations of ancestry

Verband hannoverscher Warmblutzüchter e. V.

D 2810 Verden, Lindhooper Straße 92, Telefon (0 42 31) 67 30

Abstammungsnachweis

Eigentumswechsel (nur durch die Geschäftsstelle des Verbandes einzutragen): **(14)**

Leistungsprüfungen, Zuchtwertfeststellungen und Prämierungen: **(15)**

Eintragungsbrand (linke Halsseite) **(16)**

Stutbucheintragung:
in das

(Name) _____ (Nr.)

Verden, den _____

_____ (i. A. Stutbuchführer) **(17)**

FN-Eintragung für Turnierpferde

Der Abstammungsnachweis wird nur **einmal** ausgestellt. Etwaige spätere Veränderungen in der Beschreibung des Fohlens vom Landbeschäler sind beim Landgestüt, 3100 Celle, des Fohlens vom Privatbeschäler beim Verband zu beantragen. Eigenhändige Eintragungen sowie Änderungen sind Urkundenfälschung und werden strafrechtlich verfolgt. Der Abstammungsnachweis gehört zum Pferd und ist bei Besitzwechsel mitzugeben.
Dieser Abstammungsnachweis ist Eigentum des Verbandes hannoverscher Warmblutzüchter und bei Tod oder notwendig werdender Tötung des Pferdes an diesen zurückzuschicken.

Abgang am:

Ursache:

12. Registration of the date of foal branding and the kind of the foal brand signed by the branding deputy
13. Affirmation that the specifications made are correct by the signature of the breed director or his deputy
14. Change of ownership (to be filled in by the office of the Society only)
15. Registration of the performance tests taken (stallion performance test, mare performance test, licensing notes)
16. Official stamp confirming the granting of the neck-brand
17. Indication of the stud-book in which the horse is entered and the signature of the stud-book keeper.

CHAPTER 22

Warmblood Trends in North America

With North Americans searching for quality sport horses, warmbloods continue to increase in popularity. Riders and drivers who want to compete successfully often prefer European breeds.

Holsteiner breeder Elizabeth McElvain said, "In Europe, it's crowded with people and farms. There's no room for a backyard horse. The four equestrian sports created the horse. Here the horse created the sport. Now that the sport horse is available, the four classic sports are growing like crazy. We don't have to ride a Thoroughbred cross-country any more—we finally have a suitable horse."

Logically, not everyone will purchase and import a horse from Europe. Most buyers will look for domestic horses and buy American.

North America has developed its warmblood industry in a short time. Only a few thousand European horses are scattered across the continent, but Americans, and Europeans living in North America, agree that quality has improved rapidly as equestrians gain knowledge. Hermann Friedlaender explained, "In the old country you have so many more than

we have here. So the selection process can be so much more severe than here. If we used the same selection here, we would have none. It doesn't come up overnight."

Dietrich Felgendreher has shown in breed classes at the Dressage at Devon show since 1978. "It's a great learning process in this country. We're trying to produce great sport horses in a very short time, where it took Europe centuries. On the whole, you can see the fruit of the American breeders' efforts. At the Devon show, you can see the great improvement in the horses that are being produced in this country."

Americans are anxious to learn and to compete equally with European riders and drivers. In retrospect, they agree that in previous years importers did end up with Europe's cast-offs.

Trakehner breeder Robin Koenig: "In the early 1980s, anyone who could afford the fare went to Europe and imported horses. Now times are tough, and the true people can sell because they will buy or breed what the market needs. The Germans got ahead of us because they were in transition—we got horses they dumped."

Rider and importer Kathy Adams: "When

the whole breeding craze started, we were sold some lesser-quality horses because we didn't know better. There was a lot of compromise because there was a fad going on.

"More and more people have realized what quality is. The U.S. has a lot of top-quality young horses. The standards have improved and people have sought good advice and learned."

Trainer and breeder Uli Schmitz: "America will be a little bit different from Europe, but I think the standard is going up very fast. America is America, and that's not being negative."

Trainer Dorie Schmitz: "I think Americans are very anxious to have the same qualities as Europe—they're thirsty for knowledge. They desperately want to do it right, and I can see the standard coming up very fast."

Comparing Quality between the Old and New Countries

Authorities voice opinions on the comparison. Elizabeth Searle recognized that Americans don't easily accept the need to select, to cull animals that do not show desirable traits. She sees owners who present lesser-quality horses at *Keurings*. "They're enthusiastic breeders, but they don't know conformation or movement. Horses are presented that absolutely won't go.

"The Dutch have become stricter, a lot stricter than when they started, with the acceptance of Thoroughbred mares." She noted that with the judges' experience in seeing American Thoroughbreds over the years, they can better evaluate the range of quality.

Trakehner breeder Anita Hunter said, "All of the American breeding is originally of German stock. Horses here are equal to horses there. They grow differently here because of our climate and nutrition."

How do American Holsteiners compare with the German? According to breeder Elizabeth

McElvain, "In Germany, what is 'in' is elegance, because they have so much substance. Substance is very much 'in' in America, because we still don't have the substance that we want."

The mare populations of the two countries also differ. Germany has a base of Holsteiner mares to breed to its Thoroughbred-influenced stallions. America continues to cross Holsteiner stallions with its population of Thoroughbred mares.

Guenter Bertelmann, a successful Trakehner breeder said, "I would say in the weanling to six-year-old mares there is quite an improvement, and through importation of the right stallions came different bloodlines. We have some excellent Trakehner stallions over here in North America. Breeders found out that you only can sell quality. If you select for quality, there is always a market."

American Trakehner Association Secretary Helen Gibble noted, "We have good bloodlines here, some that are extinct in Germany. We have the material here. We don't have the expertise."

When asked if buyers could find the same quality Dutch horses here, Elizabeth Searle answered, "You bet you can. They don't have to go to Europe now. If I went over to Europe to buy something, it would be strictly to bring a line in that I had lost or never had. It would be on the mare side to get that particular line. As far as bringing in a potential performance horse, no."

She added that some North American horses are being exported to Europe. Kathy Adams agreed, saying, "The Europeans are starting to come here to buy horses. You always get that before the Olympics. They're looking at the Prix St. Georges horses, and buying trained horses."

Do horses in this continent match the European trend of the lighter, more elegant horse? Louis Thompson of the American Hanoverian Society sees a continual improvement in the quality of mares. He noted that the old-style mares imported in the 1970s have been replaced by improved mares. "A good many of the stallions in this country, compared with the ones being approved in Germany, are more on the heavier side. But some of the exceptional, refined ones are the stallions we approved last year. The combination of these stallions and good mares results in very nice babies."

Some breeders find that Americans prefer the older types. "Americans still like those big, important horses," said McElvain. "A lot of the Thoroughbred owners want the old-fashioned type stallion, because they are reacting against the refinement of the Thoroughbred. They want more bone and better disposition."

Jayne Ayers, who breeds Hannoverians and Westfalens, has also found that Americans tend to avoid too much Thoroughbred. "They say, 'Let's stick with what we want in the warmblood.' But I find the average buyer wants a pretty horse, and doesn't want it to behave or move like a Thoroughbred."

Dressage trainer Gerhard Politz imported a Westfalen stallion, Anstand, which he anticipated as a successful cross—not too far removed from warmblood mares. He described how Anstand's parents were both half-Thoroughbred: "His sire, Angriff, and Angriff's dam are of the Angelo xx line, and his dam is by a son of Cottage Son xx. He has all the good warmblood characteristics, and all the good points you seek in every horse—good Thoroughbred characteristics like an excellent shoulder and saddle position."

Politz noted how this stallion can cross with either old-style warmblood mares or Thoroughbred mares. "His breeding is not that alienated to the Thoroughbred. He will improve topline and bone."

In general, the American market seems to prefer the "middle" horse—a balance between the very light and the old-fashioned warmblood. Dressage trainer and Oldenburg breeder David

Bonjour Bonuit, sired by the Selle Francais Bonjour, combines an athletic background with pinto coloring. Owned by Tahna Curtis.

Wilson described this horse as medium in every way. "If you've got all the *'gummi'* [energy] in there, and with the quiet horse that's not too hard to maneuver around the ring, then you have the ideal sport horse. If a horse is a very good, medium-boned type, the results come quicker. The whole breeding program improves because the horses do better."

Douglas Mankovich also mentioned the medium horse. "With more and more introduction of Thoroughbred lines, you see in Germany it's the middleweight type they're looking for. The aesthetically pleasing athlete is what's being bred. The modern sport horse is not the heavy old agricultural or war horse."

He added that the older types aren't outdated, but the suitability of size influences riders' choices. "The aesthetic is very important—the type of the horse for the rider. That's where there's a man's horse, or a lady's horse."

Elizabeth Searle agreed, noting, "We have some very good performers, but I don't think it's the horse we're looking for, for dressage. The lightness, the elegance needs to be more. Women riders are too light and need to be exceptionally good riders [with the old-style warmblood]."

Do the Europeans keep the best horses? The U. S. and Canada have imported World and Olympic Champions. Abdullah, bred in Germany, was foaled in Canada. Yet authorities contend that the best horses will remain in Europe because breeders intend to maintain their domination of the sport horse market. Why should they assist the competition?

Importer Hans Schardt said, "You cannot get 1000 years of knowledge and horsemanship into 10 years. What they sell to the U.S. are horses that never produced, that have no performance behind them. If you get 10 offspring from one breeding of the same stallion and mare, maybe two are top, one average, the others nothing. To Americans they sell the horses that aren't at the top—the average or the bottom 50 percent."

Breeders first imported European stallions, planning to profit from stud fees. As a result, both superior and average stallions represent European breeds in North America. The influx of stallions has resulted in a ratio of one stallion to five warmblood mares. European breeders consider this high, as most of their breeds stand about one stallion for every 50 mares.

Comparing stallion populations between the U. S. and Germany, Jayne Ayers said, "Overall, the stallions here are much lower in quality. There are a handful of very good stallions, but a lot of others that wouldn't get approved in Europe, or would stand a year or two and then be removed."

European officials on breed inspection tours concur about the assessment of the overall stallion population. As an example, in 1989 the American Hanoverian Society licensed one of eight stallion candidates. Authorities politely described the others as average in quality.

In the Dutch breed, North America is home to 22 stallions of Registered status. Some Dutch

sport horse stallions have been presented at *Keurings*, but failed to qualify for Approval. Searle noted how some riders and trainers seem unconcerned about a stallion's credentials. "They don't care as long as it's a good stallion and a good producer, that produces the talent they want. I don't think it makes any difference [to the owner] because maybe the horse himself is a very good jumper, or good for the sport."

About the Swedish Warmblood, Linda Zang expressed concern for the quality of American stallions. "The testing is so much harder in Sweden. It worries me because it's easier to get approved over here. Will the quality of American-bred horses be the same as the Swedish? I'm for breeding in the U. S., but I'd be very careful to stick with the hard, regimented testing they do in Sweden."

The Warmblood Mare Population

Breeders who aim to replicate European warmblood breeding find the American mare base to be limited. They note the difficulty in importing quality mares. Trakehner breeder Judy Yancey said, "The Germans allowed probably too many good stallions to come over, but they hold tight to their good broodmares. The good broodmares are here because they were bought as young horses. A good breeder doesn't sell his good mares until they're of a particular age."

Thompson, a Judge with the American Hanoverian Society, has toured German studbook inspections. He contends that in this breed, North America has a higher average quality of mare. "Germany has the wide numbers. The finest mares there would probably top the exceptional ones here, but the average here is higher. Now people import the best horses, with the cost of importing. What we've imported over the last 7-8 years is a higher quality mare which produces good offspring."

Stallions here match the mare base. For instance, Germans originally sold North Americans old-style, heavier Hannoverian stallions, to breed to the Thoroughbred mares. Now, with the trend toward the modern horse, lighter mares have come to this continent. Owners of the more refined, modern warmblood—and those with Thoroughbred mares—will want to cross with the more substantial stallions.

In the Trakehner breed, Guenter Bertelmann explained a similar situation. He sees breeding as significantly improved on this continent. "In the beginning, 15 years ago, the mares were the older Trakehner type, first-class foundation mares. Now we have a lot of modern type stallions, and those guys really appreciate good solid mares. We are getting a little bit more size. The reason to get maybe a little bit more elegance in for North American people is the influence of Thoroughbred blood—not only coming from North America, but also from imported stallions."

To compete, America has to breed its own sport horses. This continent has bred talented athletes, and breeders want to prove that domestic stock can fill the needs of American equestrians. They predict success for the cross between domestic Thoroughbreds and European champions.

Dr. Roland Ramsauer of the International Sporthorse Registry said, "North America can be a special partner to Europe. We have in this country such special horses. We are serious competition, as AI has changed the situation." He mentioned a young stallion that exemplifies the Thoroughbred-warmblood cross—Special Memories, by Abdullah out of the dam of Olympic jumper Touch of Class.

The Thoroughbred Cross

Like Europeans, Americans cross the Thoroughbred with the warmblood for improved temperament, more substance, and a better chance

Ladies Man is an Anglo-Trakehner, owned by Jill-Marie Jones.

for long-term soundness. Buyers from the Continent have purchased some quality Thoroughbred stallions for European studs.

With a substantial population of Thoroughbred mares, breeders foresee a product that meets American needs. The cross provides an affordable warmblood, and supporters recognize the positive contributions of Thoroughbred blood.

"Our sport horse of the future will be half-Thoroughbred and half warmblood," said Elizabeth Searle. "It's the best of two worlds, with the lightness, spirit, elegance, and forwardness of the Thoroughbred. Each has so much to offer, and the combination is going to be what most people can deal with, ride successfully, and look good on."

She noted how the Europeans do not generally use Thoroughbred mares, but stallions. "I've taken a 180° turnaround, because realistically we breed a Thoroughbred mare to a warmblood stallion. So I go to Thoroughbred sales, looking for mares of substance with the neck coming out correctly and that move right."

Douglas Mankovich praised the cross. "That is what the American market can produce. It's almost forming a new breed—the American version of the warmblood. Even the Europeans are beginning to realize that this has potential, as they recognize the fact that we have wonderful Thoroughbred bloodlines here, not just racing bloodlines, but sport bloodlines. This potentially can be a very important part of the market, for the Americans who can't afford a $50,000 three-year-old."

He added that this horse will increase in popularity with the dollar's reduced buying power overseas. As a stallion owner with 10 years' experience, he noted, "I've seen a time when it was very tough for stallion owners, because you didn't get the breedings. A lot of stallions changed hands, and they still are. We haven't crossed the road yet, completely."

Opportunities to Expand Knowledge

Learning means studying, to gain the experience. In evaluating horses, the horseman needs to see a broad cross-section of animals and develop an eye by evaluating as many horses as possible.

Such opportunities do exist in North America, although the serious student will have to travel. Major breeding farms can showcase a breed or type. Helen Gibble of the American Trakehner Association advised, "It's easier for a large breeder to cull and be selective. Ask questions, and compare the answers."

Breed associations will distribute names of respected breeders who can share objective viewpoints on sport horses. Guenter Bertelmann said, "We are lucky that we have quite a lot of breeders who like to teach newcomers. They give a clear and honest opinion, and that's the most important thing. Also see where you are

standing by taking your horses to evaluations and breeding shows."

With an individual horse, Searle suggested asking a European judge for his or her opinion. These authorities frequently visit North America to judge at shows or inspect breeding stock on tours, and a buyer could arrange to present a horse to the judge at a location on his or her itinerary.

Searle advised corresponding with an open-minded judge, who is not oriented to a specific breed or society. "Ask if he has the time during his rounds to give you an opinion on a horse. You don't have to tell him what breed it is." As examples of judges with good eyes and no breed favoritism, she recommended Major-General Jonathan Burton, Col. D. W. Thackeray, and Marianne Ludwig.

Breeding stock approvals offer a formal occasion to learn from European experts. By following a mentor, who has a strong foundation in a breed, the equestrian can develop knowledge. Directors of breed associations who tour the continent include such authorities as Dr. Ramsauer (International Sporthorse Registry), Dr. Haring of the FN, Dr. Wilkens (Hannoverian Verband), and Dr. Maharens (Westfalen).

At the approval, close observation educates spectators who can compare opinions with an expert's insights. Helen Gibble advised, "Watch as mares are being inspected. See why they get what marks."

Judy Williams said, "Go to a large inspection, where there are a lot of horses gathered together. You can see offspring from a lot of different stallions, You can see mares, you can see the mother and many times the sire and the offspring—and you can hear the comments from the committee about the offspring. That's the only way to learn, as far as the breeding is concerned."

Trainers can be a source of information. Authorities recommend to find a trainer who

Warmbloods as Hunters

Americans have developed a mindset about the warmblood as a show hunter. In general, they label European horses as unqualified, saying that the large warmblood can't compete with the classic Thoroughbred. Surprisingly, hunter authorities do accept the modern warmblood of "Thoroughbredy" conformation and smooth jumping style.

Willie Arts said, "People say they don't like warmbloods for this or that, and it's just because they look at the wrong horses. They see the kind that's not suitable for that particular event and say, 'Yeah, they're not good.' Now they can go with the light, pretty horses—the old ones are just one generation behind."

Although some authorities still contend that only Thoroughbreds can win these classes, warmbloods have succeeded in the hunter ring. The legendary Ruxton, AHSA Regular Working Hunter Champion, was one-half Hannoverian. Bavaria has taken many honors in both working and conformation hunter classes, and the stallions Werner-Wettstreit and All the Gold continue to win championships.

The Trakehner and Anglo-Trakehner have won several national honors in recent years. Baron Palazzo was the 1986 AHSA Champion First Year Green Working Hunter. Hunters sired by Abdullah include Home by Dark (AHSA Horse of the Year, Second Year Green Working Hunter), Gabriel (AHSA Horse of the Year, First Year Green and Regular Working Hunter), and Elfin Magic (AHSA Horse of the Year, First Year Green Working Hunter). Abdullah's son Bier Meister and daughter Kirin were Grand Champions of the International Hunter Futurity in 1989 and 1990, respectively.

To win as a hunter, the warmblood or the Thoroughbred-warmblood cross has to have the expression of a Thoroughbred, with a long neck and pretty face. It must jump correctly, arcing smooth over every fence.

Hunter trainer Frank Madden felt that a warmblood had to have Thoroughbred blood to make a hunter. "The worst thing is to buy a horse on the cold side. Hot blood is better for jumping. An athlete has to have quality to its blood, and you want a fair amount of Throughbred qualities in a Hannoverian or Holsteiner."

Unfortunately, the popularity of the straight hind leg in the hunter ring has made some Europeans consider such a horse as "a hunter type for the American market." The overly straight hind leg is associated with OCD (Osteochondrosis dessicans), a disease affecting young horses.

The hunter class is unique to America. Some European nations have recently initiated a similar event, called style jumping.

Hilda Gurney shows the American-bred Westfalen Chrytique in Fourth level dressage.

understands European horses. This would be a person who has studied in Europe, gained an education, and teaches a European system.

Shopping Domestic

In some ways, domestic shopping for a sport horse is easier. The process is clear, without the confusion caused by differences in language and culture.

Elizabeth McElvain noted how buying a horse here involves the same observations as buying in Europe. "You can visit to watch the horse in different stages of training. You won't buy it under auction conditions, but actually in a way it is better for you. The horse won't be driven up in value by seven other people who want the same one you do."

Distances pose the major barrier to horse shopping. The size of North America is its biggest disadvantage. If buyers find it a challenge to locate good horses in a portion of Europe, they agree it is harder still to search across an entire continent.

Breeder Dale Bormann noted how prices compare for three- and four-year-olds. "In Europe, I can look at horses in the $20,000 range. Why isn't it that people in the U.S. will come to look at my good three- and four-year-olds for 6, 8, $10,000?"

Buyer's Checklist

Associations. Officials of North American associations naturally recommend these groups as sources of information. Many publish names of breeders and farms. Some also prepare sales lists, although their marketing activities are minimal compared to European breed societies. Most organizations concentrate on registering rather than helping breeders.

Breeding Farms. Visiting large farms gives the opportunity to see a variety of animals. North American farms vary according to the breeder's expertise. The manager of one of the country's top farms said, "Americans need to rely on farms like this, that have done the footwork and are absolutely comparable to farms in Europe. Our nutrition and horse management is better here. We have fewer problems on vetting horses born here than the mature horses from Germany. Our care is better—some imported horses had never been wormed before."

Videotapes. Sellers disagree on the usefulness of this sales tool. Videos help market horses across the continent, and the medium does attract buyers. Tapes especially help sellers who are located inland from either coast.

A video can be useful for general impression of a horse, but it can be misleading. The horse might look worse or better than in real life. The buyer still needs to see the horse in person.

"The horse can look completely different," said Dale Bormann. "So basically it's an illusion. If the buyer likes the illusion, they'll come buy the horse. Some horses I've sold off tapes, people knew they would buy the horse before

Warmbloods as Hunters (continued)

Guenter Bertelmann explained how Germans appreciate the hunter style of riding. "It's basic for all the jumpers. In the hunter class, you have to ride in perfect style, to become later on a jumper. They don't have hunters there, and they would be very happy if they would have it. Style is everything—if you don't learn it as a 14-year-old girl, you never will."

On the course, a hunter gallops and jumps in a careful, graceful style. The horse has to use itself, but not to excess. The hunter generally moves flat—like a Thoroughbred—rather than round like a dressage horse. A horse that gallops with too much movement or springs too high loses the desirable hunter style of arcing over the fence.

European stallions have been selected for their jumping ability—to jump with scope, bascule, and power. A powerful jumper does not necessarily jump in the pretty hunter style of skimming over fences. In a way, a hunter is a type of "reduced" jumper that does not show the ability to clear high and wide fences.

Should a hunter meet the market demand and be a less-capable jumper? Ludwig Christmann of the Hannoverian Verband suggested that in America, the mare's performance test could be modified to demonstrate hunter ability. "The Abglanz line is suited for the hunter type, pretty and with good style. They are maybe not high jumpers, but good for lower fences."

Breeder Judy Williams said, "We're trying to produce a super athlete, whether it's a super jumper or dressage horse. The dressage horses have to have a lot of movement—too much for the hunters, by and large. The jumpers have to have a lot of scope and a lot of jump—it's more of an aggressive jumper than they want for the hunters."

Can hunters be bred? Yes, but some breeders consider it an "accident." "You can breed a horse with a lot of Thoroughbred," said Ayers. "I bred one that didn't work out as a dressage horse. He didn't like flat work, and I sold him to a local hunter trainer." The horse was later sold for a substantial sum and carried an equitation rider to place in the Maclay Finals.

The Thoroughbred cross can "dilute" the warmblood's rounder movement. The offspring may excel in the hunter ring, but most judges in dressage breeding classes consider flat movement less desirable.

Finally, the influx of warmbloods in hunter classes can subtly influence the judging of the discipline. As judges see substantial, calm hunters compete with the more temperamental, lighter Thoroughbreds, they may prefer the former. Classes today already emphasize more jumping form rather than galloping ability. Warmbloods which are bred to jump will naturally show form over fences.

they stepped off the airplane. It's unrealistic, and it aids in people getting the wrong horses."

Sellers complain about the time and expense of producing good tapes, and the need to update the tape to present the horse in its current condition and training ability. Some buyers seem to collect videos, browsing through horses, so sellers must require cash deposits.

Advertising. Responding to published advertisements brings a potential owner into the buying mix. Hermann Friedlaender recommended to investigate horses advertised in a publication like *The Chronicle of the Horse*. "If you don't care what breed, see what's being offered. From there, one step leads to another. There are usually more horses offered than there is a demand for."

He noted that the buyer must realize that some sellers are ethical and others are not. The buyer must recognize the disreputable sellers and sort through the hyperbole. By becoming familiar with an association's registration process, the shopper can verify a horse's credentials.

Auctions. A few prominent events have attracted interest, but in general, North America won't compete with Europe's gala auctions. Unfortunately, horse auctions in this country have the reputation as an outlet for stock that the seller can't market any other way. Impatient riders won't buy youngsters, which would be the most likely stock.

Trainers. To sell a riding horse, many breeders send horses to trainers' barns. Those seeking a highly-trained horse would probably concentrate on this source. Such a horse would rarely be stabled in the owner's backyard.

Whatever opportunities the buyer pursues, she will network with breeders and sellers. Breeder Kyle Karnosh recommended, "Know what you want to use the horse for, and your own personal preferences. People have to be

honest with themselves. They say, 'I want a 16.1 chestnut gelding' and fall for a 16.3 bay filly.

"Go and look at a lot of horses to gain experience. You start to develop an idea, if you're not sure what you want. You get an idea of what you like. It's a really personal decision."

She recommended patience during the search, which could last months or even years. "Scour all the material. Look at publications, farms, individual horses. The horses are there, but the one- or two-horse owner won't spend a lot of money advertising. It's easy to miss that one classified ad."

The price range also affects the search, depending on the buyer's desire for a nice horse, one with world-class potential, or a proven performer. A young prospect can be less expensive, because the buyer doesn't pay for its training, yet it's a riskier purchase. The rider aiming for dressage doesn't know the horse will have the mind and ability.

Trainer Jan Ebeling said, "With a young horse, all you can see is he's a big mover. You never know if he can piaffe or passage. That is an advantage with buying a 6 or 7 year old, that has been trained to a single flying change. You can see how 'crazy' he gets—you can find out more about the horse's abilities."

Support for the Sport Horse Industry

Documentation has made European breeds great. Tracking and reporting statistics on bloodlines—and financial incentives—encourages breeders to continue to improve the sport horse. The measurable results of matings benefit sellers and buyers.

In the Americas, concerned breeders fear that the lack of such historical data will limit the success of American-bred sport horses. Horse-breeding in North America lacks the authenticity of a valid agricultural pursuit. Breeders and

Amerens

The Dutch mare Amerens is a winning hunter in both amateur/owner and working hunter classes. Owner Patty Arnett explained, "Even though she doesn't move like a Thoroughbred or look like one, she jumps a hunter fence in absolutely perfect hunter form. That's why we did so well in the hunter ring."

Arnett imported the mare from Holland. She bought Amerens as a three-year-old through a dealer, off a breeding farm. "She was not broke and was 14 days pregnant when I saw her. I saw her free and free-jumped." The mare had been shown at the National Mare Show as a two-year-old, representing the province of Zuiderzeeland. She was said to have been the unofficial national champion at that show.

By the stallion Nimmerdor, Amerens is out of the mare Syolita, sired by the Thoroughbred Erdball who was out of a model *preferent* mare. She was bred by M. Terpstra.

Arnett started the mare as a jumper and went through preliminary and amateur/owner classes. "But she's so typy with her form that I switched to the hunter ring." In 1989, the mare won the high point hunter award at the Zone VIII championships. For Zone VIII AHSA Horse of the Year, she placed third in Green Working Hunter, Second Year, and sixth in Amateur Owner Hunter, Over 30 years old.

Arnett presented Amerens at a North American *Keuring*, achieving the *Keur* predicate. The NA/KWPN awarded Amerens the *Keur* mare of the year award for all North America, along with Dutch Sport Horse of the Year for amateur/owner hunter and second year green working hunter.

Along with her show career, the nine-year-old Amerens has produced five foals. Her oldest son won a *Star* at a *Keuring*. In 1991 she foaled two colts and two fillies by Arnett's stallion Arthos, carrying one herself and producing the others through embryo transfer.

Arnett said, "It's interesting getting to know the foals—they're four distinct individuals. Amerens and Arthos produced two grays and two bays—two fillies and two colts, one of each color."

Amerens, shown by Ben Wade.

owners enter and leave the industry rapidly.

Without statistical information, breeders lose track of their horses' offspring. They cannot prove a stallion's production record. They find it difficult to compete with the European market, because they lack the documentation that European associations maintain.

Germany and France both compile and report winnings of competition horses, and track data by bloodline. The FN database includes all competitors, who must register in order to show in Germany. Breeders pay a set fee to keep their stallions listed in the FN Yearbook. The FN database and SIRE provide valuable information to the industry, and these facts give the horse show industry a credibility it lacks in North America.

In 1984, Canadian authority Dr. Peter Birdsall organized the Horses in Sport Federation. This non-profit organization attempted to compile such information for North America—to record information on sport horse bloodlines and to help breeders keep track on their horses. It planned to develop competitions and incentives. Unfortunately, the experiment did not continue.

Long-time breeders agree that documentation will help the American industry progress. Data will educate competitors about bloodlines and build a permanent market for horses. Breeders could make decisions based on facts, and they would be less likely to choose a stallion that appeared attractive due to advertising. Because stallion owners have to compete for breedings, often the owner with the largest advertising budget gains the most breedings.

Stallions also have to combine performance with a stud career. (In Europe, most stallions never compete. Their offspring build their reputations). Douglas Mankovich noted a common misconception: "If a stallion competes now, he must be the best stallion around. People think it the horse isn't at Grand Prix, he's no good.

That's a big mistake."

Breeder and trainer Lilo Fore said, "Here our breeding stallions are performance horses. That's the first question I always hear: 'What has he done?' It's not important [to them] that he's been a breeding stallion and he's fully licensed."

Although many authorities agree on the importance of this task, supporters realize the size and expense of compiling a database. Germany's extensive network of breeding and riding clubs helps support its information system. Dr. Roland Ramsauer explained, "In Germany a staff of 20 maintains the FN database, from show records and all registries. Each year, it costs DM 10 million for this program."

Supporters suggest varied approaches. Many believe that AHSA should assume this responsibility, compiling data from entry forms.

Other ideas:

- Breed associations can contribute information.

- Associations can fund a university project to build a database. Students could gather data from AHSA, USDF, and breed associations, to compile all information in one file.

A major obstacle is the apathy of the average equestrian. How can breeders convince the industry that this is important? Benefits:

- Market sport horses as animals, equal to livestock industry.

- Add credibility to the sport, less hype.

- Promote shows, as competitors seek to enhance reputations of their horses, and relations.

- Validate domestic horse-breeding.

- Reduce the reliance on imports.

- Equalize the balance of trade.

Two incentive programs currently benefit the industry—The International Hunter Futurity (IHF) and the International Jumper Futurity (IJF). Both programs aim to increase the market for young horses by awarding cash prizes to horses' owners and breeders.

The IHF's performance futurity began in 1986. Three-year-olds compete in two performance classes in three regional competitions (East, West, and Midwest). Horses perform over fences (3' 3" maximum height) and under saddle, and their final score includes 25 percent judged on conformation. The regional shows also add in-hand classes for yearlings, and two- and three-year-olds. In the year's Finals, the horses show in conformation over fences (conformation judged as 25 percent), hunter under saddle, and another over fences class.

Payments by owners of nominated stallions, along with owners' payments to maintain the offspring's eligibility, make up the purse. The IHF annually distributes to breeders and owners a purse in excess of $150,000.

Open to all breeds, the major percentage of the 150 nominated stallions are Thoroughbreds. However, stallions such as Abdullah (Trakehner) and Best of Luck (Dutch) have sired class winners and finals champions.

Begun in 1989, the IJF showcases jumper prospects. Four-year-olds demonstrate their abilities over low, inviting courses. These horses must not have competed for prize money as a jumper.

Judges score horses on their potential in three classes at the three regional competitions (East, West, Midwest). In the Suitability class, horses perform under saddle and over cavaletti. They are judged on movement, balance, and attitude, along with conformation. Horses jump two rounds, with the first course of 8 to 12 fences (maximum 3' 6" height, 4' spreads) and the second 10 to 12 fences (maximum 3' 9").

The International Event follows the regional schedule and adds a third round. Fifteen finalists compete over a course of 8 to 10 fences of 3' 6" to 4' high, with maximum spreads of 4' 6". At all events, judges score horses' potential as a jumper.

In 1990, 105 stallions were nominated for the IJF. Warmbloods predominated, especially Dutch and Hannoverian stallions. The four 1989 regional and international champions were warmbloods. Owners of foals sired by these stallions nominate their foals as yearlings. The 1989 purse was $150,000, with $16,000 going to the International Champion, the Holsteiner, Calvin. Breeder Awards total 15 percent of the total prize money.

CHAPTER 23
How Warmbloods Differ

O verall, warmbloods are different from the breeds Americans usually ride—Thoroughbreds, Arabians, and Quarter Horses. Centuries of selective breeding influence their physical appearance, mechanisms, and behavior, yet every horse is an individual. There are quiet, lazy Thoroughbreds, and "airhead" warmbloods. Conformation and temperament depend on a horse's heredity and environment rather than its country of origin.

Warmbloods in general share certain distinguishing traits. With the increased popularity of warmbloods, owners, riders, and trainers have noted how these horses differ and suggest ways to treat them differently.

Physical differences

Size is the most obvious. Although the European trend is toward horses in the 16-16.3 hand range, many Americans still consider warmbloods to be larger in height and breadth. For instance, the cannon bone of an average Thoroughbred could measure seven inches. A warmblood, known for substantial bone, could measure nine inches.

Some observers argue that the warmblood lacks the prettiness of the more delicate Thoroughbred. A warmblood can have a large head, appropriate to the size of its body. With more substantial bone, the warmblood has larger feet to match. Some horses require oversize shoes to fit.

Due to its conformation, movement characterizes the warmblood. Warmbloods generally show rounder, more expressive gaits with more knee action. Dressage trainer Lilo Fore noted, "Thoroughbreds are not known for their best trots. They have good walks and gallops, but they're not bred to have the trot. They are bred to be flat on the ground, to be fast on the ground, not to jump up in the air and have suspension."

Elizabeth Searle said, "In getting a warmblood instead of a Thoroughbred, you'd have a very expressive, strong trot. I hope the horse would preserve the gallop of the Thoroughbred, and the big, reaching walk." She mentioned that overall, more warmbloods show an impure walk than do Thoroughbreds, and she has noted the tendency toward a lateral walk in some breeds.

The contemporary European horses are built to engage, in a uphill conformation. They naturally work off their hindquarters. Many riders claim that the average Thoroughbred tends to lean on the forehand, making it harder to collect. This horse has to be taught to work from the hocks.

Dressage rider Julie Sodowsky explained, "A good warmblood is born and bred to do dres-

The sport horse's neck is set more upright than the Thoroughbred's. Generally the Thoroughbred is built more on its forehand, for forward rather than upward movement. A low, horizontal neck is undesirable in a dressage horse, but a jumper could compensate for this conformation.

sage. They have power and suspension in their gaits. With a Thoroughbred, you have to train that in. It can end up being a very nice dressage horse, but because it's not bred for it, you have to take time and don't hurt the horse physically in the process. You have to spend years putting

the strength in them so they can collect, whereas the warmblood, it's bred into them."

Holsteiner breeder Elizabeth McElvain said, "Under saddle, the warmblood feels really powerful. You can really sit down on them because they push."

Behavior

Again, owners mention how warmbloods tend to demonstrate certain traits. These generalities do not apply to all warmbloods.

Quiet. The warmblood is not as quick to react as the hotblood. Trainers find that many Thoroughbreds, especially those bred and trained for racing, require a more tactful riding style than the average warmblood.

The Thoroughbred tends to be a fast-reacting horse. It responds quickly to a stimulus. The Thoroughbred usually has a high proportion of fast-twitch muscle fibers. Briefly, horses have two muscle fiber types that move the horse and influence its speed, length of stride, and duration of stride: fast-twitch and slow-twitch. Fast-twitch muscles produce speed and power through rapid, forceful contractions. Slow-twitch muscles expand and contract more slowly. These muscles can maintain their effort over a longer period of time, giving the horse endurance. Breeds like the Arabian tend to have more slow-twitch muscle fibers.

Muscle fiber types influence the horse's performance in sport. Breeder Kyle Karnosh explained, "In a sport like eventing or jumping, that fast reaction time of the Thoroughbred is an advantage. In dressage, steadiness is more important."

With their breeding, different types of warmbloods can excel according to the sport. Breeder Dr. Richard von Buedingen recommended the fast-twitch muscle types for jumping today's courses with large, technical fences. "The horse has to turn quickly and jump off its haunches."

Dressage training requires the horse to handle a different type of discipline. A horse with fast-twitch muscles tends to be more sensitive. It feels and reacts to the rider's motion. Von Buedingen said, "Dressage came out of a military origin, and with the army teams, there was importance more on lengthening. You could do dressage on a Thoroughbred then—now it's different, because so much collection is called for. The horse has changed with dressage, so warmbloods meet the requirement."

The disciplines of show jumping, three-day eventing, and combined driving require a combination of stamina and speed. Riders generally consider the warmblood lacks the galloping speed required for the upper levels of eventing, unless it has a concentration of Thoroughbred blood. The warmblood's dependability and soundness make it a reliable choice for those riders who compete through the intermediate level.

Dressage trainer Jan Ebeling explained that the more sensitive horse required a tactful rider. "You can't muscle them into work, but you think more about what you're doing. You think about doing another extension, or maybe walk for a few minutes."

He added, "You ride a more hot-blooded horse differently than an old-time warmblood." As an example, he described one Hannoverian as "a little bit of a couch potato." Of another warmblood in his barn, a predominately Thoroughbred horse, he said, "You've got fire and power. If you know how to control it, that's super. It's something that's working for you."

The warmblood tends to be more mentally stable than the Thoroughbred. Karnosh said, "People who talk to us say, 'I'm tired of Thoroughbreds,' speaking of the disposition. 'I want a horse I don't have to fight with all the time.' That's one of the attractions of the warmblood."

"Warmbloods have a little bit easier temperament to work with," said Searle. "They don't

The sturdy warmblood is ideal for combined driving. Herbert Cassidy, Jr., drives a pair of Dutch Warmbloods.

have the flightiness. When you put the pressure on at higher levels, they don't have the tendency to blow up, not nearly as much as the Thoroughbred."

A reputation for placid dispositions has made some riders complain that warmbloods are dull. Sodowsky noted, "A warmblood is more physical to ride. It has a quiet that doesn't react to outside influences." She considered her Hannoverian, Tamino, "not as nervous or spooky as a Thoroughbred. New things intrigue him—his reaction isn't to get nervous. He has a certain sparkle."

Searle described warmbloods as not as impulsive, and she blamed riders for labelling warmbloods as dull. A rider who hangs on the horse's mouth will discourage forward movement. She said, "Warmbloods can more easily have their desire killed. They're not like the Thoroughbred, which is bred to go forward and has a stronger desire. Riders and trainers tend to blame breeds for riders' faults.

"With a warmblood, a rider who's used to a Thoroughbred's always wanting to go has to develop what I call the 'go' button. Laziness is easily overcome if it's done in the right way. You can teach them to go just as quickly from a light aid as anything else, but it has to be taught very patiently, very consistently, very repeatedly right along."

Lilo Fore noted that some people don't know how to handle warmbloods. "I don't have a horse in the barn that isn't just as sensitive as the Thoroughbreds I rode. If you ride them from the beginning, ride them forward and allow them to move forward, I don't think you'll have that problem." She said that some European lines are lazy, and some are hot—just like there are quiet and hot Thoroughbred lines.

Persistence. Describing warmbloods as basically kind, Kathy Adams said, "Once they learn your size, you're dead meat. You can never let them learn that they're bigger than you are. Never allow the horse to know anything different from perfect behavior."

She recommended to handle a warmblood assertively. Many of these horses have strong, independent personalities, and some tend to be pushy and invade the handler's space by crowding. Handlers need to reinforce their aids with consistent discipline and be persistent and strong-willed in return.

Although warmbloods have been selected for reliable, responsive attitudes, some horses do demonstrate a strong, willful personality that can result in a "says who?" behavior. The horse might resist going forward. It may not blow up or get mad, but it can get stubborn—especially if the handler tends to "spoil" the horse.

About this stubborn attitude, Kyle Karnosh said, "It depends on the bloodlines. Certain lines are known for that tendency. A lot of Polish Trakehners have that reputation. Others have a reputation for an outstanding temperament—such as the [Hannoverian] A-line and the D-line."

A willful attitude can develop into a lack of

respect. Again, the handler cannot allow the horse to learn its own strength. A horse that gets stubborn under pressure may not show this behavior until advancing to more sophisticated levels of competition. Over a Grand Prix course, or performing FEI-level dressage movements, the horse must be a cooperative athlete with the desire to please.

Interior Qualities

Experts agree that these horses take longer to reach maturity. Yearlings might grow taller faster than Thoroughbreds of the same age, but horses finish growing later. Compared to a three-year-old Thoroughbred, the young warmblood often looks less mature.

Holsteiner breeder Elizabeth McElvain noted, "Fillies grow up faster than colts. Then colts catch up and go past. First they grow tall, then they get big."

At the Trakehnen stud, authorities advised to wait until the age of six to ride a horse. Today, Trakehner breeders realize that the horse achieves its growth between the ages of five to seven. Breeder Anita Hunter does not start young Trakehners on flat work until they are three years, three months—or three years, nine months if X-rays indicate the need to wait.

Because of their large size at a young age, many feel the horses are ready to start. Yet their muscles are not as strong as they look, especially the back muscles.

Willie Arts explained a common mistake about preparing a young stallion prospect for inspection. "Work comes easy for him, and he accepts it. But you can make the work too much for him. You have to be careful not to overask him or overwork him. A young stallion can have a big engine, but he's still not all the way developed. The engine gives power, but everything else has to do it, too."

He noted that a horse that's large for its age may lack strength. "A smaller horse, that's more compact, is usually stronger at a younger age than the bigger one."

Uli Schmitz has observed problems with Americans starting youngsters too early. "People think, 'This horse is big, he is strong.' He's not. His legs are weaker than smaller horses—he needs more time to strengthen and develop. We start our horses under saddle about three and one-half to four years—even older with large horses."

Some breeders question the demands of the performance futurities. They feel that preparing a three- or four-year-old for these events asks too much of a youngster. However in Europe, horsemen routinely send young stallions and mares through the performance testing.

Easy keepers. For centuries, these breeds have lived under northern Europe's extreme climate conditions. Caretakers have not babied these horses.

"Horses grow differently here," cautioned Anita Hunter. She noted that the climate and nutrition in North America affected how young warmbloods develop. "I have to be careful with the young horses—I keep them ribby. They get so big so fast, that you cannot feed them [too much]."

Abnormally high weight for size, or too much size at a young age, puts stress on joints. OCD can occur in domestic breeds, which affects as many as 25 percent of U. S. Thoroughbreds.

European authorities recommend that Americans avoid feeding excess protein to young horses. Too much protein can cause enlarged joints, rarely seen in Europe. In Germany, horses spend the warmer months on pasture, with no additional feed. Ludwig Christmann said, "Horses need protein only when they nurse, the last four weeks of pregnancy, or when they're started in training, to build up muscles. When they muscle up, they need carbohydrates to burn energy."

He advised Americans to turn young horses out to pasture. Like all other youngsters, young warmbloods need regular, free exercise. Horses raised in groups grow naturally. Youngsters have the opportunity to stretch their legs in free gallops, to develop strong joints, tendons, and cardiovascular systems.

Durability. Warmbloods have been selected for their soundness. With speed a primary trait, Thoroughbreds have a reputation for less-durable legs. Breeders have sought to breed speed rather than correctness and durability.

Equipment

Warmbloods' conformation does require certain tack. In fitting bridles, the large heads of some horses make it difficult to find a bridle that will position properly. The browband and throatlatch of a full-size bridle might be too short on a horse with large jaws and a deep head from forehead to throat.

Some manufacturers now market specially-designed bridles to fit the warmblood head. These are sold as "Oversize" models.

In some breeds, horses inherit a round wither. A wide, fleshy wither might not hold a saddle in place. A foregirth can maintain the saddle's position as it prevents the saddle from sliding forward.

CHAPTER 24
Breeding for a Warmblood Foal

North American observers recommend that American horsemen breed sport horses on this continent, and breeders contend they can produce horses equal in quality to the European market. With the weak dollar and European efforts to retain the best stock, few American buyers can continue to import outstanding horses. The existing breeeding stock can produce winning homebreds.

Traditionalists from established European breeding areas question whether a nation or an individual can produce horses of quality without a centuries-old background. How can a breeder succeed without learning careful selection through generations?

One American breeder, judge, and trainer (who did not wish to be identified) noted that breeders here lack an eye for breeding. "Here we don't have knowledgeable people or the tradition of horse breeding. In Germany, every other farmer knows more than all the breeders here put together."

New breeding philosophies have arisen in the mid-20th century. North America has not yet bred a warmblood Olympic or World Champion, but hundreds of farms large and small do breed sport horses. With the new European Community restrictions, Americans see a freer market for their animals.

Anyone breeding for a sport horse foal contributes to the breed. "I hope in the U.S. we will get more people who breed with a purpose," said Dr. Richard von Buedingen of Graf Bae Farm. "Americans have a laissez-faire attitude about breeding. They haven't paid attention to things the Europeans have considered important for so many years."

Although breeding sport horses is new on this continent, as an individual you can produce quality by analyzing the successes of Europe. You should be willing to learn and to pursue a lifelong education—beginning with realistic goals.

Set Breeding Goals

American breeders can learn from Europe's breeding successes. European breeders tend to look at the breed as a whole. Most aim to profit by marketing their produce, and they consider how an individual will affect the breed.

Before a horseman breeds a mare, he should determine the purpose of the produce—to sell specific offspring, to obtain personal performance horses, or to improve the breed through generations. "You have to know what you want to breed," said Hans Schardt. "A good athlete is a good athlete, but only the exceptions can do both dressage and jumping. Don't expect to make a bad jumper into a dressage horse, or a bad dressage horse into a jumper."

Hannoverian breeder Judy Williams noted how the Hannoverian breed emphasizes breeding along jumping or dressage lines. "It's breeding for a purpose, not just breeding a pretty mare to a nice stallion. Jumping and dressage are different kinds of movement."

She advised mare owners to consider what they want to produce—not just "a horse." The mare owner should match abilities of stallion and mare. "What is your mare good at? Is she a good jumper? If you don't jump but want to breed dressage, get a mare that's a really good mover. Don't try to make a horse that's talented in one area try to be something else."

In any breeding program, breeding implies selection, not sentiment. To achieve success, breeders must adopt the European selection of superior horses. Selection controls genes within a population, with the aim of perpetuating good genes. The breeder retains superior parents which can produce offspring that meet current market demands—and culls inferior animals that fail to meet standards of conformation and movement.

Kyle Karnosh of Con Brio Farms said, "There's nothing magic about the European system. People have to buy into the system—to believe it and not breed, even if it's their prize mare. It's a very difficult thing to go to this system, but you see the results this system gets."

Follow Established Practices

In matching stallion and mare, the breeder must consider how to perpetuate good qualities, while not passing on faults of either parent. Gert van der Veen explained, "Ideally you match a top horse to a top horse. But the strength is determined by the weakest link, and what if both have the same weak link? The offspring won't be as good as either parent.

"Top horses must complement each other's weakest factor. Strengthen the weak link without weakening the strong one."

Breeders also use the compensation principle, as practiced at Trakehnen. Directors mated lighter mares to heavier stallions, and the stronger mares to more elegant sires. Goodall wrote, "A certain weakness in the mare must be offset by the strength of the stallion...One must bear in mind when considering a pairing, not only the mare and stallion, but their parents and grandparents."

Others follow the practice of breeding animals of similar type. They recommend homogeneous matings, which can increase the predictability of results.

Douglas Mankovich advised, "Don't breed something that's completely different—you run the risk of producing something that's much farther from what you would like to have. Go for a subtle change, not a dramatic change. If the mare is light-boned and you want a little more substance in the offspring, yes, look for a stallion with correctness of bones and angles."

Estimating heritability isn't a definite task. A horse can have a superior phenotype (observed appearance and behavior), but lack a genotype (genetic factors that influence phenotype) that will pass on to its offspring. And the opposite is also true, with a average animal producing outstanding offspring. The horse with high heritability—that passes on desirable traits to a minimum of 30 percent of its offspring—would be a dominant sire or dam.

In sport horses, most breeders would consider desirable traits to be temperament, correct conformation, and quality of gaits. A stallion that has and passes on these traits, the prepotent sire, breeds true to type. He produces animals like himself, and his foals inherit his fixed traits. One way to can predict dominance is to study the offspring of a stallion. They should represent his desirable characteristics.

Linebreeding has produced many superior sires. To intensify genetic merit, breeders cross back to a particular ancestor. Some horses' pedigrees trace two, three, or four times to one prominent sire.

Inbreeding mates horses that are closely related, with one or more common ancestors close up in the pedigree. This method increases the proportion of gene pairs that are homozygous (alike). The breeder concentrates genes for desired traits.

However, a population needs genetic variation, with new lines introduced through outcrossing. Breeders bring in new lines, which might be distantly related many generations back, in hopes of increasing variation in succeeding generations. The resulting hybrid vigor can succeed in influencing offspring, or it might produce horses of lesser quality than the parents and grandparents. Hybrid vigor is usually a product better than the mean quality of both parents.

Dr. Roland Ramsauer commented how German breeding managers recognize the importance of introducing new lines. "You don't want to get too narrow with your bloodlines. We call that from the genetic side the heterozygous effect—that you're not coming too close in relation to all the bloodlines."

After the first outcross, the first filial generation, European breeders generally cross back to the original breed. As an example of this backcrossing, a Westfalen breeder would breed a

mare by a Thoroughbred back to a Westfalen. The breeder aims to improve the breed by bringing in genetic variation and retain the benefits gained in the first filial cross.

Jan Ebeling noted how European breeders can estimate the breeding value of a stallion. "They can see the potential in a stallion. After one year or the second year, they know that an average stallion breeds really well with a certain type of mare. You cannot have only a super stallion or a super mare, and think that no matter what you breed it to it will be super. A lot of times, an average mare and average stallion can produce an incredible offspring."

Only a few great sires emerge from a breed's gene pool. Usually such stallions make their names by crossing with mares whose traits complement the stallion's.

Ebeling mentioned the tendency in this country for breeders to miss such a stallion. Many concentrate on the best-known sires, expecting it to complement any mare. "Maybe if you're lucky you'll have one mare that crosses well with that line, but more than likely all the others will not. The combination doesn't necessarily have to be the super mare and the super stallion."

Breeder Dale Bormann cautioned amateur owners about the risks in breeding. "When people breed, even more so than when they buy, they're looking at a dream. They look at a stallion and say, 'I want one just like that.' They don't realize that they won't be able to ride a horse like that. They're better off getting a horse that has a reputation for producing good amateur horses, that they can actually ride."

A superior individual might not reproduce its qualities. An animal could look outstanding, yet be of a mediocre family. Breeders would not expect this animal to breed true, as it is of heterozygous genes.

Douglas Mankovich criticized the assumption that the most expensive stallion produces

The Dutch mare Alona typifies the quality of mares needed to produce competitive sport horses in North America.

the best. "After getting mediocre results, breeders wonder, 'How can this be?' Because they didn't find the best stallion that complements their mare—they breed to what's in vogue." He noted that he stands three stallions of different types. To the mare owner, he recommends which horse will best complement that individual mare.

The stallion's line generally passes on its qualities. By studying inherited characteristics noted on pedigrees and in stallion books, the horseman can see how consistently a line reproduces itself. Pedigrees useful for such study must include performance data, so breeders can predict animals that will likely transmit important traits. With horses, this is usually show placings and prize money won.

Mankovich emphasized the scientific, thoughtful approach practiced by Europeans. "The European way is to do research," he explained. "Look at the bloodlines, look at the type, go back a few generations and see what's been produced. Is it jumping—is it dressage? Look at some offspring and then decide."

Breeders in America lack the advice and counsel that European organizations share with their members. A German Verband, national stud, or selection index assists breeders by publicizing the breeding values of stallions and mares.

For example, the Hannoverian Verband recommends which horse cross best with which lines. From experience, breed authorities know that a particular heavier stallion produces better foals when bred to mares with refinement. A stallion himself may not look heavy, but history proves that his bloodlines nicks best with certain types of mares.

Progeny testing has not been feasible in North America. With such a small number of offspring sired by individual stallions, breeders cannot assess how parents pass on traits. The more samples that breeders examine, the more accurate is the assessment.

Yet chance also influences the results of any mating. "Bloodlines are important, but not the most important," said Willie Arts. "It's not true that you can say that certain bloodlines give 100 percent chance that you will get the right horse. That never works, but it makes a chance that your offspring is good. You have to make that chance as big as possible."

Each animal inherits half its genetic makeup from each parent. Breeder Judy Williams noted, "There's a tremendous variation that's genetically possible. In breeding the same mare with the same stallion over and over again, you could get a tremendous difference."

"It's important to find the proper mate for your mare, to build up the breed," said Hermann Friedlaender. "Quality doesn't come up overnight, and horse breeding is only a part of knowledge—the other part is luck."

Breed only Better Mares

With some excellent sport horse stallions in North America, breeders can match these with good mares. Carefully breeding the right mares with the right stallions will improve the quality of American-bred sport horses, and make breeding progress.

"Start out with mares that have some other offspring that have proved to be good horses," advised Willie Arts. "Not only good horses to look at, but horses that perform in the ring—that makes it just that much more possible to breed the right ones."

European authorities note that Americans tend to use unproven or unsound mares for breeding. A mare lame due to navicular can pass on the predisposition toward that unsoundness. A more reliable choice is the mare who has proved performance ability in jumping or dressage. The mare does not have to be a winner in FEI-level competitions, but the breeder should have an impression of her talents. This will aid in matching her to a stallion of the same sport type.

Uli Schmitz said, "Only the best are good enough for breeding. Breed only the best mares who have proven themselves. If injured, it depends on what the injury comes from. If it's because of conformation, don't use the mare for breeding."

Some stallion owners will discourage mare owners, when they estimate that the offspring will not enhance the stallion's or the breed's reputation. Others stand their stallions to all mares.

Elizabeth Searle said, "People think if they're going to put out that much money for a warmblood, they'd like it to be a mare. They're cutting their losses to have a breedable horse. But they don't necessarily select the mare that way. Is this going to be a top broodmare and a riding horse?"

The successful broodmare displays a defi-

The imported Hannoverian mare Wanderer's Gold, sired by the state stallion Wanderer, has the desirable feminine expression of a broodmare. Her attitude reflects motherliness and a definite sex type.

nite sex type. She looks and acts like a mother. Her ability to carry a foal and her maternal instinct affect the offspring's phenotype.

Kathy Adams advised to study a mare's produce. "Analyze the mare's conformation, her strong and weak points. What sort of babies does she throw? What qualities does she carry strongly with her? Then match her with a stallion, where you see continuity in his qualities."

Mankovich commented how breeders underestimate the mare's contribution. "Having stood stallions to a variety of mares over the years, the stallion is not going to wave a magic wand. He can't produce a magnificent baby when the mare's a chunk. The stallion won't

A Dutch foal by the stallion Wanroij and out of a Quarter Horse mare.

completely change the conformation and overrule the mare."

He does see that the stallion can exert a significant impact on correcting certain traits. He has found that the stallion especially influences the offspring's temperament—probably the most important trait of a sport horse.

"To me, temperament is absolutely the top of the list. My stallions had to have a proven, demonstrable quality of temperament or we wouldn't even consider them. I've seen stallions with temperament I consider atrocious passing that on to their offspring, time and time again.

"You see the stallion with more influence on the temperament. The mare has more contribution to the conformation and size."

Soundness is another important factor in matching sire and dam. Gert van der Veen advised, "Only use a stallion tested for soundness as well as performance potential. Don't judge a stallion just because he has a good sport record."

How to Start?

The owner of a potential broodmare should evaluate her honestly. Breeder Kyle Karnosh advised, "If you're not sure, take her to a breed inspection. You can get scores and feedback on her weak and strong points."

In choosing a Thoroughbred mare, the horseman would look for one with substance and correct angulation. Because OCD affects a substantial percentage in the breed, investigate the line to ascertain whether the disease would be likely to affect offspring.

Helen Gibble recommended, "Buy one or two fillies, not a stallion. Talk to people about the horses you breed, to keep or geld them." She suggested ATA's voluntary inspection program as a way to receive opinions on a mare's possible contribution to the breed.

Judy Yancey agreed, saying, "I recommend to start with top quality fillies. It depends on what your goals are. If you really want to preserve, promote, and protect the Trakehner breed and all its history, then obviously the best choice is with a nice young mare."

Respected breeders often share objective advice with newcomers. Trakehner breeder Guenter Bertelmann explained, "When I give advice, I am very honest. I tell them, that mare, get rid of her. Every horse needs the same size stall, eats the same grain. It's better to have one good one than three average mares."

Judy Williams advised, "I look most at the mare in front of me. The next important thing is the pedigree, probably the first generation. After the third generation, it doesn't really matter. Then I try to match the stallion."

The breeder also analyzes the results of the crosses selected. Oldenburg breeder David Wilson has found that some breeders rely on crossing the same stallion with the same mare. "The

Graf Bae Farm

Dr. Richard von Buedingen first encountered Hannoverians while a young show rider in the late 1940s. These horses, offspring of Hannoverian stallions brought to the U.S. after World War II, were bred at the Army's remount stations.

As a hobby, he started crossing Hannoverians with Thoroughbreds in the 1970s. He aimed to breed a sturdy horse for riding and jumping—similar to the cavalry horses. "I said, 'What we need here is the remount back.' My purpose was to breed another good riding horse, with temperament, size, and character. The Thoroughbred horse was inappropriate, not bred to go around a little ring."

Von Buedingen breeds horses for the market, and he produces horses of consistent quality. His stallion, Domingo (Duerkheim-Bleep xx), sires foals praised by German officials. Ludwig Christmann of the Hannoverian Verband said, "He is very successful as a sire. He was bought by Dr. Bade, but was a late developer and was not accepted [by the Hannoverian breeders] at first. So Dr. von Buedingen had a chance to purchase him."

About Domingo, von Buedingen said, "It's unusual to get a world-class competitor and an incredibly prepotent stallion. He is probably one of the most prepotent stallions in the world today. He is the ideal stallion—he has pair-dominant genes everywhere you want them. His pedigree says he should have these characteristics, and his selection was one that was very carefully thought out." Domingo has already sired two Elite Mares of the American Hanoverian Society, and he won five Grands Prix in 1990.

Von Buedingen sees a need for more "legitimate" breeders to develop a valid sport horse industry. He noted that the U.S. lacks serious, lifetime breeders. "People lose interest and don't understand the program or the processes. You learn from your mistakes. Unfortunately, by the time you get good at it, it's time to quit—now that we've got it down to an art and a science."

mare produces the same bad characteristics in the conformation or the performance or the attitude. I think people should be more open— 'Well, maybe this didn't work for me. Maybe I should sell my mare, or pick another stallion."

The foal's registration possibilities also affect the choice of stallion. The various associations' regulations specify a range of acceptances for mares. Choosing a stallion registered in the same breed usually simplifies registration, but the best stallion for that mare may be of another breed.

Those who plan to cross a warmblood with a Thoroughbred, Arabian, Quarter Horse, Appaloosa, or other domestic breed, should study the rules of the association. Some accredit Jockey Club or Arabian Horse Club mares, while others will accept the offspring in a secondary studbook or issue only proof of pedigree. In general, most associations do not involve horses of the stock type. They consider the Western riding style separate from the Olympic disciplines.

Fees also vary. Costs can accumulate if they include joining the organization and paying an inspection fee, registration, and an annual mare fee. Some organizations, usually branches of European associations, have the reputation of multiple charges.

Buy or Breed?

Breeding is expensive in money and time. To raise a foal up to riding age can cost from $8,000 to $10,000. The owner saves money only if the mare passes on good qualities.

The economics of horse breeding tend to discourage breeders who aim to show a profit. To succeed, it takes knowledge, capital, and willingness to adjust to the market. In recent years, even major farms have gone under due to the uncertainties of the industry. This affects the market by decreasing the value of other breeders' animals.

"It's much cheaper to buy a two- or three-year-old," said Willie Arts. "With a two-year-old you can tell already quite a bit about how the horse will turn out. It's much better to buy than breed a mare you don't know about, or might be lame or no good for competition."

Dressage trainer Guenter Seidel noted, "I think it's best to buy a talented young horse, if you are with a trainer to help you through each level. If you have the money, buy a schooled horse that you can learn on."

Rider Dorie Schmitz also recommended buying a young horse. "You buy a known product. You have something you can start working with, fairly soon. Breeding, you don't know what you're going to get."

Hannoverian breeder Judy Williams advised mare owners not to breed a mare they don't like.

She recalled owners who cite their mare's faults, yet want to breed her. "If you don't like your mare, you really don't want to perpetuate that. Your mare could be old or broken down, but she should be quality."

Marketing the Offspring

To show a profit, or just to break even, American breeders must produce what the market demands. Sellers agree that buyers tend to want horses old enough to ride, which requires the breeder to raise the animal to a certain age.

Breeders must sell animals without the middleman, the raiser. If they sell a foal, they earn a profit with minimal investment. A yearling represents an increasing investment, with limited saleability.

Jan Ebeling said, "Nobody knows anything about how to judge a two-year-old that doesn't look like a finished horse. The colt is long and looks ugly. It's not easy to judge its gaits, because it just grows. It's very difficult to judge that age group—in fact, a lot of people in Europe don't know how to do that."

Elizabeth Searle noted, "When warmbloods started, people would buy a foal and wait. Now they're smarter and want a three-year-old. Breeders spend more time and money, for a higher overhead."

Because breeders lack a venue for marketing, here they share some ideas to help sell young sport horses:

- Compile an information packet with information about the horse's bloodlines. Photocopies from a stallion book will establish the worth of the horse's ancestors. Educate buyers on the importance of the horse's background.
- Coach family members on dealing with buyers—emphasize that they communicate only actual facts.
- To show a young horse, keep it in a stall before a potential buyer arrives. Turn the

horse loose in an arena, and it will display its best movement.

- Show a yearling only when it looks good in its uneven growth. Don't show it when it's in a gawky stage, or has grown too much in the hind end. The horse's appearance influences your reputation.

Source List

North American Associations

Belgian Warmblood Association
Koen Overstijns
PO Box 8123
Rancho Santa Fe, CA 92067

American Hanoverian Society, Inc.
Judy Hedreen, Secretary
14615 NE 190th Street, #108
Woodinville, WA 98072

Purebred Hanoverian Association of
American Breeders and Owners, Inc.
Robert Bollentin, Secretary/Treasurer
Box 429
Rocky Hill, NJ 08553

American Holsteiner Horse Association
Janice Scarbrough, Executive Director
222 E. Main Street, Suite 1
Georgetown, KY 40324

North American Selle Français Horse
Association, Inc.
Sheryl Akers
PO Box 646
Winchester, VA 2260

International Sporthorse Registry
Margaret Schrant
PO Box 957045
Hoffman Estates, IL 60195

Swedish Warmblood Association
Kristina Paulsen, West Coast Representative
PO Box 1587
Coupeville, WA 98239

American Trakehner Association, Inc.
Joan M. Schlimme, Executive Director
1520 W. Church Street
Newark, OH 43055

North American Trakehner Association
Frank LaSalle, Public Relations
1660 Collier Road
Akron, OH 44320

Warmbloed Paardenstamboek in Nederland
North American Department
Mary Giddens, Secretary
PO Box 956
Winchester, OR 97495

American Warmblood Registry, Inc.
Alexandra L. Dunaif, Secretary
PO Box 395
Hastings, NY 10706

American Warmblood Society
Jean R. Brooks, President
Route 5, Box 1219A
Phoenix, AZ 85009

Westfalen Warmblood Association of America
Lucy Parker, President
18432 Biladeau Lane
Penn Valley, CA 95946

Bibliography

American Trakehner Association, *Stallion Selection*.

Baranowski, Zdzislaw, *International Horseman's Dictionary*. Pitman, 1975.

L'Éperon, Spécial Cheval de Sport Français. Issy-les-Moulineaux Cedex, France, 1989.

Flade, Johannes, Erich Tylinek, and Zuzana Samkova, *Compleat Horse*. London: David and Charles, 1987.

Goodall, Daphne Machin, *Flight of the East Prussian Horses*. New York: Arco, 1973.

Goodall, Daphne Machin, *History of Horse Breeding*. London: Robert Hale, 1977.

Goodman, Patricia L., *Trakehner Horse*. Newark, Ohio: American Trakehner Association, 1981.

Hanford, Priscilla L., ed., *American Hanoverian Society 1990 Yearbook*. Woodinville, Washington: 1990.

Jepsen, Stanley M., *Coach Horse: Servant with Style*. Cranbury, New Jersey: A. S. Barnes, 1977.

Kidd, Jane, *Horsemanship in Europe*. London: J. A. Allen, 1977.

Kidd, Jane, *Illustrated International Encyclopedia of Horse Breeds and Breeding*. New York: Crown, 1989.

Köhler, Hans Joachim, *Pferdekenner und Fehlergucker*. Excerpted in *NATA Trakehner Tales*, March, 1984 and April, 1990.

Köhler, Hans Joachim, Monique Dossenbach, and Hans Dossenbach, *Grossen Gestüte der Welt*. Bern: Hallwag, 1978.

Lindner, Nils-Olof, and Fredericson, Ingvar, *Flyinge, 1661-1986*. Swedish Equestrian Breeding and Sports Foundation, 1986.

MacGregor-Morris, Pamela, *World's Show Jumpers*. London: Macdonald, 1955.

Marcenac, Louis-Noël, and Henri Aublet, *Encyclopédie du cheval*, 14 edition. Paris: Maloine S. A. Éditeur, 1980.

NA/WPN, *1990 NA/WPN Stallion Directory*. Forest Grove, Oregon: 1990.

Rossow, Dietrich, *Stallion Book of the Holsteiner Warmblood Breed*, Volume 2. Federation of Breeders of Holsteiner Horses and Riding and Driving School, Inc., 1988. Translated by Kaye Norment Smarslik, Sun Treader Farm, 1990.

Stenglin, Christian, *Hanoverian*. Translated by Christina Belton. London: J. A. Allen, 1990.

Summerhays, R. S., *Observer's Book of Horses and Ponies*. London: Warne, 1961.

United States of America. *Code of Federal Regulations*, 1990.

Verband hannoverscher Warmblutzüchter, *Member's Guide*. Verden: 1989.

Williams, Dorian, *Great Riding Schools of the World*. New York: Macmillan, 1975.

Index